CRIME AND PUNISHMENT

IN

MUGHAL INDIA

Crime and Punishment in Mughal India

Dr. Satya Prakash Sangar

RELIANCE PUBLISHING HOUSE
NEW DELHI-110008

Crime and Punishment in Mughal India

ISBN: 81-7510-022-2

Published by ·
Dr. S.K. Bhatia *for*
RELIANCE PUBLISHING HOUSE
3026/7H, RANJIT NAGAR
NEW DELHI-110 008
PH. : 5722605, 5737377

Composed by :
COMPUTRA COMMUNICATION
9, GOPALPUR, DELHI-110 009
PH. : 7652321

Printed at : Print Line New Delhi

Dedicated to
My Revered Teacher
Professor Sri Ram Sharma
F.R.H.S

PREFACE

Crime and Punishment in Mughal India was originally submitted as a Ph.D. thesis to the University of Poona in 1957. The interval between the acceptance of the thesis in the same year and its publication has been utilized in adding further matter and subjecting the manuscript to a thorough revision. As a result, the original thesis has assumed almost double its former size.

My approach to this intricate subject has been, by no means, that of an expert. I have dealt with it in the spirit of a keen student of Mughal history, whose only endeavour has been to present a coherent picture in an objective, accurate and unbiased manner.

My grateful thanks are due to my revered teacher, Professor Sri Ram Sharma, under whom I had the privilege to study during my university days at Lahore. His able guidance and mature advice enabled me to surmount numerous difficulties and avoid many a pitfall.

I am deeply indebted to my esteemed friend, Principal Kanhaya Lal Kapur of D.M. College Moga, for many of his useful suggestions.

I am grateful to Dr. Raghubir Singh of Sitamau for permitting me the use of his library. I am equally thankful to the Librarian, National Library, Calcutta, and his staff for having provided me facilities for work there. I am obliged in particlar to Shri A.B. Sen Gupta, Deputy Librarian, and to Shri S.M. Hasan, Assistant Librarian. Shri O.P. Gupta of the Panjab University Library Chandigarh deserves my gratitude for the assistance rendered in preparing the bibliography.

Satya Prakash Sangar

CONTENTS

I
MUSLIM LAW

(A) SOURCES OF MUSLIM LAW

The four sources of Islâmic law are the Qur'ân, *Sunna, Ijmâ'* and *Qyiâs.*[1]

THE QURÂN : According to the celebrated Sunni Imâm, Abû Hanifa, the "Qur'ân is the word of God, and His inspired Word and Revelation." "It is written in a volume, it is read in a language, it is remembered in the heart."[2]

The Qur'ân is also termed as *al-Kitâb* and contains collected revelations of Mohammad in a definitive written form. These revelations 'came from heaven and were taken from a well-guarded tablet' or a concealed book. The book is called "an admonition on noble, lofty, pure leaves through the hands of noble scribes." The revelations which existed completely in the heavenly book were taken piecemeal to Mohammad in Arabic dress through the intermediary of the trustworthy spirit (the angel Gabriel).[3]

In the early days of Islam memory was used as a channel for the transmission of the Qur'ân. During the life-time of the Prophet only a part of the revelation was recorded. It was the Caliph Abû Bakr who decided to have a written text prepared and entrusted Zaid bin Sâbit, the favourite secretary of the Prophet, with the task. Caliph 'Usmân appointed a commission to co-operate with Zaid. Their combined efforts resulted in putting together a definite Qur'ân in four copies.[4] The final recession of the Qur'ân was produced by 'Usmân twenty-five years after the death of the Prophet in 632 A.D.[5]

There are 114 chapters or *šûras* in the Qur'ân and each *šûra* is divided into a varying number of verses or *âyât*. Out of these there are about 100 *šûras* which can serve as a sort of preamble to a code of conduct and which simply seek to reform the existing customary law. The scholars of the Medina and 'Irâqi schools aimed at the elaboration of the *Sharî'a*, a system of the law for the Muslims, based on the common stock of the Qur'ânic principles.

"The basic of Mohammad's legislation was not legal, but ethical. He does not lay down legal formulas but indicates what is right conduct and what wrong."[6]

2. *THE SUNNA:* Literally Sunna means a "path or way; a manner of life."[7]

In the Qur'ân the sunna usually occurs in two connections : *sunnat-awwalîn* and *sunnat Allâh*. In *Hadîs* by sunna is commonly understood Mohammad's sunna comprising his deeds, utterances and his unspoken approval. "Mohammad's sunna in the sense of his words, actions and silent approval is fixed orally and in writing in the Hadis. In theory the conceptions of *sunna* and *Hadîs* are different but in practice they often coincide."[8]

The sunna or tradition is a real storehouse of material for the life of the Prophet and of Muslim institutions.[9] During his life-time the Prophet had decided many questions from case to case and his words and deeds and silent approval were reduced to writing and came to be termed as sunna.[10] "These traditons of what the Prophet said and did, "gradually laid the foundations of what is now called Islam." And "it is to tradition rather to the Qur'ân that *we* must refer for Mohammadan law."[11]

The group of Muslim jurists called *Ašhâb al-Hadîs* as opposed to those known as *Ašhâb al-Râ'y*, attached greater importance to sunna as a source of law in preference to *Rây*. The zeal of *Ašhâb al-Hadîs* led them to forge a number of traditions called *Hadîs* alleged to have been said or done by the Prophet. Most of these traditions were invented in the 8th century A.D. in order to justify innovations and tendencies which were very foreign to the intentions of the Prophet. Eminent Muslim jurists and scholars made compilations of the traditons in the 9th century either according to the chronological order of the successive authors or on the basis of their subject matter.[12]

IJMÂ' is the third source of Muslim law. Literally it means "agreeing upon." Al-Shâfi'î defines *ijmâ'* as the view held by the majority of the Muslims and uses it as a secondary source of elucidation on questions which cannot be decided from the Qur'ân and the sunna of the Prophet.[13] Later on, it was defined as the 'agreement of the *mujtahids* of the people (i.e. those who have a right, in virtue of knowledge, to form a judgment of their own) after the death of the prophet, in any age, on any matter of the faith'. *Ijmâ'* thus did not signify the opinion of the mases. The agreement was not arrived at by a council or a synod but was reached 'instinctively and automatically.' As a result of the agreement the points in dispute got settled and each settled point became the essential part of the faith; and disbelief in it came to be regarded as an act of unbelief (*kufr*).[14] Thus *ijmâ'* did not remain as supplementary to the Qur'ân and sunna, but was regarded as confirming them. Later on it received the power even of cancelling prescriptions of the Qur'ân and sunna. "Important sections of the system of the Muslim law are based on *ijmâ'* alone......In the last resort, in this view the whole of Muslim law owes its authority to the infallible *ijmâ'* alone.[15]

Ijmâ' was regarded as a major source of law and helped in overcoming the difficulties arising from the disputes among Muslim jurists about the rulings and methods of interpretations. "By means of *ijmâ'* what was at first an innovation, and as such heretical, has been accepted and has over-ridden the earlier sunna......*Ijmâ'* (in certain cases) has not simply fixed unsettled points, but has changed earlier doctrines, of the greatest importance. It is thus regarded by many, within and without Islam, a powerful instrument of reform."[16]

AL-QIYÂS, the fourth source of Muslim law, literally means "to compare" or deduction by analogy. The analogical reasoning with the learned in regard to the teaching of the Qur'ân, hadis and *ijmâ'* is known as *al-qiyâs*.[17] Al-Shâfi'î says in his *Rîsâla* that *qiyâs* is used in the cases which are not dealt with in the Qur'ân, sunna or *ijmâ'*. He regards *qiyâs* is of two kinds, *qiyâs-i-jali* or evident and *qiyâs-i-khafi* or hidden.[19]

For the commentator Fakhr al-Din al-Râzi Qur'ân and sunna have precedence over *qiyâs*. The use of *qiyâs* was permissible only when it was impossible to use these sources or "roots". "If traditions require to be verified by the sacred text, *qiyâs* does still more so. Qur'ân is the word of Allâh, while *qiyâs* is the work of feeble intelligence."[20]

(B) ISLAMIC JURISPRUDENCE OR FIQH

Fiqh meaning 'intelligence, knowledge', denoted Muslim jurisprudence. The term covers all aspects of religious, political and civic life. It includes criminal laws regulating the administration of the state and the conduct of war.[21]

When Islam spread beyond the confines of Arabia and came in contact with more advanced civilizations, it could not but be influenced by them. The most patent influence upon the development of Islam was that of the Roman law which was adopted in a "thorough-going" manner by the jurists of Islam. Goldziher holds the view that "even the names of legal speculation (*fiqh*—intelligence) and of its students (*fuqahâ*—intelligent) have been influenced by the Latin term (juris) *prudentia* and juris (*prudentes*) in their special application to the study of law and teacher of law."[22] the borrowings from Jewish Law also played a part in the formation and development of Islamic law. Kremer is of the opinion that even many of the provisions of Roman law adopted by Islam found a place in the Muslim jurisprudence through the intermediary of the Jews.[23] The extent of Persian influence in the development of *fiqh* is yet a subject of investigation.[24]

In the older theological language *fiqh* was considered synonymous with *râ'y* or opinion which is arrived at by independent exercise of judgment of legal points. Both the terms *fiqh* and *fuqahâ* (masters of the science, i.e. jurists) were originally limited to deductions not based on tradition. With the gradual recognition of the four sources or "roots" of Islâmic law (the Qur'ân, Sunna, *Ijmâ'* and *Qiyâṣ*), as methodical principles for laying down the legal prescriptions, this limitation no longer remained valid. *Fiqh* next became a science which co-ordinated and included all the branches of knowledge derived from the four sources.[25]

CODIFICATION OF ISLAMIC LAW

Attempts were made, sporadic during the Umaiyad and systematic in the 'Abbâsid period, at a condification of the law. The theologians who made the first serious efforts in Medîna, Syria and 'Irâq to evolve a regular system of law always accepted the four sources as authoritative. "According as they made limited or free use of one or other of the "roots" or selected one in preference to another of the contradictory traditons, they attained different results on particular points of law."[26]

The first such attempt said to be on record to codify the Islâmic law was the *Majmû'a of* Zaid bin 'Ali (died 740 A.D.), founder of the Shî'î sect of Zaidiya.[27]

The *Muwatta'* of Mâlik bin Anas (715-95 A.d.) is recognized as the oldest *corpus juris* of the Sunni branch of Islam. This was a condification of the *fiqh* as it developed in the theological centre of Medîna in Hijâz. In 'Irâq, Hammâd bin Suleimân became the pioneer of another school of *fiqh*. Imâm Abû Hanîfa belonged to this ('Irâqi) school which was placed on a firmer footing by his two great pupils, Abû Yûsuf (died 795 A.D.) and Mohammad bin al—Hasan al-Shaibâni (d. 804

A.D.). Almost at the same time *fiqh* was being systematically developed in Syria by 'Abd al-Rahmân al-Awzâî'î (d. 774 A.d.). Sufyân al-Thâwri (d. 778 A.D.) was yet another important teacher belonging to the 'Irâqî school of *fiqh*.[28]

In the 'Irâqî school of *fiqh* râ'y had a predominant influence and in comparison with it, the Hijâz school made a moderate use of this source of law. The jurists who believed in the validity of *râ'y* came to be called as *Ašhâb al-â'y*. Opposed to them were those who were termed as *Ašhâb al-Hadîs*.

Between these two extremes appeared a mediator in the person of Mohammad bin Idrîs-al-Shâfi'î (d. 820 A.D.). He systematized the method for the deduction of the laws from the sources of law (*ušûl al-fiqh*) and laid down the exact limits within which each might be used.

Thus during the second and third centuries of Islâmic era, Muslim jurisprudence had been codified by the individually developing schools of the above-mentioned founders of the law. And it is to these codifications of the law that all the present (four) orthodox Sunni schools of law trace back their origin. The development of the *fiqh* has taken place in four directions resulting in the establishment of the four schools or *mazâhib*. These four schools prevail even today in different parts of the Islâmic world and are called after the *Imâms* on whose teachings they are founded.

(C) SCHOOLS OF JURISPRUDENCE

1. *THE HANAFÎ SCHOOL* has been named after Imâm Abû Hanîfa, the patriarch of the 'Irâqi school. He was born in 700 A.D. at Kûfa where his grandfather, Zûtâ, taken prisoner in Kâbul, was brought as a slave by the Muslim conquerors and received his freedom in that town. His father, Sâbit, was a silk-dealer at Kûfa. Abû Hanîfa devoted the whole of his life to the study of the sacred science. He came to be regarded as a leading *fiqh* scholar and a great logician and oracle of Sunni jurisprudence.

Although the authentic writings of Abû Hanîfa are not extant, his influence as an authority on legal questions led to the rise of the 'Irâqî school. In the Hanafî system of *fiqh râ'y* played a predominant part. The doctrines of Abû Hanîfa and his two pupils, Imâm Abû Yûsuf and Imâm Mohammad bin Shaibâni are followed in by far the greater part of the Muslim world (Turkey, Central Asia and the Indian mainland). Abû Hanîfa died in Baghdâd at the age of 70.[29]

2. *THE SHÂFI'Î SCHOOL* The founder of this school or *mazhab* was Mohammad bin Idrîs al-Shâfi'î. He was a Hâshimite belonging to the tribe of the Quraish and was thus remotely connected with the Prophet. His father, an inveterate foe of Mohammad's, had fought at the battle of Badr, taken prisoner, released on ransom and was subsequently converted to Islam.

Shâfi'î was born at Askalon in Ghazza (Palestine) in 767 A.D. and lost his father early. His mother brought him up in very humble circumstances in Mecca. He was endowed with an extraordinary talent. He learnt the whole of the Qur'ân by rote at the age of seven, and at 10 he committed to memory the *Muwatta'* of Mâlik and at 15 attained the rank of *mufti.* His works are more voluminous than those of any Muslim doctor, although they were published between the age of 47 and 54 when he died.

At 20 he went to Medîna to Mâlik and remained there till the latter's death in 796 A.D. After going to Yemen, Baghdâd and Mecca, he settled in Egypt in 815 A.D. and died in 820 A.D.

Shâfi'î was an eclectic who acted as an intermediary between the independent legal investigation and traditionalism of his time. He is regarded as the founder of *Ûsûl al-fiqh* or Muslim jurisprudence. He did a great deal to advance the systematization of Islâmic law.

The Shâfi'î teaching is still eagerly studied in the Azhar mosuqe. It is even now predominant in South Arabia, Bahrain, the Malay Archipelago, the former German East Africa and some parts of Central Asia.[30]

3. *MÂLIKÎ SCHOOL* is named after Mâlik bin Anas. He probably was born in about 710 A.d. Because of his ugliness he was not in particular admired by any one. There is not much reliable information in regard to his early life and studies. At Medina where he spent most of his life, he got in trouble with the government, received flogging at the hands of the governor and suffered a disloation of shoulder. He died in 795 A.D. at the age of 85 in Medîna. Many details of his life are buried in fiction. His fame rests chiefly on his *Muwatta'* which work received a surprising success. One of the main objects in the juristic thought that appears in *Muwatta'* 'is the permeation of the whole legal life by religious and moral idea.....'. This work recorded the usual consensus of opinion in Medina and became authoritative as the expression of compromise.

Mâlik's main achievement lay in the development of the formation of the Islâmic legal system. The *Muwatta'* can be regarded as evidence of the stage reached in the general development of Muslim law of this time.

4. *THE HANBALÎ SCHOOL* received its name from Ahmad bin Mohammad bin Hanbal, the celebrated Islâmic theologian. Ibn Hanbal was born at Bagdâd in November 780 A.D. In that city he attended the lectures of al-Shâfi'î and received from him instructions in the traditions. He attained great fame from his profound knowledge of both civil and spiritual law. He suffered corporal punishment and imprisonment at the hands of the Caliph al-Mu'tsim whose son and successor Mutawakkil made amends by conferring on him honour and distinction. The *Musnad* was his main work which acquired great fame. This encyclopaedia of traditions was compiled by his son 'Abd Allâh and contained about 30,000 traditions. Another of his works, *Kitâb al-zuhd,* was also supplemented by his son.

Ibn Hanbal was an adherent of *Ahl al-Hadîs* and as far as possible derived every law from traditional sources and occasionaly admitted very feeble traditions as the basis of his decisions.[32]

His *mazhab* was much more widely spread in the countries of Islam till the 14th century A.D. The rise of the Ottomon power dealt Hanbalism a very severe blow and set it on its way to decline.

(D) MUGHAL PRACTICE

It was not possible for the Mughals to govern the country in strict observance of the law as described in the *fiqh* books. The Muslim law as detailed in the law books had grown to maturity outside of India. No monarch could be blind to the peculiar features of the country. The orthodox Muslim law was bound to undergo changes. Even the Sultans of Delhi had recognized the futility of governing the country in strict accordance with the Muslim law. Aurangzeb who attempted a rigid adherence to the tenets of Islâmic law did not meet with success.

Still the observance of the main forms of the orthodox law was essential. The Indian rulers and judges had always looked for guidance to the decisions of the eminent Muslim jurists outside India. They themselves did not feel competent and authoritative enough to set precedents. The Indian rulers and judges, like their counterparts in other Muslim countries, based their decisions on any one of the four schools of jurisprudence.

As a matter of fact the Indian kings and the majority of the Sunni Muslims regarded the Hanafî school as orthodox. It became necessary for the Indian judges to have at their elbow a digest of Islâmic law compiled from the accepted Arabic writers and such digests were prepared from time to time. Aurangzeb appointed a syndicate of theologians to prepare such a digest in India. The result was the Fatâwâ-i-'Âlamgîrî prepared in Arabic at a cost of two lac of rupees.[33] It was 'an authoritative work on Muslim Polity, Law and religious usages.'[34]

REFERENCES

1. Dictionary of Islam, pp. 400; 548;
   Shorter Encyclopaedia of Islam, p. 614;
   Muslim Institutions, p. 61;
   Islam by A.S. Triton, pp. 62-63;
   Medieval Islam by Von Runebaum, pp. 148-53.
2. Dictionary of Islam, p. 48.
3. Shorter Encyclopaedia of Islam, pp. 273-75.
4. Muslim Institutions, pp. 63-64.
5. Dictionary of Islam, p. 400.
6. Origins of Islamic Jurisprudence by Joseph Schacht, p. 384.
7. Dictionary of Islam, p. 622.
8. Shorter Encyclopaedia of Islam, p. 552.
9. Muslim Institutions, p. 66.
10. Encyclopaedia of Islam, IU, p. 556.
11. Dictionary of Islam, p. 400.
12. Muslim Institutions, pp, 65-66.
13. Shorter Encyclopaedia of Islam, p. 613.
14. Encyclopaedia of Islam, II, p. 448.
15. Shorter Encyclopaedia of Islam, p. 614.
16. Ibid.; p. 158.
    Encyclopaedia of Islam, II, p. 448.
17. Dictionary of Islam, p. 482.
18. Ibid.
    Shorter Encyeclopaedia of Islam, p. 226.
19. Dictionary of Islam, p. 482.
20. Shorter Encyclopaedia of Islam, p. 267.
21. Encyclopaedia of Islam, II, p. 101;
    Shorter Encyclopaedia of Islam, p. 102.
22. Encyclopaedia of Islam, II, p. 102;
    Shorter Encyclopaedia of Islam, p. 103.
23. Encyclopaedia of Islam, II, p. 102;
    Shorter Encyclopaedia of Islam, p. 103.
24. Ibid.
25. Shorter Encyclopaedia of Islam, pp. 104.
    Encyclopaedia of Islam, pp. 103.
26. Ibid.

27. Ibid.
28. Encyclopaedia of Islam, II, pp. 103-4;
Shorter Encyclopaedia of Islam, pp. 104-5.
29. Encyclopaedia of Islam, I, pp. 90-91;
Shorter Encyclopaedia of Islam, pp. 9-10;
Dictionary of Islam, pp. 7-8.
30. Encyclopaedia of Islam, IV, pp. 252-53;
Shorter Encyclopaedia of Islam, pp. 512; 613-14;
Dictionary of Islam, p. 570;
Neel J. Coulson : The Thought Quarterly, No. 40, p. 20.
31. Encyclopaedia of Islam, III, pp. 205; 206, 208;
Dictionary of Islam, p. 312;
Shorter Encyclopaedia of Islam, pp. 320-23;
32. Encyclopaedia of Islam, I, pp. 188-89;
Encyclopaedia of Islam, II. pp. 102-3;
Shorter Encyclopaedia of Islam, p. 20;
Dictionary of Islam, p. 188.
33. Mughal Administration, p. 101.
34. A Bibliography of Mughal India, p. 130.

II
FACTS ABOUT AURANGZEB'S COURTS AS REFLECTED IN THE JAIPUR NEWSLETTERS

The contemporary foreign travellers of the 17th century make us believe that the Mughal Emperors used to hold the court of justice (*adâlat*) once a week. This, however, is not borne out by the *Akhbârât-i-Darbâr-i-Mu'alla'* or the Jaipur newsletters of Aurangzeb's time. They are supposed to be the most authentic, original and unpublished Persian documents of the last twenty-seven years of that Emperor's reign. It is not easy to challenge the veracity of these important documents which were daily recorded in the royal' court by qualified writers expert in the Persian language. A careful persual of these records leaves us in no doubt that the different courts held then were termed as '*Adâlat, Diwân-i-khâso-'âm* and *Ghuslkhânah.* For some time the court was named as *Diwân-i-mazâlim.*

We have a detailed account of these courts right from July 1681 to the last days of Aurangzeb's reign in 1707. In July 1681, he happened to be at Ajmer and for two weeks of August at Pushkar. No court or *'adâlat* was held from July 20 to 30; *Dîwâni-i-khâs-o'âm* was held for two and *Diwân-i-Ghuslkhânah* for all the eleven days. In August the *'Adâlat* took place only for one day on 27th, *Ghuslkhânah* for 13 and both this and *Khâs-o-'âm* for five days. In September, *Diwân-i-Ghusalkhâna* met for 13 and *'Adâlat* for 8 days. No *Khâs-o-'âm* held. But in October it did meet though only for a day; *'adâlat* for 16 and *Ghuslkhâna* for 12 days. In November, *Diwân-i-khâs-o-'âm* took place on six *'Adâlat* on ten, and *Ghuslkhânah* on 19 days; both *'Adâlat* and *Dîwân* for two days and both *Dîwân* and *Ghuslkhâna* for one day.

Another point worth nothing is that for almost half the month of September. The whole of October and November, Aurangzeb was on march from Ajmer to Burhânpur. During this period he held the courts at temporary halting places, although with perfect regularity. When he was at Pushkar in August, he held the *Ghuslkhânah* court there also.

Dîwân-i-Ghuslkhânah—It is interesting to note that during these months (with the exception of August), the Friday holiday was not strictly observed on all occasions as far as the holding of one or another court was concerned. In July, the *Ghuslkhâna* was held on two Fridays, in September the *'Adâlat* took place on Friday (9th); in October, *'Adâlat* was held on all the four Fridays (7th, 14th, 21st and 28th); in November, on two Fridays (4th and 11th) there was the meeting of the *Ghuslkhânah* and on 18th of the *Dîwân*. On the last Friday of the month no court was held formally, although the Emperor performed the duty of the office and issued orders on important matters of state. On Fridays usually, Aurangzeb, while in a city, went to the *Jâmi' Masjid* for prayers. On October 4, no court was held because of the *Id-ul-fitr*.

Although Aurangzeb had ordered on November 24, 1681, that the *Ghuslkhânah* court would be held after the *Diwân-i-khâso-'âm*, no regularity in this connection was ever observed.

From the entries of July 1685 in the *Akhbârât* or newsletters it is clear that from 24th to 30th of the month, during the king's stay at Sholâpur, the *Ghuslkhânah* court was held everyday excepting on two days.

From the entries of the court proceedings for April and July to November 1688, during the king's stay at Bijâpur, we find that the three courts were held without any regularity or order. Out of 45 days, the *Dîwân* was held for 6 days, both *'Adâlat* and *Ghuslkhânah* for 20 and only the latter for 29 days.

There is no entry of the *Ghuslkhâna* for 1692 and 1693 in the Newsletters, nor from April 12, 1695, to March 1696. From November 1701 till the third week of March 1702, the daily courts held by the Emperor on the halting stages during his march, were termed as *Diwân-i-Mazâlim*. After that *Mazâlim* was dropped, meetings were held of *'Adâlat* or the *Dîwân*, but not of *Ghuslkhânah*. Aurangzeb was usually on march on the revolving throne and held the court in the villages where he halted. The last court of his reign was the *Dîwân-i-Adâlat* held on February 14, 1707. And he breathed his last on Friday, March 3, in Ahmadnagar.

An important fact worth observation is that the matters dealt at these courts were almost identical. Below are detailed the proceedings of the *Ghuslkhâna* court held on May 26, 1685, when the day had passed one *pahar* and 4 *gharis* :

The Emperor awarded one *bâzuband* (armlet) costing Rs. 7,000 to Prince Shâh, Âzam Bahadur.

In connection with transportation, it was ordered that fodder should be procured wherever it was found surplus.

Ibrâhîm and others who arrived from Haidarâbâd were taken into service. (The ranks conferred on each one are mentioned.)

Bahâdur Khân and Dâûd Khân etc, etc., troopers from the army of Khân Jahân Bahâdur, were posted with Ruh-ullah Khân as before.

A certain person named Qaisar brought forward a suit against an official Mohammad 'Ali who had put up his quarters on his land and garden. The Emperor ordered that officers who perpetrated oppression on *ryots* and the poor should be punished. Ihtimâm Khân was ordered to assess the amount of damage caused to the complainant's agriculture, charge it to the concerned officer to be paid to Qaisar. The tents forcibly pitched in his land were also ordered to be removed.

Earlier, complaints had been received that one Mohsin Khân had been inviting to his house some Persians who created noise and made disturbance. The Emperor had orded Ihtimâm Khân to ask Mohsin Khân to stop this practice. Learning of its continuance, the Emperor ordered the diminution of 100 *zar* in the rank of Mohsin Khân.

One *kara* (Gold bracelet costing Rs. 10,000, and one set of dress was entrusted to Mohammad Sâbar to be given to Aurangâbâdi.

Sayyid Abu Zamân, commandant of Sholâpur, was ordered to come to the *Ghuslkhâna* court.

A letter was received from Sâbar Khân, the commandant of Badr that the Haidarâbâdis were collecting forces although he was keeping vigilance. The *harkâra* reported verbally that they had not accepted the offer made to them. A *farmân* was issued to Râja Kishan Singh and Hamzah Khân to ravage their country.

Below are noted the proceedings of the *Dîwân-i-Ghuslkhânah* held on May 27, 1685 :

Mohammad Nâzim *Faujdâr* was absolved from supplying provisions for the beasts of burden.

Rewards in cash and kind were conferred on certain officials; titles were granted to some and promotions to others. A few appointments were made. Applications of two officials were presented to the Emperor.

In the *Dîwân-i-Ghuslkhânah* held on May 29, 1685, rewards, robes of honour and promotions were conferred on some officers. A commandant's request for permission to come to the royal court to pay respects to the King was accepted. The news of the death of the daughter of Khânzâd Khân was reported to the Emperor.

In the *Ghuslkhânah darbâr* held on August 8, 1688, Râja Kishan Singh was rewarded for having killed the rebel Râja Râm Jât. A report was received from Amîr Khân, the governor of Kâbul against the oppressive deeds of Hasan Beg Kakkar *Faujdâr,* of Fatehpur. His recommendation for the appointment of another person in his place was accepted.

In the *Dîwân-i-Ghuslkhânah* held on August 10, 1688, presents were received from Ruhullah Khân, Governor of Haidarâbâd, and one appointment was ordered. A complaint was made against a Superintendent by an official. Orders were issued to the *Dîwân* of Bengâl to investigate into complaints against a *jâgîrdâr.* Money was granted for new buildings in Bijâpur fortress. Orders were issued for the despatch of 100 *kahârs* to fetch guns.

I other meetings of the *Ghuslkhânah* also the usual proceedings were appointments and transfers, promotions and demotions of officers, *mansabs* and rewards to fresh converts to Islam, awards of *jâgîrs,* news about the activities of the rebels and orders for the suppression of their activities. No *Ghuslkhânah* sessions were held from April 12, 1695, to March 1696, from October 7 to December 1692, from January to December 1693, and from January to April 1694.

DÎWÂN-I-KHÂS-O-'ÂM

The matters taken up at the court, according to the *Akhbârât* or newsletters, used to be the following :

Presents received from various persons were shown to the Emperor. Approval was granted for the solemnization of marriages amongst the sons and daughters of officers. Leave was also granted to the concerned officers for this purpose. Presents were sent by the King on such auspicious occasions. Petitions were received from officers for their transfer or retirement. Reports were made about the mutual recriminations and fights among officers. Orders were to be issued for stopping the *Holi* and *Dîwâli* festivals among the Hindus, against their riding horses or using *pâlkis* and indulgence in image worship.

Cases of forgery and official corruption were reported and punishments announced. Titles were conferred on royal princes and officers, *jizya* was fixed and *jâgirs* were awarded. News was received about the death of some *mansabdâr* or about breaking of fire. Mace-bearers were ordered to be sent to fetch officers against whom some complaints had been received. Orders were issued for the celebration of the birth of the king's grandsons. Officers were ordered to go and bring *ghee* or mangoes for the king. Permission was granted for the purchase of elephants and parading those already purchased.

Presents of gold *muhrs* or pearls, horses and elephants and of the Holy *Qurâ'n* were made by or to the Emperor. Occasionally news was brought about stopping of Muslim prayers in the mosques by Hindu *zamindârs.* Fruits like pomegranates or grapes, mangoes and pears, sent by the Superintendent of Gardens and others, were presented to the Emperor and distributed under his orders to various Princes and officers. Sanction was granted for the repair of gardens and forts. News was received by Aurangzeb and recorded i the proceedings of the court of the breaking of rains, birth of lambs to a single goat (and utterance of God's praise for this by him) and of the details of engagement with the enemy. Orders were issued for the chastisement of enemy forces.

In the *Dîwân-i-khâs* of November 7, 1695, the following matters were taken up :

The news of the death of Mohammad *Bâqar* was reported to the Emperor. It was ordered that the *janâza* of the officer be brought next day to enable him to offer the *janâza* prayers. Condolences were offered by the Emperor to the sons of the deceased.

Permission was given to Khânzâd Khân for apprehending Dhanna rebel. Promotion was granted to an officer and rewards to another. News of the death of another officer was announced to the King, and also about the enemy raids. Despatches were received from Haidrâbâd and orders were passed on them. Orders were given to Yâqût, Superintendent of Gardens, for the repair of Sholâpur gardens and for the supply of fruits to the Bukhâra refugees.

'ADÂLAT

The time for holding the *'Adâlat* was usually one *pahar* and 3 or 4 *gharis.* The place of the *wazîr* or *dîwân* was in front of the silver pillar. The usual business performed was the appointment and transfer of officers, promotion and demotion of *mansabdârs,* receipt and award of presents and decisions on the petitions received in the court. News was received about the activities of the Marâtha rebels and orders were given for their suppression. Robes and rewards were conferred on the new converts from Hinduism to Islam. Orders were given for the demolition of Hindu temples and stopping of image worship.

Detailed below are the proceedings of the *'Adâlat* held on April 13, 1695 :

Yâqût reported that Khânjâhan had sent 400 *qalams* of grapes from Aurangâbâd. A petition of a woman was received to the effect that the *gumâshta* of Râja Kishan Singh of Chânda had wrongfully arrested her son. The *gumâshta* was ordered to be sent to the court.

In the, *'Adâlat* of June 3, 1695, the dismissed *zomindâr* of Bhopatgarh was ordered to come to the court.

In July, August and November, 1689, there are a number of entries when the Emperor held the *Ghuslkhânah* after the *'Adâlat.* The usual time was one *pahar* and one or two, six or seven *gharis.*

Courts were not held on the last Thursdays of the month, on the *Ids* and usually on Fridays, although Aurangzeb did hold *Dîwân* or *'Adâlat* on same Fridays as well. Whereas the Hindu festivals were banned, the Muslim festivals were celebrated at the court. The Superintendent of *Naqqârkhânah* (Bands) would inform the Emperor that people had viewed the new moon, and received the permission of informing others by ordering the *naubat* to be played upon. On the occassion of *Îd-uz-zuha,* the Emperor would cancel the holding of the court, go to the *Îdgâh* and sacrifice a camel and a goat with his own hands.

From June 1702 to the end of the year only the *Dîwân-i-'Adâlat* was held with occasional sessions of the *Dîwân-i-Khâs*. It appears from a persual of the newsletters that before going to attend the *'Adâlat,* Aurangzeb used to ask for and change his clothes (*Akhbârât*, April 13, 16, 1696).

The *'Adâlat* was not held once a week as suggested by the contemporary foreign travellers. There could be a daily session of this court or it could be held at irregular intervals. There were no fixed rules, at least, according to these newsletters, for the holding of the *khaso-'âm, 'Adâlat Ghuslkhânah* or *Mazâlim* courts. If there were any regulations about them, they were observed in their breach alone. All depended on the sweet will of the Mughal Emperor. Nor were there only criminal cases decided at these courts. Cases of theft and robbery were reported from the districts and sub-divisions and orders for the apprehension and punishment of the culprits issued. These criminal cases, however, came up along with so many other cases of absolutely different nature.

DÎWÂN-I-MAZÂLIM

From November 1701 to March 1702, the courts held by Aurangzeb were termed as *Diwân-i-Mazâlim.* During this period he was usually on march and covered a distance of a few miles every day on the revolving throne known as *Takht-i-rawân.* The court was held on the halting places. In December 1701, the *Mazâlim* was held for 21 days, in January 1702 for 3, in February for 7 and in March for 11 days. After 23rd March there is no mention in the newsletters of this court, although there were frequent sessions of the *'Adâlat*. The recorded cases that came up before the *Mazâlim* court were as mentioned below :

Orders were issued for the suppression of the Marâtha enemies, about the execution of the Marâtha prisoners of war and about the inquiry of the rates of grain from the Superintendent concerned. Appointments and promotions were ordered, robes of honour and rewards were conferred. At one session of this court, news was received of the death of 'Abdur Rahmân *Bakshi* and of the mourning of his death by his sons. The Emperor ordered that four big dishes of food be sent to his house. At the *Mazâlim* court mostly news was received of Mughal wars with the Marâthas.

On various occasions the sessions of the *Dîwân* were suspended. Even then the business of state was transacted the details of which have been duly recorded in the *Akhbârât-i-Darbâr-i-Mu'alla'*. Appointments and dismissals were ordered, promotions and demotions took place, rewards and punishments were announced. News about the Marâtha warfare was reported to the Emperor. The routine of work was regularly performed even when he was on march.

Proceedings of the last 'Adâlat of Aurangzeb held on February 14, 1707 as recorded in the Akhbarât :

The Emperor held the court (*'Adâlat*) at one *pahar* and four *gharis* and left at noon.

Bakshi-ul-mulk Mirzâ Sadr-ud-dîn Ahmad and Dayânat Khân Dîwân attended the court after recovery from illness and presented gold *muhrs* to the Emperor.

Sâbar Khân, Bakhshi *Shâgird-Peshân* was given promotion and robe of honour. Dilâwar Khân, the son-in-law of 'Inâyat Khân, was appointed Bakhshi *Shâgird-Peshân.*

Fateh-ullah Khân, son of Habîbullah and son-in-law of Mastân Khân, was appointed Superintendent incharge of hunting on the transfer of Qâlib 'Ali and promoted. Mohammâd Hâdi, Superintendent of Stables and Farrâsh-khânah, was appointed Superintendent of another department on the transfer of Mohammad Nafar. On the previous night, a *farmân* had been entrusted to Sarbrâh Khân Kotwâl to be delivered to Prince Mohammad Kâm Baksh. The said Khân brought the answer from the Prince and presented the same to the Emperor. The petition of Ghâzi-ud-dîn Khân Bahâdur Feroz Jang Chin Qulich Khân was presented to the King. Prince Mohammad Kâm Baksh had sent rewards to a number of *mansabdârs*. Every one among them presented himself before the Emperor and paid respects. (Names are mentioned along with the rewards).

PROCEEDINGS OF THE LAST DIWÂN : FEBRUARY 16, 1707

The petition of Prince Mohammad Kâm Baksh was presented to the Emperor by Hidâyat Keesh Khân *Vekil*. Orders were issued about the governorship of Bijâpur and *Faujdâri* of Karnâtak. It was reported from Aurangâbâd that Khushâl Khân was defeated and captured near Ausa. The petition of Prince 'Âzam Shâh was presented by his *Vakil*. Tâj, the son of Fateh Jang Khân, was granted sick leave for six months for treatment. Orders were passed on the petition of Chin Qulich Khân Bahâdur. Jamdhar Khân was given a horse and cash. Sarbrâh Khân *Kotwâl* received a horse and a robe of honour. Mohammad Hâdi was given a robe and an elephant. Khwâjah Mas'ûd Khân was permitted to go to Aurangâbâd to present fruits to the Prince there. The petition of Prince Mu'azzam Bahâdur Shâh was presented by his *Vakîl* Mohammad Ikhlâs. The petition of 'Inâyat Khân commandant was presented to the King. Fakhruddîn Khân was permitted to come to the *Dîwan-i-'Adâlat*. Sayyid Mohammad, son of Nasrulla Khân, presented himself before the Emperor and received promotion. Qâlib 'Ali, son of Rahmat 'Ali Khân, Superintendent *Sazâwalân,* and others were appointed to accompany the horse of Prince Mohammad Mu'azzam. Mohammad Ja'far was appointed to the rank of 100 zât.

Towards the close of his reign, Aurangzeb adopted a novel method of dealing with petitions. He would call the Chief Secretary to his presence and ask him to present only five petitions in his retiring room. The entry of October 4, 1700, reads as follows :

When the day had passed one *pahar* and two *gharis,* the Emperor opened the window of his bed room, ordered Mun'im Khân in the royal presence and asked him to present petitions. Accordingly, five petitions were placed before him. After that the *Dîwân* and '*Adâlat* were suspended.

The entry of July 27 reads :

"When the day had advanced one *pahar* and five *gharis,* the Emperor set aside the curtain of his retiring room and Chief Secretary Siâdat Khân presented five files to him."

There is an almost similar entry for 31st July.

The entry of 18th September reads :

"The said Khân presented to His Majesty five files of five persons. After that the Emperor put up again the curtain of the retiring room."

There is an exactly similar entry for 19th September, 1704.

On September, due to the illness of Siâdat Khân, files were ordered to be presented by Bâqar Khân, *Tan Bakhshi* of the *Ahâdîs.* When he entered the room, the Emperor set aside the curtain and received the five petitions from the Khân.

September 23, 1704

The Dîwân was cancelled on that day. After the *Zuhar* prayers, the curtains of the retiring room were set aside and Siâdat Khân put up the files. Hamîd-ud-dîn Khân Bahâdur and the Chief Bakhshi, Mirzâ Sadr-ud-dîn Mohammad Khân, came to the Emperor under orders. After 1 ½ *gharis* the curtains were drawn again.

SEPTEMBER 30, 1704

When the day had advanced one *pahar* and 7 *gharis,* the Emperor set aside the curtains of the retiring room. Tahawwar Khân, Mir Tuzk, presented before him, as ordered earlier, Mansur Khân, Superintendent of Artillery of the Deccan.

The same entry as of July 27, is there for October 9, 1704. Three days later, Mohammad Amîn came to the retiring room after the curtains had been set aside, and presented his five-year old son to the Emperor.

JANUARY 8, 1706

On that day the *Dîwân* was cancelled. The window of the retiring room was opened and Hamîd-ud-dîn Khân Bahâdur, Siâdat Khân and Banda Khân, Mîr-i-Sâmân, came to the Emperor under orders. Siâdat Khân presented five files to the Emperor.

On January 24, after the window of the retiring room had been opened, a number of high officers, including the Superintendent of the Court of the Grand *Dîwân,* came to the Emperor, under orders.

Last entry is of December 1, 1706. His Majesty had ordered the cancellation of the *Dîwân.* After the *Zuhar* prayer, the window of the retiring room was opened and the Chief Bakhshi, Mirzâ Sadr-ud-dîn Mohammad Khân came to the royal presence and reported important matters of the state. The Emperor sat there for 1 ½ *gharis* and then retired.

Every body was not allowed to attend the various courts held by Aurangzeb. The entry was restricted only to the grandees who had earlier received his permission. He ordered on the night of July 1, 1703, that Jumdat-ul-mulk Amîr-ul-umarâ and Chief Bakhshi Ruhullah Khân and Hamîd-ud-dîn Khân Bahâdur, Mohammad Amîn Khân, Khânzad Khân, 'Abdur Rahim and some other officers, in all two dozen chief nobles, should come to the *'Adâlat* via *Dîwân-i-khâs* None else should be allowed entry. On July 10, Hamîdullah Khân Bahâdur, *Dârogha-i-Diwân-i-khâs,* submitted that a number of nobles had come to the *Dîwân-i-khâs* for audience. The Emperor ordered the submission of their names and after a careful scrutiny, he permitted not more than a dozen nobles to attend the court.

He issued orders on September 24, 1703, that whenever Jumdat-ul-mulk Amîrul Umarâ came to the Chief *Dîwân* on the *'Adâlat* day, Tahawwar Khân, Mir Tuzk, should go and arrange for twenty mounted mace-bearers.

Steps were always taken to control noise in the courts. On September 1, 1696, the Emperor told Tarbiat Khân, Mir Tuzk, that there being excessive noise in *'Adâlat,* Bhâskar Râo *harkâra* and two servants should be ordered to stop people from coming to the court. On September 25, 1703, an enclosure was ordered to be fixed to stop unauthorized entry in the court. A wooden enclosure was ordered to be prepared within the *Dîwân-i-khâso-'âm* and was shown to the Emperor on September 12, 1703, for his formal approval.

III
ADMINISTRATION OF JUSTICE IN MUGHAL INDIA

In Mughal India, there were three agencies in general charge of judicial administration. The Emperor and his agents like the provincial governor, the *faujdâr* in the *sarkâr* and the *kotwâl* usually administered political cases. Robbers and rebels working in organized bands would claim the attention of and receive punishments from these secular officers.

The *qâzî* administered Shar'î or sacred law. His jurisdiction was confined only to questions connected with religion. He decided disputes concerning family law and marriage, inheritance or *auqâf* and also criminal cases.

For the Hindus and the village people there were the courts of the Brâhmin Pandits and the caste elders. They administered the common (unwritten) law or codes of tribal traditions. They were not subordinate to the *qâzî,* nor had anything to do with the Shar'î law.

THE EMPEROR AND HIS COURT

In respect of criminal justice, the Sharî'a had left a wide field to the discretion of the sovereign.[1] The Emperor was the highest authority in the kingdom and was the fountain of justice. It is wrong to say, as alleged by the foreign travellers, that his will was always law in all affairs.[2] There was the Islâmic law and he dared not transgress the boundaries of the Sharî'a without provoking misgivings in the hearts of the orthodox. It was particularly true in the case of Shah Jahan and Aurangzeb who were staunch *Sunnis* and based their decisions as far as possible on the orthodox law. The Mughal Emperors, however, were subject to no other religious authority in or outside India.

Extraordinarily hard-working as the Mughal monarchs were,

they kept an eye on all departments of the State including that of law and justice. The Emperor himself was the highest court of appeal as well as the court of first instance. It seems, however, improbable that he had time enough to dispose of all the cases that came up before him. A large number of appeals from distant parts of the country could not be filed in his court. The innumerable inconveniences that attended long travels in the Middle Ages might have made the people hesitant to go to the imperial court.

The Mughal Emperor used to hold his court everyday where ordianry cases were decided. Akbar held his court after prayers and administered justice there.[3] Every Mughal Emperor, however, set apart a day of the week for administration of justice. In the case of Akbar it was Thursday,[4] for Jahangir Tuesday[5] and for Shah Jahan and Aurangzeb Wednesday.[6] As regards Akbar, Ab'ul Fazl has recorded : "In the investigation of cases of the oppressed, the Emperor placed no reliance on testimony or oaths. He drew his conclusions from the contradictions in the narratives, the physiognomy, and from sublime researches, and noble conjectures."[7] Father Monserrate has praised Akbar's regard "for right and justice in the affairs of Government."[8] He was by nature kindly and benevolent and was 'sincerely anxious' that offenders should be punished.[9]

William Hawkins who visited India during Jahangir's reign (1608-13), remarked that the Indian kings sat "daily in justice every day."[10] Nicholas Withington (1612-16) observed that Jahangir sat in his court at Agra three times a day to do his 'great justice."[11] Edward Terry (1616-19) confirms this and adds that any complaint there could hold up his petition and was sure to receive a hearing.[12] We learn from the account of William Hawkins that Jahangir came to the Audience Hall at 3 o' clock and took his seat on the royal throne while his nobles and *mansabdârs* kept standing. For two hours he 'heareth all cases in this place."[13] According to another eye-witness account he came to the court between 3 and 4 o' clock in the afternoon and did not leave till the evening.[14]

The foreign travellers have also referred to the golden chain of justice during Jahangir's time. He had a bell or bells hanging in his seraglio 'with a cord which reached out into an outer room.' Any complainant who had failed to secure justice could ring the bell. The emperor sent up for him, examined the case and pronounced judgement or took any other appropriate action.[15] In spite of this evidence, it cannot be believed that many people could make use of the chain of justice.

"Shahjahan upheld the maxims of his father that true justice must be enforced."[16]

Aurangzeb was "desirous of appearing a great lover of justice."[17] He maintained that a king should apply himself unweariedly and painstakingly to the dispensing of equal justice to every body.[18] He endeavoured to "maintain in the eyes of the world that he is zealous in the cause of justice."[19]

The Mughal emperors even when out of the capital, did not neglect the cause of justice. While embarking on the Bengal expedition, Akbar held his court in the boat and decided cases there.[20] During his stay in Ahmedabad in 1618, Jahangir appeared in the *jharoka* every day for about three hours to administer justice and award punishment to the guilty.[21]

Even while he was on march the King failed not to hold the court in a tent and administer justice. 'The kings of Hindustan seldom fail, even when in the field, to hold this assembly twice during the 24 hours, the same as when in the capital. The custom is regarded as a matter of law and duty, and the observance of it is rarely neglected."[22]

No court was held on the special day reserved for the administration of justice. Straight from the *darshan* window, the Emperor, followed by officers, *qâzîs, muftis,* scholars and the *kotwâl*, went to the Private Audience Hall. From 8 o' clock in the morning till noon the Emperor continued deciding cases. As a court of first instance he got the details of the complaints from the plainiffs, tried to ascertain the facts by inquiry, consulted the lawyers about the law and then pronounced judgment. Appeals were also filed in his court. This was the case when the plaintiff had either been refused a hearing in the local courts or had received an adverse judgment. Most often when it was not possible for the Emperor to ascertain the facts, he would send the case back to the court of its origin. The court made full investigations and delivered judgment. In certain cases the matter could again be referred to the Emperor.[23]

Besides the special day reserved for the administration of justice, the Mughal Emperor used to hear cases in the *Dîwân-i-'Âm* also on almost all the days of the holding of the court. The petitions of the aggrieved concerning different matters were presented before him. The persons involved were ordered to present themselves before the Emperor who heard their complaints and delivered judgment usually on the spot. In certain cases he ordered full investigation, sent for detailed report and then gave his decision. According to Bernier, Aurangzeb devoted two hours on another day to hear in private the petitions of ten persons selected from the lower order. One day he fixed to attend the justice-chamber, called *'Adâlat Khâna,* where he was assisted by two principal *qâzîs.*[24]

As a court of first instance and as the highest court of appeal, the Emperor was supposed to dispose of a large number of cases. This, however, was not possible. Many plaintiffs could not reach his court for fear of the provincial or local authorities, long distances and unsafe roads. One thing is clear. Trials in Mughal India by the kings were speedy and so the punishments.[25]

EXECUTIVE OFFICERS AND ADMINISTRATION OF JUSTICE

Governor—The governor, like the Emperor, set apart a day for administering justice in person.[26] The *qâzî* and other law officers attended the court and helped the governor in deciding cases. The procedure followed could not be different from that of the imperial court. The governor took the law from the law officers and pronounced judgment. In case, however, there was not sufficient legal evidence, but the governor and the officials of the court were convinced of the offence, the accused was sentenced.[27] Against the organized bands of robbers and rebels, the governor used to despatch armies. In Mughal India it was obligatory on the part of the executive officers to ensure the safety of the people from robbers. For all cases of thefts and robberies in their jurisdiction the responsibility lay with the respective executive officers.[28]

The governor inquired into the cases of the captives that were sent to him by the local officers and dealt with them in accordance with the law.[29]

The governor was 'an absolute lord, in the strictest sense of the term.' He was 'in his own person the intendant of justice, the parliament, the presidial court......"[30]

Faujdâr—The *faujdâr* was responsible for the maintenance of law and order in the district. He took measures to guard the roads against the activities of the robbers. It was his duty to traverse the country along with his armed guards and hunt out the culprits. Whenever a robbery took place in his jurisdiction, he was to trace the robbers find out the lost goods, or compensate the sufferer.[31] He sent the captives to the governor[32] for investigation and punishment.

Kotwâl—The *kotwâl* was an important officer and the cheif of the city police. He was required to attend the court of justice held by the Emperor or the governor. From a *farmân* issued by Akbar it is clear that the *kotwâl* was required to perform multifarious duties.[33] In Aurangzeb's *farmân* his duties had been made very clear. Whenever his men arrested a culprit and brought him to his *chabûtra,** the *kotwâl* was personally to investigate the charge against him. If he was found innocent, he was forthwith to be released. If some body had any charge against him, the *kotwâl* was required to direct that man to resort to the court against the alleged culprit. When the *qâzi* sent a culprit to him for detention, the *kotwâl* was to carry out the *qâzî's* orders and keep the person concerned in prison. He was to send the detenue to the *qâzî' 's* court every day so that his case could be decided quickly. If the *qâzî* had fixed the date for his trial, the prisoner was to be sent to his court.[34] Manucci defines the *kotwâl* as the 'chief magistrate ruling over the whole city."[35]

Thânedâr—In the *pargana* there was the court of the *thânedâr,* at least during the reign of Aurangzeb. The *thânedâr* was entitled as *Tahawur Sha'âr* or '*Tahawur Dastgâh.* The *gumâshta,* news-writer, biographer, *chaudharis,* and *qânûngos* were the officials usually present at the court of the *thânedâr.* In the 49th year of the reign of Aurangzeb, *Tahawur Dastgâh* Udai Singh, *thânedâr*, of Pargana Bhaurâsa in the *sarkâr* of Sârangpur, held court in the village Sahiya. The *muqaddams* of the village invited the *thânedâr* and his soldiers to a feast. There used to be a *nâib* or assistant *Dastgâh.*[36]

Aurangzeb had ordered that local cases should be tried by local officers in their courts.[37]

THE QÂZI AND HIS COURT

The Qâzî—The word *qâzî* philologically means consideration of a matter and determining it. Its literal rendering is "consummation." Among other things it means the office of a *qâzî* or judge, and the sentence of a *qâzî.*[38]

The *qâzî* had an important place in every Muslim country. In the Ottoman Empire he exercised judicial functions and also a sort of general supervision over the conduct of administration.[39]

In Muslim countries the *qâzî* was appointed by the Caliph or his representative, the *Sultân,* the Governor or the *Grand Qâzî.* The *Grand*

---

* Chabûtra was a raised platform, usually rectangular. The word is often used as meaning a 'court, judicial office''. Such courts were frequently held in the open air, the officer sitting on a square-shaped raised platform, (See Manrique, p. 424.)

Qâzî was appointed by the*Sultân* and was required to be of full age and understanding, free, a male, a Muslim, equitable, possessed of hearing, sight and knowledge.[40]

The Muslim rulers regarded it as their duty to do justice personally. The Umaiyad Caliphs were the first to create the post of the *qâzî* together with other judicial appointments. They had a *qâzî* for each province. Later on, his duties multiplied and he had delegates for their performance. He was a 'Chief Justice, sitting on the high seat of judgment."[41]

It was necessary for the *qâzî* to know the Qur'ân, the Sunna, what the community had agreed upon by *Ijmâ'* and the divergent opinions held by the earlier doctors. He must have the capacity to comprehend the various aspects of *qiyâs* when need arose. He must be intelligent, alert, reliable, firm and clement. He must possess reasoning powers. Above all, he should be chaste, an abstainer, just, upright, truthful in speech and resourceful. It was best if he belonged to the *Quraish.*[42] He was required to be an adult, a free man, a Musim, sane and unconvicted of slander, and a scholar of blameless life.[43]

In case there was only one man capable of holding the office, it was his duty to accept the post and the king could compel him to undertake it.[44]

In ancient times the *qâzî* was expected to have a perfect knowledge of the canon law. Later on it became a matter of secondary importance. Honesty and good sense came to be recognized his only essential qualifications. He could make up for his want of knowledge of the law by choosing learned counsellors or could rely on the reasoned opinion of an acknowledged judicial expert. He was required to possess a perfect behaviour and avoid participation in over-sumptuous feasts and gatherings for singing and gambling.[45]

The *qâzî* was required to sit for justice in an open place in the middle of the town, one well-known to the people. It was not to be in a mosque. According to the *Fatâwâ-i-Âlamgiri* and the Dictionary of Islam, he could, however, sit in a mosque. He could, if he so desired, decide cases in his house. It was preferable if the house, like the mosuqe, was situated in the middle of the town.[46]

In case of non-Muslims, special magistrates could administer justice. If, however, a Muslim had an interest in the case, the *qâzî* alone was competent to deal with it in accordance with the Muslim law. A *Shi'a* or a non-Muslim could not decide the case of a *Sunnite.*[47]

In Muslim countries outside India, the great bulk of ordinary disputes did not come into the court of the *qâzî,* as the village, corporation and social groups had their own organization. Certain offences like unchastity and adultery were punished almost automatically with death without the necessity of *qâzî's* intervention.[48]

Jurisdiction of The Qâzî's Court—The *qâzî* was regarded as an arbiter settling disputes between persons who appealed to him.[49] He pronounced sentence of the law on delinquents against whom charges were brought by private persons. His business was to pass decrees merely on the opinion of others.[50] The *qâzî* could decide all cases involving civil and criminal law.[51]

Muslim jurists did not recognize the distinction between civil and penal, personal and other divisions of law. They considered the *qâzî* competent to administer in his court every branch of law. The existence of customary usage and group tribunals, however, imposed many limitations upon the range of their functions. The limitation of a more serious nature resulting in the weakening of judicial administration was the abuse of penal authority by military and administrative officers, who, without the necessity of a trial, ordered punishments. In Muslim countries like the Turkish Empire the rulers tried to put down these practices and also their evil results by empowering the *qâzî* to administer justice according to the Islamic law. The military and police authorities, however, again resorted to arbitrary conduct and showed complete indifference to human life.[52]

The courts were held in official buildings specifically meant for the purpose. The *qâzî* at Agra used to hold his court in the *katchery* situated outside the gate of the Fort. The gate came to be known as the *katchery* gate.[53]

There was a judge's court inside the Fort palace of Shahjahan at Delhi.[54]

According to Manrique, the *katchery* was also termed as *chabûtrâ*.[55]

The *qâzî* was concerned not only with the settlement of disputes, but with civil contracts also.[56] In respect of criminal cases he had a wide field to his discretion under the king's instructions.[57] The *qâzî* and his *nâib* acted as notary public, registrar, procurator, officiated at marriages of notables, and looked after the property of orphans and minors.[58] He was also concerned with the administration of religious foundations.[59]

The business of the *Shar'î* courts was extensive and complicated. Even then there was no provison by law and usage for more than single judge in each court.[60]

Decison of the first court was regarded as final. No one court in theory had a higher status than another, though such a court did exist in Egypt. Taking of one case for re-trial in another court was strictly contary to Islamic law.[61]

Evidence—The *qâzî* was to announce judgment on the evidence of two witnesses. The evidence was in general to be oral.[62] Testimony of close relations was generally not accepted, nor that of a master in favour of a slave. Evidence of two women was equal to one man and that of non-Muslims was admitted occasionally though grudgingly.[63]

Two witnesses were required to testify the real existence of a disputed undertaking. The *qâzî* must give unlimited credence to their evidence, both in civil and criminal cases. Every man could not be a witness. It was the duty of the *qâzî* to draw up a list of men whose perfect probity in the legal sense. (*'adâla*) has after investigation been vouched for by a person whom he trusts. Persons thus chosen were then alone qualified to give evidence before the *qâzî*.[64]

The two legal witnesses came to fill the role of assessors of the *qâzî* and occupied the position of counsellors. In certain circumstances, in criminal cases, for example, the *qâzî* might be compelled to accept the evidence of eye-witnesses, even of women.[65]

The principles regarding witnesses, though respectable, 'sometimes amounted in effect to a denial of justice, especially as the taking of oath was very lightly regarded in all except pious circles.' A more frequent abuse was the suborning of false witnesses. In Egypt, provisions were made 'to prevent such miscarriage of justice through the manoeuvres of dishonest persons on pain of the *kâdi's* dismissal and punishment.' The conduct of certain judges towards litigants was not always above reproach.[66]

Manucci has remarked that in spite of Aurangzeb's "exertions to be justice-loving, his kingdom is over-run with men whose only profession is to act as false witnesses or to forge signatures."[67] Tavernier observed that witnesses could always be had 'in great numbers, at a cheap rate, and never punished."[68]

Qâzî's Remuneration—The *qâzî* was paid for his work. Although the law forbids him to accept any present, yet the acceptance of gifts by the *qâzî* was a common practice.[69] Later on he was given a salary.[70]

The *qâzîs* had ample means at their disposal to amass wealth which they did not grudge to utilize.[71]

Usually the *qâzîs* did not enjoy good reputation. In handbooks of the law of all times 'the *qâzîs* of our times' are represented as unscrupulous beings whose unreliable judgments were chiefly directed by their greed.[72]

'Bad *qâzîs* were there always in all times and most *qâzîs* were corrupt and ignorant.[13]

The same was true in Mughal India. The contemporaries are one in their opinion as to the covetousness of the *qâzîs*. Money was their main consideration. Those who could appease their greedy natures, were sure to receive favourable decisions. Aurangzeb's first Chief *Qâzî*, 'Abdul Wahab Borah, was notorious for corrupt practices and within sixteen years of his office had accumulated a fortune of over 33 lacs of rupees. Mohammad Rashid, the corrupt *qâzî* of Burhanpur, was removed from his post and put under arrest on account of corrupt practices. Legal proceedings were ordered against him in 1681.[74] Some *qâzîs* were known for their honesty. 'Abdul Wahab's predecessor had the courage to refuse the proclamation of Aurangzeb to the throne while Shahajahan was still alive for which he was removed from his post.[75] Sheikh-ul-Islam, son and successor of 'Abdul Wahab, was the rare example of an honest *qâzî*. He showed no concern for the ill-gotten money of his father. Rather he gave away his own share of it in charity. He avoided corrupt practices to such an extent that he refused to accept even the customary presents and gifts from his nearest relations and friends.[76]

Muftis—The *qâzîs* were to be assisted by the *Muftis*. The *muftis* were those who gave the *fatwâ* by a judicial consultation based on one or more precedents. The *mutis* expounded the law and supplied the *qâzî* with fatwâs or decisions.[77] As their usual counsellors were inefficient, the *qâzî* and most Muslims with them, had recourse to a few men who enjoyed a reputation for learning, and who gave legal consultations (*fatwâ*)...Those givers of *fatwâ,* those muftis, became by princely decisons, official interpreters of the canon law.[78] A *mufti* must be acquainted with the *Qur'ân*, the *Sunna, Ijmâ*' and *Qiyâs.* He must be learned in *Hadîs* and in the Muslim works of law besides the *Qur'ân.*[79] He must be a Muslim, chaste and intelligent.[80]

Although the office of the *mufti* carried with it no salary, the *muftis* exacted a fee for delivering *fatwâ* proportionate to the wealth of the petitioner. This was supplemented by income from teaching or other minor religious offices in case of lesser *muftis.* The chief *muftis* in the Islamic countries were granted pensions and administrative posts.[81]

Position of the Qâzî in Mughal India—Like other muslim countries, the *qâzî* held a prominent place in Mughal India as well. The Chief *Qâzî* was appointed by the Emperor and he could appoint his subordinates. The practice of administering justice by the *qâzîs* was the same in the provinces as at the centre. In 1671, Aurangzeb learnt that the *qâzîs* of the province of Gujarat enjoyed holiday for three days in the week, held their court for two days and on other two days attended the governor's *darbâr*. A *farmân* was issued to the Diwân of Gujrat that such a practice was contrary to the convention followed at the centre and in other provinces. The *qâzîs* were ordered to discontinue their previous practice and follow in line with others. They were ordered to have only Friday as holiday, to attend the governor's *darbâr* on Wednesday and hold their court on all the other five days. The Emperor even fixed the timings of the court. The judges were required to sit in their courts for doing justice from two *gharis* after daybreak to a little after mid day and retire to their houses at the time of *zuhar* prayer.[82]

Bernier lamented that the Indian judges were not armed with sufficient powers to redress the grievances of the oppressed subjects.[83] Cases of oppression of the subjects at the hands of the officials and of official corruption do not seem to have worried the *qâzî* much. They had, however, their inalienable sphere of jurisdiction. All the cases that lay under canonical law were to come before the court of the *qâzîs*. Aurangzeb's *farmân* of 1672 throws a flood of light on the working of the *qâzî's* court. There were very few criminal cases which did not engage his attention, perhaps such as those where the criminals were an organized band of robbers or rebels. Against them large armies were sent and the punishment was inflicted at the hands of the royal generals or *faujdârs*. Otherwise, almost all other cases were to be tried in the *qâzî's* court. The crime was to be established by him and the punishment to be carried in his presence. A crime could be established after legal evidence in the *qâzî's* court. He was to inflict appropriate punishment on the robbers and highway robbers. He was to take cognizance of the offences of the adulterers and sodomists, courtesans and drinkers and apostates. He ordered the offenders requiring detention to be taken to the *chabutrâ* of the *kotwâl* and sent for them when their cases were to be tried in his court.[84]

SHAR'Î VAKÎLS

Every *zamindâr* and *mansabdâr, faujdâr* and commandant, used to have a *vakîl*. These *vakîls* represented their cases to the Emperor. The princes royal also had their own *vakils*. There are constant references to the presence and function of these *vakils* in the News Letters of Aurangzeb.

He had, moreover, ordered the appointment of *Shar'î vakîls* who sat with the *qâzî* in his court. Khâfi Khân has termed this as an evil which became current in the Mughal territories.[85]

Vakîls also used to appear in the *qâzî*'s court on behalf of the parties.[86]

OFFICERS AND HOLDING OF COURTS

The Mughal Emperors were particular to see that the governors, *dîwâns* and other officers held their respective courts at fixed times and places. During Aurangzeb's stay at Burhanpur in September 1681, it was brought to his notice by Sayyid Sharf Khan Bayu'ât that Mohammad 'Ali Khan, *Khân-i-Sâmân,* did not sit in the court (*'adâlat*) and did his office work in his house. The Emperor declared this to be irregular and ordered both Sharf Khan Bayutât and Mohammad 'Ali to do the office work in the court.[87] (*'adalât.*)

On 12th June, 1693, it was reported that officers at Odni (renamed Imtiazgarh) did office work sitting in their houses. An order was sent to Raja Anup Singh commandant and *faujdâr* of the place, to do the office work sitting at one place and at the gate of his house.[88]

A report was received from Hoshangabad on 17th May 1695, that Mohammad Khan Bîjâpuri, *faujdâr* of the place, did not come from his house to offer Juma prayers; nor did he hold the court. Bahrahmand Khan, the Chief Bakshi, was asked to write to the said Khan that he must always be particular in holding the court.[89]

On 23rd March, 1702, it was brought to the notice of Aurangzeb in the *Dîwân-i-Mazâlim* that a provincial *dîwân*, Mir Kalân, was doing office work at his house. His plea was that he was not strong enough to come to the court. Ruhullah Khân, the Chief Bakshi, was ordered to write to the governor of the province in this connection.[90]

OATH-TAKING

Thevenot found in Surat the prevalence of oath-taking in civil cases. If a person sued another for debt, 'he must either shew an obligation, produce two witnesses, or take an oath.' A Christian swore upon the Bible, a Muslim upon the Holy *Qur'ân,* and a Hindu upon a cow. The Hindus however, avoided taking the oath. Most of them chose rather to lose their case than to swear, 'because they who swear are reckoned infamous among them.'[91]

TRIAL BY ORDEAL

Trial by ordeal was common in civil and criminal cases in India. The common form was the ordeal by fire, but more common was ordeal by water. Thevenot found this sort of ordeal prevalent in Cochin. There was a small tank on the river side where crocodiles were kept. The accused was required to cross the tank on the back of a crocodile. If he was truthful, the crocodile brought him back safe. If he had told a lie, it carried him in the middle, took a dive under water with the man and drowned him. Thevenot had heard this story from the people though he did not find the crocodile in the tank during his visit to the place.[92]

Agra to Surat : April 1633. On the way a number of mountainous thieves attacked Mundy's men and killed one of them, Piru, by hitting an arrow through his neck. Others, thinking them many fled away. (It was dark). Next morning, his men brought and buried him. The thieves took also another of his party and got from him his arms and clothes, i.e., sword and buckler, shash, coat, dupatta, girdle, breeches and shoes. Mundy complained to the Raja of the place, who brought with him the Chief of the next town. As the incident had taken place at night and there was no proof thereof, Mundy suggested to the Chief the trial by ordeal. 'It was concluded that those whom we thought Culpable should thrust their Armes into hott BOYLINGE oyle', and if they were guiltless, no harm would come to them from the boiling oil. 'This belike is the countrie manner of Try all in doubtfull matters'. But it was not put into execution.

ff. Trial by ordeal was recognized in early Hindu law. the ordeal of boiling oil was used only for persons of inferior degree. See Crooke, Things Indian, vs. Ordeals.

The penal code for the Hindus appears to have been the same as for the Muslims. In the villages, however, criminal as well as civil cases were decided by the village *panchayats* and also the revenue cases.

Sir Henry Eliot has given an apt description of the *Panch* and *Panchâyat* courts as they existed before the introduction of the Indian Penal Code in 1861. That naturally may have been the continuation of the Mughal system of the rural administration in India. The learned author remarks that though the origins of the *Panchâyat* are lost in antiquity, its popularity has remained unimpaired throughout the ages. The popular saying in India was that is "in the *Panch* there is God." The *Panch* consisted of five persons, of the same village, or of the same caste and rank in life as the parties concerned. Prior to 1861, the district officers, particularly in the Punjab, utilized to a great extent and advantage the institution of the *Panch* not only for criminal, but for civil and revenue suits. The plainiff and the defendant named two men each, and exercised the right of challenging the other's nominees. "The magistrate or other presiding officer then chose a head or *sarpanch;* the point in dispute was clearly stated to the *panch,* all the necessary papers were handed over to them, and they were sworn to decide fairly and honestly, and to return a judgment in a certain number of days. The particular value of this mode of trial was that in intricate points of native customs, often depending upon a state of feeling which it was difficult for the English officer, as being a foreigner, to enter into, the members of the *panch* were thoroughly at home in their subject and were able to give due weight to a variety of minor considerations which none but a native could perfectly understand. Even in the older provinces, where the regulations are in force it is found at times convenient to have recourse to this time-honoured method of decision, and the result is so satisfactory, that one is tempted to wish it were more largely resorted to."[93]

Tavernier perhaps was referring to the administration of the *Panchâyats* when he remarked : "In Asia, if justice be ever administered, it is among the lower classes, among persons who being equally poor, have no means of corrupting the judges.'[94]

CASES OF THE FOREIGNERS

According to an agreement of 1618 between Prince Khurram, the Mughal Governor of Gujarat, and Sir Thomas Roe, the English Ambassador at Jahangir's court, the East India Company had been permitted to decide cases of dispute between the English themselves.[95]

Nicholas Withington was accused of wronging the Company and was ordered to be brought in chains from Agra to Ajmer by two Englishmen and presented before Mr. Edwards, "our would-be ambassador."[96]

PUNISHMENTS : MUSLIM LAW

According to Muslim law, there are two categories of crime. The first includes crimes of human and private nature and are subject to the law of talion and ransom. In the second category are the crimes of theft, brigandage, extra-marital sexual relations, apostacy and wine drinking. In neither case will the penalty wipe out the offence. It may, however, be expiated by a course of conduct *kaffârâ* which no earthly authority can enforce.[97]

In Muslim law, punishments are divided into *Hadd, Qisâs, Diya and Ta'zîr.*[98]

Hadd—Hadd signified boundary or limit, barrier or obstruction. In the *Qur'ân,* it is always found in plural, meaning the limits laid down by God, i.e. the provision of the Law.[99] *Hadd* is that punishment which has been exactly defined in the *Qur'ân* or the Hadis by the Prophet.[100] This is an unalterable punishment prescribed by canon law and is considered *haqq allâh* or right of god.[101]

Under this category were included the crimes of adultery, fornication and false accusation of adultery (*qazf*), apostacy, drinking of wine, theft and highway robbery.[102]

The *Qur'ân* declares all extra-material sexual relations to be criminal. For *muhsans* or adulterers who had lived in the bonds of legal matrimony, and for sodomists, lapidation was the punishment. For fornication (sexual) relations between unmarried persons) the offender had to receive one hundred strokes of the whip.[103]

In practice, however, the law of *zinâ'* could not be operative because it was not easy, as required by the *Qur'ân,* to prove the charge. Four witnesses were required to give evidence that they were present when the act charged was committed and a false informer was liable to a penalty of hundred strokes of the whip himself.[104]

The false accusation of a married person with adultery was known as *qazf* for which the offender was awarded eighty stripes.[105]

For theft (*sariqah*) an offender had to lose his right hand, for robbery (*qatu'l-tarîq*) both hands and feet, and for robbery with murder he was awarded death punishment.[106]

Although for apostacy no legal, *hadd* or *Qur'ânic* punishment was prescribed, yet it was punished with death.[107] An apostte or *murtadd* could be excused if the crime was violently forced on him and he remained faithful at heart.[108]

Drinking of wine was a crime meriting punishment.[109] According to the Sunnites the offender was to receive eighty strokes of the whip and the Shi'tes prescribed forty.[110] During the 'Abbâsids, it was a favourite drink both at the court and in the city.' In the history of Muslim social life the campaign against wine is one of the repeated themes of reformers, who, in the name of the *hisba,* seek out the drinkers and break their jars.[111]

These offences being against God, the offender could hope for

His mercy. The judges were advised to give every opportunity to the criminals to clear themselves and not to press them further if they could deny the deed and refute the accusation.[112]

Qisâs—*Qisâs* means retaliation. It was of two kinds. *Qisâs fi'l-nafs* or blood vengeance which is applied in cases of killing. The other is called as *Qisâs fi-ma dun al-nafs* and applied to cases which do not prove fatal.[113]

If a person committed a wilful murder or inflicted a wound which did not prove fatal, he was liable to *qisâs* or retaliation. *Wali* or next-of-kin of the slain person, had the right to kill the offender under certain circumstances and under the supervision of the judge.[114] The judge had to see that the slain person was not a descendant of the slayer and that the murderer was in full possession of his faculties and had reached the age of discretion. *Qisâs* took place only if the next-of-kin demanded it. In case there are more than one claimant for the blood of the offender, all must be unanimous in their demand.[115]

Although the punishment was fixed by the law, it could be remitted by the person offended or by the heirs of the murdered person.[116]

According to Abu Hanifa, the avenger of blood was allowed to behead the offender with the sword or a similar weapon. For slaying in another fashion, he was punished with Ta'zir. Al-Shâfi'î and Malik advocated the killing of the murderer in the manner in which he had killed his victim.[117]

In occasions affecting life, retaliation is incurred by wilfully killing a person whose blood is under continual protection, such as a Muslim or a *zimmi,* in opposition to aliens who have an occasional or temporary protection. Abu Hanifa authorises the execution of a Muslim for the murder of a *zimmi,* although Shâfi'î disputes this. A free man is slain for a free man and a slave for a slave. A man is slain for a woman, an adult for an infant, and a sound person for one who is blind, infirm, dismembered, lame or insane. A father is not to be slaim for the murder of his child, but the child is slain for the murder of his parent. According to Abu Hanifa retaliation occurs if a man drowns another in water, though his two disciples do not agree with him.[118]

No retaliation was to incur if any bone excepting the tooth was broken and in offences short of life between a man and a woman, a free person and a slave, or one slave and another slave.[119]

In cases of retaliation short of life, a hand was cut off for a hand, a foot for a foot, a nose for a nose, and a tooth for a tooth.[120]

If the murderer escaped death punishment at the hands of the avengers of blood, he had nevertheless to pay compensation or blood-m l oney.[121]

Diya—*Diya* means 'a sum extracted for any offence upon the person, in consideration for the claim of *Qisâs,* or retaliation, not being insisted upon."[122] *Diya* or *Aql* was compensation paid by one who had committed homicide or wounded another.[123]

In case the legal conditions necessary to render the *qisâs* possible were not present, or when the heirs of murdered person entered into a composition with the murdered for a certain sum, retaliation was remitted for *diya* or blood-money.[124]

The indemnity for the murder of a man was fixed by the Sunna at a hundred she camels.[125] The camels were to be of definite condition and age, ranging from one to four years.[126] The *diya* for a crime committed against a woman was half of that given for a man. The *diya* of a Jew or a Christian was one-third of a Muslim's.[127]

There was no *diya* for a minor or an insane person. The law of retaliation held good between slaves as between free persons.[128]

A Muslim was not to be put to death for an unbeliever unless he had killed him treacherously.[129]

Women and children were not liable to pay diya.[130]

There was a complete fine for the destruction of a nose, or a tongue, or a virile member or for tearing out the beard, for eyes and lips, and for destroying the beauty of a man's person.[131]

Ta'Zîr—Literally *tazîr* means 'to censure or repel'. This punishment, intended to reform the culprit (*li'l-tashhîr*), was not known to the Qur'ân and found its way into Muslim law at a comparatively later date.[132] According to *fiqh*-books, *Ta'zîr* was inflicted for such offences which had no *hadd* punishment or *kaffârâ* prescribed for them, whether it was a question of disobedience of God or of crime against man.[123]

The main object of this punishment being reformation, the degree of punishment varied with the social status of the accused.[134] According to one writer, men were classified systematically for this purpose : 'In the case of great men and notabilities it was discreet warning uttered by a delegate of the *qâzî; fuqha* and such like were called into his presence and admonished; merchants went to prison, and the common people received the lash.[135]

While awarding punishment for this crime, the judge exercised his own discretion. It could be any thing from a public reprimand to whipping or banishment. In case of the divine law he could even remit the *ta'zîr,* but not in case of crime against man.[136]

Personal confession by the offender or the evidence by two witnesses could be sufficient ground for awarding the punishment.[137]

This punishment left vast discretion in the hands of the *qâzîs* and provided opportunity to the offenders to win them over by bribery. In order to curtail the powers of the judges, Muslim rulers devised ways to lay down definite punishments for a series of offences.[138]

MUGHAL PRACTICE

In Mughal India provincial governors and other executive officers were not allowed to inflict capital punishment in an arbitrary manner. A *farmân* of Akbar in 1582 forbade the provincial governors to award death punishment without his permission,[139] although Manucci observes that the governor was empowered to confirm death sentences.[140] When Akbar himself acted as a judge, the guilty was given death penalty only when the order had been issued for the third time.[141] By an order of Jahangir no person against whom death sentence had been pronounced, was to be executed, until sunset. Jahangir once issued orders for the remission of capital punishment of an offender, but before the second and revised orders reached, the criminal had already been executed. It was to avoid the repetition of such an incident that he felt the necessity of giving the above orders.[142] Jahangir had reserved to himself the authority of awarding the capital punishment. Making of eunuchs was declared by him a capital offence.[143]

Thevenot, who visited India in 1666 observed that no civil or criminal judge was authorized to put any offender to death. That power was reserved by the king to himself. The case of a criminal deserving death was referred to the king through a special messenger and the punishment was executed only on receipt of his confirmation.[144] This is fully confirmed by Ovington (138) and Mirât-i-Ahmâdi (op. cit. Saran p. 388).

Death penalty could be inflicted by hanging, beheading, and impaling. Execution could take place by throwing a man down from the roof.[145] Another common method was to get the criminals trampled under the feet of elephants. Shahajahan kept an official with several baskets full of poisonous snakes for punishing the guilty.[146] Terry asserts that, among other forms of punishment, malefactors were stung to death by snakes.[147] He has quoted an instance of the punishment having been inflicted for matricide while he was at Ahamadabad. Jahangir had been much troubled about making the punishment fit the crime.[198] Yet another method was to get the criminal torn to piece by dogs. Dâ'ûd Khan, the commandant of Vellore fortess, once ordered that all the thieves caught in the army should be thrown to the crocodiles in the ditch round the fortress.[149] As the Deputy Governor of Carnatic, he kept ferocious Persian dogs which could tear off the criminal to pieces.[150]

Kokla Jât and his companion were executed at the *Chabutrâ kotwâlî* and their bodies were cut to pieces.[151]

Sambhaji and his companion were given the most cruel punishment under Aurangzeb's orders. Their tongues and eyes were pulled out and they were put to death along with ten other associates with utmost torture. The dead bodies and skulls of Sambha and his companion Kab Kalas were stuffed with grass and paraded through important towns and cities of the Deccan.[152]

Impalement was yet another form of punishment. Jahangir had inflicted it on the accomplies of Khusrow in 1606 after his abortive rebellion.

Some time an imperial officer abused his authority and inflicted a most cruel sort of death penalty. A rare ape in the possession of Dâ'ûd Khan, the deputy Governor of Carnatic, died on account of the neglect of the servant. Dâ'ûd Khan became furious, caused the servant to be put to death by driving a stake into his anus until it came out at his neck.[153]

Other forms of punishment were mutilation, flogging, banishment, imprisonment, fines and confiscations, forfeiture of rank and title, forbidding the court and dismissals.

Mutilation was also one of the penalties in Mughal India particularly for notorious and habitual robbers and rebels. The Bihar Governor Afzal Khan defeated the rebel *faqîr* who had assumed the name of Khusrow, captured him and then tore him to pieces limb by limb. By this he earned the displeasure of Jahangir. He disapproved the death penalty of a man, who, though a rebel, had expressed filial relationship with the Emperor.[154]

As mentioned elsewhere in this book, Jahangir while staying in Ahmadabad, had ordered the thumbs of the servant of Muqarrab Khân, the Governor, to be cut off. His fault may not seem very serious to us. he had simply cut down some *Champâ* trees alongside the river.[155] In the beginning of his reign Jahangir had forbidden the cutting of the noses or ears of any person.[156]

The French traveller of Aurangzeb's reign, Thevenot, is of the opinion that 'the custom in most countries of the Indias' is mutilation of both the hands for theft.[157] A *qâzî* of Aurangzeb's is said to have remarked: "In the department of justice, I award some people in accordance with Shari 'law the punishment of retaliation and on others I inflict the punishment of amputation of hand and other forms of chastisement."[158]

BANISHMENT to Mecca, Bhakkar and Bengal was a usual form of punishment in Mughal India. Humayun had punished both 'Askari and Kamran by ordering them as exiles to the Holy city of Mecca. In Akbar's time the same punishment was meted out to a number of persons including Bairam Khan and Mulla Pir Mohammad Sherwani, though in their case it was not implemented.

When the Hindus of Thânesar complained to Akbar against Hâjî Sultân for his offence of cow-slaughter, he was banished to Bhakkar.[159]

The same punishment was meted out to Sheikh Husain, grandson of Khwâjâ Muin-ud-din of Ajmer, for his unbecoming behaviour.[160]

When it was discovered that several officers had not maintained the required number of troops after the passing of branding regulation, akbar punished them by transferring them to Bengal.[161]

Shahjahan once ordered the banishment of an ordinary soldier when he wrongfully usurped the wife of a Hindu clerk.[162]

IMPRISONMENT

Although imprisonment was a very usual form of punishment in Mughal India, there were no specific rules fixed for it. That must have gone hard for the majority of prisoners. There used to be three 'noble-prisons or castles' in Mughal India. One was at Gwalior, second at Ranthambor and the third at Rohtas. Criminals condemned to death punishment were usually sent to the fort of Ranthambore. They met their death two months after their arrival there. The 'governor then bringing them to the top of the wall and giving them a dish of milk, which having drunk, he is caste down thence on the rocks."[163] To this place 'are sent traitors who are condemned to die. They make them drink a great quantity of milk and throw them down from the top of the castle upon the declining side of the hill, which is full of sharp pointed craggy stones, that tear the bodies of the wretches, before they can reach the bottom of the precipice."[164]

GWALIOR FORT

30.12.1630 : Mundy reached there on his way from Surat to Agra. Here in the fort the king kept his noblemen as prisoners ('such as deserve it'), from where they hardly got out again.

Mundy, II, p. 61.

The Gwalior fort was reserved for the 'nobles that offend'. To Rohtas were sent those nobles who were condemned to perpetual imprisonment, from whence 'very few return home'. Princes of royal blood were often sent to this place.[165]

Occasionally, the prisoners were transferred from one place to another. On 27th October, 1692, a *farmân* was issued through Siâdat Khân in the name of Shujâ'at Beg, the *faujdâr* and commandant of Asirgarh, to the effect that prisoners there be transferred to the fortress of Gwalior.[166]

According to Muslim law, the *qâzis* were supposed to visit the prisons and inquire into the conditions there, and release those who showed signs of repentance. Usually, however, they neglected their duty. The only redeeming feature for the prisoners was that orders for their release were issued on special occasions. These occasions were birth of a crown prince, recovery of the Emperor or any of his sons from long illness, or some occasional royal visit to a prison fortress. On the birth of Prince Salim, Akbar ordered that all the prisoners in the imperial dominions who were confined in the fortresses for 'great accounts' were to be released.[167]

Soon after his accession, Jahangir ordered the release of all those persons who had been imprisoned for a long time in the forts.[168] In 1610, he released some of the prisoners in the Gwalior fortress.[169] Six years later while he happened to pass by the fort of Ranthambor, he decreed that some of the prisoners confined there be set free.[170] In 1618, he inspected the condition of the prisoners in that fortress. the person confined there were produced before him to enable him to look into all individual cases. With the exception of those who had been convicted of serious crimes like homicide, he freed them all and to 'each one in accordance with his circumstances gave his expeses and dress of honour.[171]

RELEASE OF PRISONERS

Shahjahan after his accession, visited Gwalior fort and investigated the cases of the prisoners there. With the exception of those who had been kept in permanent confinement in accordance with the Shar'i law, all others were ordered to be released.

Muntakhib-ut-Tawarikh, II, p. 27 (Text).

Shahjahan had issued standing instructions that whenever he

passed by a fort, the cases of the prisoners there should be brought to his notice. When in the beginning of his reign he visited the fort of Gwalior, he ordered the release of all the prisoners there excepting those accused of very serious charges.[172] In the eleventh year of his regin, when he again happened to pass by that fort, he inspected the cases of the prisoners there, found only eleven with sentences of long duration and set them free.[173]

On the occasion of the celebrations of recovery from illness of the favourite princess, Begum Sâhib, Shahjahan ordered the release of prisoners in 1638.[174]

Mehdi Khan, commandant of the Sholapur fortress, sent Aurangzeb a message through Khwâjâ Yâqût, the royal Superintendent of Gardens, that no body had cared to inquire into the conditons of the prisoners kept there. The Emperor ordered the *Dârogha* to inquire and report.[175] In 1703, Aurangzeb ordered the release of all the prisoners there excepting one *faqîr.*[176]

Writing about Golconda that lay outside the Mughal dominions in September 1652, Tavernier records that it was the custom in that country not to keep a man in prison; 'but immediately the accused is taken, he is examined and sentence is pronounced on him, which is then executed without any delay.'[177]

When prisoners were taken to the prison, they were usually 'loaded with iron fetters on their feet and shackles on their necks.'[178]

For temporary confinement there were police lock-up in the cities termed as *Chabûtrâ-i-kotwâlî*. There are frequent references in the News Letters of Aurangzeb about the confinement of thieves, robbers and even guilty officers in these lock-ups. The officer-in-charge of the *Chabûtrâ-i-kotwâlî* used to be the Mushrif. There is a reference in a news-letter to the death of Bahadur Singh Mushrif of *Chabûtrâ-i-kotwâlî*, in November, 1693.[179]

One redeeming feature for the prisoners was the possibility of their release on bail.

Mohammad Amin Khan, the governor of Lahore, put Manucci in prison on a made-up case of theft. The governor-designate, Fidâi Khân, issued orders for his release. Manucci was told by the *kotwâl* that in spite of the orders, he was required to produce bail in accordance with the provisions of the law.[180]

When Manrique was arrested, his release was secured by a Muslim merchant of Midnapur on furnishing bail.[181]

Tapidas, an employee of Ruhullâ Khân, had been placed in

custody for having furnished surety for Ganga Ram, the *mutasaddi* of Khân Jahân Bahâdur, who had disappeared. On 11th August, 1681, Tapidas petitioned the Emperor through Asad Khan that it was not possible for him to trace and produce Ganga Ram while he himself continued in the lock-up. He would be able to go in for search only if he were set free. The Emperor agreed to release him in case he gave a security. Ten days later Ruhullâ Khân submitted that Tapidas had given an undertaking for the repayment of the entire amount due from Ganga Ram. The Emperor asked for a written bond which Tapidas refused to give. So he had again to go back to jail.[182]

The emperor accepted on 25th October, 1693, the surety of Mohammad Badî' Balkhi for Mohammad Ahsraf, son of Khushâl Beg, detained in Bijapur.[183]

Gobind Rai had been imprisoned at the *chabûtrâ kotwâli* on charge of forgery. He represented to the Emperor in writing that he was innocent and should therefore be released. His release was ordered on condition he produced a security.[184]

Nasrullâ Khân, governor of the province and commandant of the fortress of Bijapur, had been ordered to send to the court Rahmdâd prisoner. He reached there on 30th July, 1694. The Emperor ordered that he could be released in case he furnished a security.[185]

Bakht Buland, the *zamindâr* of Deogarh, had been dismissed and confined at the *chabûtrâ kotwâli.* The Emperor decreed that if the accused could give a trust-worthy surety, he be removed from the *chabûtrâ kotwâli,* handed over to Bahramand Khân and paid an allowance of two rupees daily.[186]

On 2nd December, 1703, orders were issued for the release of Saifulla, zamindâr of Rajorkah and confined in Haklobar, on condition that he gave a security.[187]

Tashhir was one of the punishments resorted to in ancient and continued in Mughal India. This punishment is mentioned in the Institutes of Manu. The guilty (woman) was mounted on an ass and paraded through the public streets. In Muslim history, Caliph 'Umr had inflicted *tashhîr* on a false witness in addition to the award of forty stripes. In Muslim histor in India, it was first inflicted on Saif-ud-din Ghori. His face was blackened and he was seated astride on a bullock with his face towards the tail. He had to endure the insults of the mob, was then tortured and finally beheaded.[188]

This punishment was inflicted on the offenders in Mughal India too. After the unsuccessful revolt of Khusrow in 1606, his two associates,

Hussain Beg and Abdur Rahim, were sewn in skins of an ox and ass respectively, with horns obtruding. They were seated on asses with faces turned to the tail and paraded through the streets of Lahore.[189]

In 1607, another plot was engineered by Khusrow's partisans to kill Jahangir. It proved abortive, however. One of the ring-leaders, Abdul Fateh, was seated on an ass with his face turned to the tail and paraded from place to place.[190]

Imperial officers, Sheikh Banârsi and Giâs Zain Khân, who had failed in their duty to suppress the revolt of Qutb in Patna at that time, were summoned to the court by Jahangir. Their heads and beards were shaved off, they were dressed in female attire, mounted on asses and paraded through the streets of Agra as a warning and example to all.[191]

Prince Shah 'Âlam inflicted this punishment on a woman in Ujjain for giving a false information about a hidden treasure. He ordered to tear her robe to pieces, mount her on an ass with her face to its tail and parade her through the city. She was then flogged and afterwards released.[192]

This punishment was prevalent in other places also. Thevenot was an eye-witness of this in Qandhar. The people of Qandhar, though great lovers of wine, were prohibited from drinking. 'If a Moore who hath drank wine, commit any scandal, he is set upon an ass, with his face to the tail, and led about the town, attended by the officers of the Cotoual, who beat a little drum, and they are followed by all the children (of the neighbourhood) who hoop and hallow after them.'[193]

IN JAHANGIR'S INDIA PELSAERT REMARK

"As regards the laws, they are scarcely observed at all, for the administration is absolutely autocratic, but there are books of law, which are in charge of their lawyers, the Kazis. Their laws contain such provisions as hand for hand, eye for eye, tooth for tooth; but who will excommunicate the Pope? And who would dare to ask a Governor 'Why do you rule us this way or that way? Our law orders thus'. The facts are very different although in every city there is a kachhahari, or royal court of justice, where the Governor (amil?), the Diwan (revenue official?), the Bakshi (Faujdar?), the Kotwal and the Kazi. (The terms are misleading). Here all disputes are disposed of, but not until avarice has had its share."

Corruption in Courts—all capital cases, such as thefts, murders, or crimes are finally disposed of by the Governor, if the criminals are poor and unable to pay, and the sweepers drag them out to execution with very little ceremony. In the case of other offences the criminals are seldom or never executed; their property is merely confiscated for the Governor and the Kotwal. Ordinary questions of divorce, quarrles, fights, threats, and the like, are in the hands of the Kotwal and the Kazi. One must indeed be sorry for the man who has to come to judgment before these godless 'unjedges'; their eyes are bleared with greed, their mouths gape like wolves for covetousness, and their bellies hunger for the bread of the poor; everyone stands with hands open to receive, for no mercy or compassion can be had except on payment of cash. This fault should not be attributed to judges or officers alone, for the evil is a universal plague; from the least to the greatest, right up to the King himself, everyone is infected with instiable greed, so that if one has any business to transact with Governors or in palaces, he must not set about it without 'the vison of angles', for without presents he need expect very little answer to his petitions.

TRIAL BY ORDEAL

For Criminal and other offences there used to be trial by ordeal. Even for debt cases. The criminal was brought to the side of the fire. On it a cauldron of ladle full of boiling water or oil, most commonly of lead. The ruler or magistrate assisting. First his had was washed clean; an ola, or the leaf of the wild brab-tree, with the accusation against written on it was girt round his waist. Then a solemnly the deity and the culprit was asked to plunge his hand in the cauldron and scoops up the boiling fluid. In case he drew it out unhurt, he was absolved of the charge; otherwise he received the punishment prescribed for the method of purgation was considered so sacred and firmly believed on the Malabar Coast that even some of the Christians and Muslims also had voluntarily submitted their cause to its decision on their own personal experience.

MAINTENANCE OF LAW AND ORDER

The maintenance of law and order was the responsibility of the governor in the province, of *faujdâr* in the district, *thânedâr* in the sub-division and of the *kotwâl* in the cities.

Governor—The governor was known as the *subedâr* or the *tarafdâr*. It was his duty to see that the strong did not oppress the weak. He was required to punish the refractory *zamindârs* and lawless elements, and keep the robbers in prison.[194]

Akbar issued a *farmân* laying down the duties of the *subedârs.*

Faujdar—The *faujdâr* was in-charge of law and order in the district or *sarkâr.* He was to control the rebellious *zamindârs* by a conciliatory policy or overawe them by a show of military force. He was required to destroy their forts.[195]

Thânedâr—In the sub-division of the district the *thânedâr* was responsible for the maintenance of law and order.

Kotwâl—The *kotwâl* was the chief of the city police. In order to guard against unlawful occurrences, the *kotwâl* was to appoint watchmen in every *mohallâ* in the city. The watchmen had to be on duty for the whole night and were required to apprehend thieves and evil-doers. Watchmen were to be appointed at places of entertainment to guard against pickpockets. The *kotwâl* himself was to patrol the streets and lanes and round up the thieves.

The *kotwâl* was required to take bonds from the professional women, dancing girls and liquor-vendors for good conduct and fine them in case they broke the bond.

Abul Fazal has given a detailed description of the duties of an ideal *kotwâl* in the *Âîn* (ii, pp. 41-43). Akbar's famous *farmân* given in the Mîrât-i-Ahmâdi, throws a flood of light on the duties of the *kotwâl.*

The *kotwâl* with the help of the clerks was to make a list of the houses and buildings of every city, town and village in his jurisdiction and take the census of the residents of each *mohallâ* (ward), and of their professions and vocations. He was to appoint a headman (*mîr-i-mohallâ*) who was to act as a spy and informer. In order to guard against possible thefts, the house-holders, while going out, had to inform the *mîr-i-mohallâ* and their own neighbours. It was the duty of the headman and the watchman not to allow unauthorised persons to enter the *mohallâ,* but to keep them separately in the inn. They had to keep strict watch on the entry of thieves and pick-pockets. In case of a theft, it was their responsibility to produce the thief and the stolen property.

The *kotwâl* was to award suitable punishments on those who were found guilty of brewing, drinking and selling wine. He was to receive the reports of the arrival of guests or kinsmen in the *mohallâ.* He was to keep himself informed of the income and expenses of every man in the city and to find out those who spent in excess of their income. He was also to fix the prices of articles and take steps against hoarding.[196] If any person earned money in an irregular manner, the *kotwâl* was to report the matter to the Emperor. The headman of the *mohallâ* was to inform the *kotwâl* of marriages and feasts, births and deaths in his ward. Trustworthy informers in the streets and *bâzârs* and on the fords of the rivers had to keep him informed of the occurrences.[197] Thus the main duty of the *kotwâl* was to keep law and order with the help of armed horsemen and foot-soldiers, to prevent thefts and to take steps against theives, drinkers and public women, to apprehend the criminals, to arrest, imprison and even flog the housebreakers and to perform rounds in the night.[198] He was to be answerable for the theft in his jurisdiction and was required to make compensation for the loss. Manucci has referred to the *kotwâl's* court as well.[199]

REFERENCE

1. Islamic Society and The West, Vol. II, pt. 11, p. 116.
2. De Laet, p. 93 : The Embassy, pp. 89, 104, 435; English Factories, 1618-21, pp. 14-15.
   'The Great Mogul is so absolute that there being no written Laws, his will in all things is law, and last decision of all causes, both civil and criminal. He makes a tyrannical use of this absolute power.' Giovanni Çareri in Indian Travels of Careri, p. 240.
3. Akbar Nâma, III, p. 717, Bev. III, p. 373.
4. *Ibid.* Bev. III, p. 1069: Text, III, 717
   Monserrate's Commentary, pp. 209-12.
5. The Embassy, p. 87; De Laet, p. 93 :
   Early Travels, Hawkins, p. 116; Finch, p. 184.
6. Mughal Administration, 4th Ed., p. 94.
7. Akbar Nâma III, p. 257, Bev. III, p. 373.
8. ***Monserrate, pp. 209-12.***
9. *Ibid.*
10. Early Travels in India, p. 115.
11. *Ibid.*, p. 225.
12. Early Travers, p. 326.
13. *Ibid.*, p. 115-16.
14. *Ibid.*, pp. 184-85.
15. *Ibid.*, (William Hawkins), p. 113;
    (William Finch), p. 184;
    (Nicholas Withington) p. 226; Manucci I, p. 174.
16. Manucci, I, p. 167.
17. *Ibid.*, III, p. 260.
18. *Ibid.*, II, p. 261.
19. *Ibid.*, II, p. 262.
20. Akbar Nâma, III, 88; Bev. II, p. 124;
    Tabqât, II, 285; e, pp. 436-38.
21. Tuzk, II; p. 234; Bev, II, pp. 13-14.

22. Bernier : Travels in the Mughal Empire (Constable), p. 360.
23. Eliot and Dowson VII. pp. 172-73.
    Studies in Aurangzeb's Reign, p. II.
    Mughal Administration, 4th ed. p. 94.
    Early Travels in India, Edward Terry, p. 326.
24. Bernier, I. p. 263;
    Manucci, II. p. 462.
25. Early Travels, p. 326.
26. Mîrât-i-Ahmadi, I, p, 275.
27. *Ibid,* pp. 279-80.
28. Manucci, II, pp. 461-62.
    English Factories, 1637-41, p. 61, Marshall p. 39.
    Ibid., 1656-60, p. 513, *Ibid.,* 1670-77, p. 255.
29. Mîrât-i-Ahmadi, I. p. 282.
30. Bernier, I, p. 268.
31. Thevenot, III, p. 35.
32. Mîrât-i-Ahmadi. I, p. 282.
33. Mîrât-i-Ahmadi, I, pp. 168-69.
    Chabutra was a raised Platform usually rectangular. The word is often used as meaning a 'Court Judicial office' such courts were frequently held in the open air, the officer sitting on a square shaped raised Platform (see manrique p. 424)
34. Badâûnî, II, p. 390; Eng. Tr. (Lowe). II, p. 404;
    Mîrât-i-Ahmadi, pp. 282-283.
35. Manucci, I, p, 292.
36. Jaipur Akhbârât, 49th year.
37. Mîrât-i-Ahmadi, I p. 257.
38. Dictionary of Islam, p. 479.
39. Islamic Society and the West, Vol. I, Pt. II, p. 125.
40. Hurgronje, Mohammadanism, p. III.
41. Muslim Institutions, p. 148.
42. Hurgronje, p. III.
43. Encyclopaedia of Islam, II, p. 606. See also Hedâya, p. 334.
44. *Ibid.,* Hurgronje, p. 11.
45. Muslim Institutions, p. 150.
46. Hurgronje, p. 111.
    Muslim Institutions, p. 151;
    Hedâya, English Translation by Hamilton, 2nd ed. p. 337.
47. Muslim Institutions, p. 152.
48. Islamic Society and the West, Vol. I, Pt. II, pp. 127-28.
49. Muslim Institutions, p. 148.
50. Hedâya, English Translation by Hamilton, 2nd ed. pp. 334-35.
51. Encyclopaedia of Islam, ii, p. 606.
    "The qâzî was the chief judge in criminal suits and tried them according to Islamic laws. All cases between Muslims as well as all suits between

Muslims and non-Muslims came before him."
(Indian Travels of Thevenot p. 290—Notes)

52. Islamic Society and the West, Vol. I, Pt. II, p. 128.
53. Finch, p. 183.
54. Tavernier, p. 79.
55. Manrique, II, p. 160.
56. Encyclopaedia of Islam, ii, p. 607.
57. Islamic Society and the West, Vol. I, Pt. II, p. 118.
58. *Ibid.*, p. 132; Dictionary of Islam, p. 255.
59. Encyclopaedia of Islam, ii, p. 607.
60. Islamic Society and the West Vol. I, Pt. II, p. 132.
61. *Ibid.;* Encyclopaedia of Islam, II, p. 606.
62. Islamic Society and the West, Vol. I, Pt. II, p. 131.
Muslim Institutions, p. 149.
63. Islamic Society and the West, Vol. I, Pt. II, p. 131.
64. Muslim Institutions, p. 149.
65. Muslim Institutions, pp. 140-50.
66. Islamic Society and the West, Vol. I, Pt. II. pp. 131-32.
67. Manucci, iii, 262.
68. Tavernier, i-269.
69. Encyclopaedia of Islam, ii, p. 606;
Dictionary of Islam, p. 255.
70. Muslim Institutions, p. 150.
71. Islamic Society and the West, Vol. I, Pt. II, p. 126.
72. Hurgronje, Mohammadanism, p. 111.
73. Encyclopaedia of Islam, ii, p. 606.
74. Akhbârât-i-Darbâr-i-Mu'allâ, 30.9.1704.
75. Tavernier, I, pp. 356-57.
76. Mughal Administration, p. 98.
77. Dictionary of Islam, p. 367.
78. Muslim Institutions, p. 153.
79. Dictionary of Islam, p. 367.
80. Hurgronje, 111.
81. Islamic Society and the West, Vol. I, Pt. II. p. 137.
Prof. P. Saran is of the opinion that the *mufti* in India was a sort of unofficial legal referee recognized by public opinion and he was not a regular official in the judicial department.
[The Provincial Govt. of Mughals, pp. 344-47. see Sarkar Mughal Administration pp. 26-28 & 114.]
82. Mîrât-i-Ahmadi, I, p. 275.
83. Bernier, ii, p. 253.
84. Mîrât-i-Ahmadi, i, pp. 278-80, 282, 283.
85. Muhtakhib-u-Lubâb, II, Text, p. 252.
86. Akhbârât-i-Darbâr-Mu'allâ, 4th Oct., 1693.
87. *Ibid.,* 6th September. 1681.

88. *Ibid.*, 12th January, 1693.
89. Akhbârât-i-Darbâ-i-Mu'allâ, 17th Sept., 1695.
90. *Ibid.*, 23rd March, 1702.
91. Indian Travels of Thevenot, p. 27. See also Ovington : A Voyage to Surat, p. 138. He confirms the viewpoint of Thevenot.
92. *Ibid.*, p. 124.
According to Achyut Menon there were several forms of ordeal by water. The 'accused had to swim across the ferry at Uzhavam in Cranganur, or that at Pilipuram in Vapin island which used to swarm with crocodiles, and if he escaped unhurt by these creatures he was declared innocent.'
Coachin State Manual pp. 339-40, 377.
Op. Cit, in Indian Travels of Thevenot, p. 326.
Col. H. Temple Drury writes on the oredeal as follows—
'A small pagoda, or heathen temple, stands on the bank of the river, in which two alligators were specially supported their daily food having been thrown into the water in order to keep them there. To undergo their ordeal the accused was compelled to swim across this river and back, which if he refused to do, he was dragged through, holding on with his hands to a boat. If the alligator pulled him under the water, it was considered a sign of guilt, if otherwise, he was released as innocent.'
Life And Sport in Southern India
Op. Cit. in Indian Travels of Thevenot, p. 326.
93. Memoirs on the History, Folk-lore and Distribution of the Races of NWFP by Sir Henry Eliot pp. 279-80.
94. Tavernier-i-269.
95. The Embassy, p. 478.
96. Early Travels in India, Nicholas Withington (1612-16), p. 226.
97. Muslim Institutions, p. 155.
98. Encyclopaedia of Islam, II. pp. 187; 1038.
Ibid., I. 980.
Ibid., I, 710.
99. *Ibid.*, II, p. 187.
100. Dictionary of Islam, p. 153.
101. Encyclopaedia of Islam, II, p. 187.
102. *Ibid.*, Dictionary of Islam, pp. 476-77.
103. *Ibid*, Muslim Institutions, p. 156.
Encyclopaedia of Islam, II, p. 187.
104. Muslim Institutions, p. 156.
105. Dictionary of Islam, pp. 476-77
Encyclopaedia of Islam, II, p. 187.
106. *Ibid.*
107. Muslim Institutions, p. 156.

Dictionary of Islam, p. 477.
108. Muslim Institutions, p. 156.
109. Dictionary of Islam p. 477.
Encyclopaedia of Islam, II, p. 187.
110. Muslim Institutions, p. 156.
111. *Ibid.*, pp. 156-57.
112. Encyclopaedia of Islam, II, p. 187.
113. Encyclopaedia of Islam, II, p. 1038.
114. *Ibid.*
Muslim Institutions, p. 151.
115. Encyclopaedia of Islam, II, p. 1038.
116. Dictionary of Islam, p. 477.
117. Dictionary of Islam, p. 477.
118. *Ibid.*
119. Dictionary of Islam, p. 477.
120. *Ibid.*
121. Encyclopaedia of Islam, II, p. 1041.
122. Dictionary of Islam, p. 128.
123. Encyclopaedia of Islam, I, p. 980.
124. Dictionary of Islam, p. 153.
125. *Ibid,* Encyclopaedia of Islam, I, p. 900.
126. Encyclopaedia of Islam, I. p. 980.
127. Dictionary of Islam, p. 153.
According to the Encyclopaedia of Islam, it was one-half. Encyclopaedia of Islam, I, p. 980.
128. Encyclopaedia of Islam, I, p. 980.
129. *ibid.*
130. *Ibid.*, p. 981.
131. Dictionary of Islam, p. 128.
132. Enyclopaedia of Islam, IV, p. 710.
133. *Ibid.* Dictionary of Islam, p. 632.
134. *Ibid.*
135. Dictionary of Islam, p. 632.
136. Encyclopaedia of Islam, IV, p. 710.
137. *Ibid.*
138. *Ibid.*
139. Akbar Nama, Bev., III, p. 559; Mîrât-i-Ahmadi, I, p. 163.
140. Manucci. III, p. 264.
141. Monserrate, p. 209.
142. Tuzk-i-Jahangiri, II, p. 242; Bev., II, p. 28.
143. *Ibid.*, I, pp. 150-51.
144. Indian Travels of Thevenot. p. 27.
145. Early Travels in India, pp. 305-6; 326; Akbar Nama, II, pp. 173-76; Manucci, i, 131.

146. Manucci, I. pp. 149; 197; *Ibid.*, II, p. 382, *Ibid.*, IV, p. 422.
147. A Voyage to East India, reprint of 1777, p. 354.
148. *Ibid.*, p. 362; Op. Cit. Manucci, IV, p. 422.
149. Manucci, III, p. 487.
150. *Ibid.*, IV. p. 255.
151. Ma'asir-i-'Âlamgîrî, Text, pp. 93-94.
152. Muntakhin-ul-Lubâb, Text II, pp. 388-89.
153. Manucci, IV. p. 256.
154. Bahâristân-i-Ghayabi, I, pp. 89-91.
155. Tuzk-i-Jahangiri, Rogers and Beveridge, I, p. 432, Text, p. 256.
156. *Ibid.*, p. 10.
157. Indian Travels of Thevenot, p. 136.
158. Akhbârât-i-Darbâr-i-Mu'allâ, 4th Nov., 1693.
159. Muntâkhib-ul-Lubâb, III, p. 118.
160. *Ibid.*, p. 300.
161. Akbar Nama, III, p. 148; Tr., pp. 209-10.
162. Manucci, i, p. 233.
163. Early Travels in Idnia, p. 145.
164. Indian Travels of Thevenot, p. 98.
165. Manucci, i, pp. 69; 183; 338; 339; 356; 380;
Manucci, iii, pp. 194; 426;
Early Travels in India, p. 293.
166. Akhbârât-i-Darbâr-i-Mu'allâ, 27th Oct., 1692.
167. Akbarnama, Text, II, p. 345; Bev. I, pp. 404-5;
Frishtâ, II, p. 350;
Badauni, Text, II, p. 120; Lowe, II, p. 124.
168. Tuzk, Text, I, p. 6; Tr., I, p. 10.
169. Tuzk, Tr. I, p. 180.
170. *Ibid.*, I, p. 345.
171. *Ibid.*, II, pp. 59-60.
172. Lâhori, I, p. 245.
173. *Ibid.*, p. 246.
174. *Ibid.*, II, p. 355.
175. Akhbârât-i-Darbâr-i-Mu'allâ; 8th Nov., 1695.
176. Akhbârât (Provincial), 46th year.
177. Tavernier, I, pp. 290-91.
178. Manucci, I, p. 90.
179. *Ibid*, Nov. 1693. (see p. 15 above).
180. Manucci, II, p. 198.
181. Manrique, I, p. 424.
182. Akhbârât-i-Darbâr-i-Mu'allâ, 11th August, 1681; 21st August 1681.
183. *Ibid.*, 25th October, 1693.
184. *Ibid.*, 22th June, 1694.
185. *Ibid.*, 30th July, 1694.

186. *Ibid.,* 5th November, 1694.
187. *Ibid,* 20th December, 1703.
188. Memoirs on the History Folk-lore and Distributon of the Races of NWFP by Sir Henry Eliot, Vol. I, pp. 315-16.
189. Tuzk, I, pp. 84-85; De Laet, 173-76.
190. Tuzk, I, p. 59; Tr. I, pp. 122-23; Iqbal Nâmâ-i-Jahângîrî, pp. 28-29; De Laet, p. 177; Eliot & Dowson, VI, pp. 315-16.
191. Tuzk, I, pp. 84-85; Tr., I, 173; Eliot & dowson, VI, p. 32; Muntakhib-ul-Lubâb, I, Text, p. 261.
192. Manucci, III, pp. 148-49.
193. Indian Travels of Thevenot, p. 79.
194. Hedâyat al-Qawâ'id, pp. 34-36;
Âin, ii, pp. 40-41;
Manucci, ii, pp. 450-51; Cf. Mughal Administration, pp. 55-56.
195. Mîrât-i-Ahmâdi, I, pp. 168-70.
196. Badâuni, Lowe, II, p. 404; Text, II, p. 390.
197. Manucci, II, 420-21.
198. Fryer, i, p. 246; Thevenot, iii, pp. 19-20.
Ovington, pp. 137-38, Manucci, ii, pp. 420-21;
Tavernier, i, p. 447.
199. Manucci; A Pepys of Moghul India, p. 147.

IV
THEFT, ROBBERY AND HIGHWAY ROBBERY

Muslim jurists make a distinction between theft and highway robbery.[1] As we shall see, different punishments are provided for the crimes. It seem, however, that in actual practice theft by single individuals was less prevalent in Mughal India than by groups of individuals operating on a large scale. They would sometime infest the roads, plunder towns, and commit robberies in the countryside. They attacked from their fortresses or from their hiding-places in dense forests and inaccesible jungles. Thus the Mughal Emperors had to take cognizance of organized robbery. This they did by providing severe punishments, sometimes going beyond those sanctioned by Muslim law. Further, they made executive officers responsible for tracing and punishing the thieves and compensating the sufferers.

According to Muslim law, *sarîqâh* signified the clandestine removal of property in the safe custody of another person.[2] Custody implied guarding an article in a house or a shop, or keeping a personal watch over it.[3]

Highway robbers, in the eyes of the law, were persons too powerful for travellers, who fell upon them with some weapons and robbed them when distant from a city.[4] They could only be punished for their offence if they were arrested before they had repented and returned the looted property.[5]

GENERAL CONDITIONS IN MUGHAL INDIA

The medieval Hindi poet, Banârasi Dâs Jain, has in his autobiography, *Ardhakathâ,* referred to the unsafe travel during a pilgrimage in 1580.[6]

Ralph Fitch who visited India from 1583 to 1591, has recorded that there were many thieves at that time. They had no certain abode, and moved from one to another place in the country.[7] While on his way to Akbar's court, the Portugese priest, Father Monserrate, came across a large number of thieves from Surat to Agra.[8] Abdul Fazl has recorded that in 1596 the one lac gold *muhars* that had been sent for the equipment of the army of the south, had remained in Gwalior on account of the unsafe roads.[9] Three years later he again complained about the unsafe condition on the roads.[10]

William Hawkins who was in India from 1608 to 1613 has observed that the abundance of the outlaws and thieves made it impossible for the people throughout the country to move out without great force.[11] Another English traveller, William Finch, came on 25th January, 1610, to Bhâdwâr, between Sûrat and Âgra, and found the town filthy and full of thieves.[12] He further records that from Gwalior to Ahmadabad it was all a "sandy, woodie country, full of theevish beastly men." From Ahmadabad to Cambay also the ways was "sandy, woodie, theevish.[13] The Bay of Cambay was extremely difficult to cross because of very dangerous thieves who looted the people or threw them to the fury of the tide, which comes so swift that ten to one you escape not.[14] In October 1613, Nicholas Withington went to Cambay and purchased commodities worth Rs. 200, "though with greate danger of robbinge."[15] The same traveller remarks that one "may goe as soone from Agra to Sinde as Surat; but there is more theeving, which the Mogoll seeks to prevent."[16] He found the Baluchi outlaws on the highways and on the river, "murderinge such as they robbe."[17]

The governor promised at their departure sufficient guard to conduct them through those territories for fear of robbers on the highways. He provided 25 horsemen and equal number of footmen for the purpose.

He desired them to give a good report about him to the king as he had been disgraced earlier by him for his failure to withstand the attack of the Portugese on Broach.

[The Voyage of Nicholas Downton, 1614-15, pp. 102-103. (the account of Dodsworth)]

Unsafe Journey—In a letter written to the Company from Ahmadabad on December 20, 1614, William Edwards informed them that he had succeeded in bringing 36,000 rials of eight from Surat to that place 'with some charge and hazard by reason of the *multiplicity of robbers in great troupes.*'

[William Edwards in The Voyage of Nicholas Downton, p. 172.]

Unsafe Journey and Encounter with Robbers—On their way

from Surat to Ahmadabad in December 1614, the governor of Broach provided an escort of fity horse and foot to Nicholas Downton and his party, the ways being unsafe for strangers.

[The Voyage of Nicholas Downton, 1614-15, p. 103. (Account of Dodsworth)]

Reaching a small aldea (village), they rewarded these soldiers with 50 mahmudis and gave presents to the captain. From there they were furnished with 50 horse an foot who conducted them to 'Chormondo', 8 kos away, it 'beinge the most theveshest waie in those partes'. They departed from this place with 25 soldiers who proved to be all notorious thieves. They escorted them to a place known as 'Danau', 10 kos further. As it was customary with them, the English pitched their tents in a plain and made a barricade round them with their carts. At supper time all of a sudden 50 horsemen came close upon them and, in case the foreigners were not well provided, they would have assaulted them.

(Ibid., pp. 103-4.)

At Baroda they went to see the governor who gave them the required license to depart and also provided a guard of 100 horse and foot.

(Ibid p. 104.)

Sir Robert Shirley found the way from Thatta to Agra "much infested with thieves."[20] Even the road from Âgra to Lâhore was dangerously full of them.[21] Sir Thomas Roe, the English ambassador to Jahangir's court, refused to agree to the proposal of Prince Khurram, the governor of Gujarât, that the English should not carry arms. That way their caravans, which went from Ahmadâbâd and other parts of the country every year, would be exposed to the danger of thieves and robbers on the way.[22] Things became more unsafe during Shahjahan's revolt. A letter written by the English factors at Ahmadâbâd in 1622 records that there was great danger on the way. It was daily on the increase and it was not possible to travel without the fear of violence at the hands of the thieves and robbers.[23] John Willoughby at Âgra wrote to the Sûrat Factory on 15th April, 1623, that the roads were very dangerous, "for heare is nothinge but killing every these parttes.[24] Yet another letter from Ahmadâbâd to Sûrat says : "Ways are so full of robbers that no one can pass."[25]

(Manrique, ii, pp. 251-52.)

Tavernier makes us believe that theft was rare during Shahjahan's reign. Although he ruled over his subjects as a father over his house and children, he was very strict in the maintenance of order. The police performed their duty with remarkable diligence. Roads were safe from the nefarious activities of the thieves.[26] Manrique was surprised to find the justice and rectitude which the Indians observed in the market places. Property was quite safe and fear from thieves was absent.[27] The great solicitude evinced by Shahjahan, writes Rai Bhara Mal, towards the promotion of the national weal and the resultant tranquillity was instrumental in restraining the people from committing offences against one another and breaking the public peace.[28]

The evidence of Peter Mundy, Mandelslo, and the English Factory records, however, is to the contrary. Mandelslo gives an account of his fight with the highway men, and the Factory records complain about the looting of their caravans. As regards Peter Mundy, our main authority on the subject, we have to remember one thing. Most of the evidence recorded by the traveller revolves round the years 1630-33. The western part of India at that time was in the throes of a terrible famine. Human beings died in their thousands for want of food. Tormented by pangs of hunger, the people grew oblivious of frail human relations. Father distrusted son, child feared mother, brother hated brother, friends became hostile to one another. Mutual confidence had receded into a far corner. Struggle for existence was at its worst. Unable to find for the maintenance of their lives, the inhabitants began to prey upon their fellow beings and did not show any repugnance against taking human flesh. Rather they looked forward to every opportunity to get it by any means.[29] Now, under such circumstances, it is not surprising to find theft or highway robbery as rampant as Mundy declares it to be. Bernier fails to cite particular instances of the crime. He only records that as robberies were often committed, it was prudent always to be on the alert.[30] Robbers, says he, often waylaid and murdered travellers.[31]

Robbers had a free hand during the Wars of Succession. After Dara's defeat and Aurangzeb's occupation of Agra, 'the villagers and thieves were plundering on the highways, and created good deal of tribulation to travellers, robbing and slaying them.'[32] Many of the defeated followers of Dara who fell to the rear in the hope of getting some security and relief, were set upon by 'robbers who plundered every one and killed many.'[33] Bernier who was in India from 1656 to 1668 records that there were frequent cases of robberies in the country.[34]

Things were particualrly not happy during Aurangzeb's reign though Ovington assures us that the Indians in the city of Surat always refrained from heinous crimes such as murder and robbery.[35] The situation grew worse in the latter half of the period. The wars in various places gave the malefactors a free hand in the interor of the country.[36] According to Manucci, thieves infested the whole kingdom, and particularly they abounded in the woods near Burhanpur.[37]

Dr. John Francis Careri, the Italian traveller, who visited India in 1695, remarks that there was no safety in India from thieves, nor were there *caravanserâis* at convenient places for the travellers.[38] The French traveller Thevenot who had come thirty years earlier, had found inns, particularly between Agra and Delhi 'from stage to stage for lodging travellers.'[39] At Burhanpur he saw a spacious and square one, 500 paces long and 300 paces wide.[40]

Manucci has also referred to such *caravanserâis* which accommodated and assured safety to travellers.[41]

Writing about the conditions in the south, Careri observes : 'By a Privilege granted them by their (Queen) they (Nair women) accompany Travellers through those Parts that are infested with Robbers, and if they happen to presume to Rob any Man, they all Meet, and pursue the Felons till they utterly Extirpate them. Thus one Boy with a Rod in his Hand makes it safe Travelling throughout all Canara, tho' it be through woods and over Mountains; and a traveller for a small Matter may have one from one Village to another.'[42]

In his letters, Aurangzeb complained of the bad condition of the roads and of the activities of the highwaymen. He wrote to Prince A'zam that the road from Bahadurpur, near Burhanpur, to Aurangabad was full of danger. Highwaymen fell upon merchants and travellers and looted them of their goods. Wayfarers could not travel in security. When such conditions, lamented the Emperor, existed near his own and A'zam's headquarters, the conditions on the far-off roads must have been appalling.[42a]

In another letter the Emperor wrote that he failed to understand the cause of disorder prevailing in the districts of Hâjipur and Miyânpur. The Kolîs had plundered the town of Mîrganj, situated close to the quarters of the royal army. They bound the inhabitants of the town and carried them away.[43]

Aurangzeb complained that the roads between Chamar Gundeh and Kadirâbâd in the Deccan were in bad condition. Highwaymen prepetrated tyrannies freely, and the travellers found it extremely difficult to traverse the road in safety.[44]

Thevenot records that crafty thieves (or *thugs*) harassed travellers on the road linking Agra and Delhi. They would strangle a man through the agency of a beautiful woman. She used to cast a spell on some innocent traveller and lure him to get her on the horseback behind him. Sitting there she would throw the snare round his neck and strangle him, till her robber companions came to complete the process. Some wily highwaymen would cast a snare round the neck of a traveller from a distance. When Thevenot reached a village seven miles from Broach, he suspected the inhabitants from the manner of their dress to be thieves.[45]

"This is the condition into which the saintly rule of this king has fallen", remarks Manucci flinging a jibe at Aurangzeb's rule. According to him, travellers setting out from his army were not protected against the Marathas and other robbers. If one was lucky enough to be delivered from this peril, he fell into the hands of the customs-officials or publicans. "They take what they please, unjustly and by force, and if they know that any one has money on him, they rob him, cut his throat and bury him."[45a]

In the Deccan wars during the last years of Aurangzeb's reign, roads became unsafe and travelling was dangerous. Travellers setting out from the Mughal army were not protected against the robbers.[46]

Despite the picture drawn by the contemporary European travellers, we are to be on our guard against their generalisations. Those were not the times of adequate communications, and, if a rebel *râjâ* or a disgruntled *mansabdâr* took it into his head to resort to robbery and oppression of the people with a view to pestering the Mughal authorities, he could do so easily and successfully, so long as sufficient forces were not sent against him. Even then the rebels would turn to the mountains where dense forests provided them with inaccessible spots. The failure of the Mughals to surprise and extirpate them can be easily understood if we keep in view similar attempts on our part to deal with the notorious dacoit gangs in these days of vast mechanised forces and improved communications. The travellers who have left us accounts of the unsafe conditions prevailing during Mughal times, forget to mention the situation in their own countries during those days. The conditions there were perhaps worse than they were here. The modern methods of communications and vastly developed machinery have not been able to put an end to the activities of the robbers even in the best administered countries of the world such as the U.S.A. Moreover, the foreign travellers could not always make distinction between the Mughal territory and that of a local chief and the conditions in the latter were usually more disturbed than in the former. There were certain areas, as in these days, which, because of their peculiar situation, were more frequented by robbers.

Manucci has drawn the picture of the contemporary Goa which he visited in the seventies of the 17th century. the conditions in this Portugese colony were horrible, indeed. He found there many houses 'robbed by bodies of masked men entering them.' The merchants closed their shops with the setting of the sun, otherwise they would be plundered. This is because the soldiers and kâffirs, dying of hunger, are forced into such conduct.' The merchants kept the doors of the shops closed, sold their wares and received the payment through the holes in the shop-door.[47]

ROBBER TRIBES

Besides the individual thieves and organized bands of robbers, there were in Mughal times certain tribes notorious for their nefarious activities. They were the Ghakkars, Kathûrs and Dalzaks, Kolîs and Grâsias, Râjputs and Pathâns, Balûchîs and Marâthâs.

Rohtas in the Punjab was the stronghold of the Ghakkars and they inhabited the country around it. They were warlike people much given to theft and brigandage. "They lie in wait for, and intercept free travellers, shave their heads, hamstring them, take them to Persia, and there sell them as slaves."[48] Father Monserrate who came to India in Akbar's time, found them very sturdy, though of medium stature. Jahangir in 1607 described the men of this tribe as 'wonderfully like animals.'[49]

The Kathûrs and Dalzaks who lived in the West Punjab, were notorious for mischief, oppression and highway robbery. On his way to Kabul in 1607, Jahangir found, in the village of Amrohi, beyond Hasan Abdal, about 8,000 households of these tribes.[50]

The Grâsias, who lived in the hills of Malwa, were 'theevish', and often looted caravans. Some hundred of them could have looted a caravan had William Finch (1608-11) not reached there along with their caravan.[51] According to the same authority, the Pathân thieves infested the forests between Lahore and Kabul, 'often sallying from the mountains, robbing caravans and ransacking towns.[52]

According to Nicholas Withington (1612-16), the Rajputs lived by 'robbinge and spoylinge poore passengers by the way.'[3] Pater Mundy has recorded that during Shahjahan's reign, the Rajput highwaymen frequented the country and committed robberies. They most often lived as outlaws in the jungles.[53]

Nicholas Withington found the Balûchîs of Sind mostly robbers who looted and murdered the people.[54]

During Aurangzeb's reign, Kolis, Marâthâs, Râjputs and other plundered and ruined the people in Gujarat.[55]

AREAS WHERE MUGHAL AUTHORITY WAS UNCERTAIN

The European travellers have mentioned that they often had to pass through territories where authority of the Mughal Emperor was uncertain but the robbers made their presence felt.

While on his way to the Mughal court during Akbar's reign, Father Monserrate had to pass through the Satpura range which was full of dense forests. 'The inhabitants of these mountains are always at war with the Mughals'. The robbers killed one of his guards and they could take no revenge against them.[56]

According to Nicholas Withington, between Nagar Parker and Juno (half a days journey from Thatta) lived a people who paid no tribute to the Mughal Government. When any Mughal general came and attacked them, they burnt their own houses which were built of 'straw and mortar' and fled to the mountains. After taking from the travellers what they pleased 'under colour of custome', they guarded them so long as they were in their territory. They considered it a disgrace if any other person from outside looted them.[57]

At another town, Gundajaw, on 9th January, 1614, Withington and sixteen associates along with ten camels were set upon by thieves. They tried to defend themselves and give the thieves a regular fight. They thought it advisable, however, to come to terms with them on payment of five lairs.[58] After travelling for three hours, they were again set upon by many thieves. They treated them in a similar manner and bribed them. At another town, Sarrune, the Rajput chieftain proved very kind to them and entertained them at night in his castle. Next day, along with fifty of his horsemen, the chieftain, in order to guide Withington and his party to the gates of Thatta, misled them to the jungles. There they looted the caravan of goods worth Rs. 20,000. the chieftain ordered his men to tie the camels' ropes round the necks of the three unfortunate merchants and five of their servants who formed part of their caravan. Then they gave such a twist as to strangle all the eight of them. They stripped them naked and threw them together into a hole which they made in the ground. After that they took from Withington eighty rupees that he had upon him and that belonged to the Company, deprived him of his horse, gave him the two horses belonging to the dead persons, and sent him and his men along with four of his, to his (chieftain's) brother, some twenty *kos* away in the mountains. His brother kept them as virtual prisoners for 22 days. After that they had a terrible journey in which his men had to beg food and fodder. At one place the six soldiers who had been sent by one of the chieftains to accompany them, stripped him of a very good apparel of the country fashion and a quilt of *chhints* and of many other things. They deprived his men also of every thing, till they were left only with their breeches. It was on about 5th of March that they reached Parker in a wretched condition. There a merchant of Ahmedabad recognized Withington, felt pity for him and provided him and his men with food, clothes and money and accompanied them upto Paddingpore on 19th March. From Paddingpore Ahmedabad was a week's journey.[59]

During his march from Ajmer to Mandu in 1617 along with Jahangir's army, Sir Thomas Roe found that after crossing the pass of Mukandwârâ, they came to a country full of thieves. It belonged to a Raja, who was not completely under the authority of the Mughals, but was kept under by force. Jahangir attacked their town at night, and made them run to the woods. They 'set upon a company of stragglers behind, slew divers and robbed them'.[60]

CASES OF ROBBERY IN MUGHAL INDIA

AKBAR'S REIGN

During their journey on a pilgrimage from Jaunpur in 1580, the parents of Banarasi Das Jain, the author of *Ardhkathâ,* were completely looted by thieves.[61]

Jamal-ud-din, son of Mahmud Barah, who had a love affair with Siyâh Yamin, a dancing girl at the court of Akbar, fled to the mountains. He collected a force and gave himself up to looting the *parganâs* of the neighbourhood and robbing on the highways.[62]

Mirza Mâ'sum Khafi, an imperial officer under Akbar, had, a year before joining the service, gone to Gujrat, accompanied by a number of companions. They were attacked by robbers on the way. Many of them were killed or wounded and rifled of their belongings. The Mirza himself and his father also received injuries.[63]

JAHANGIR'S REIGN

Nicholas Withington mentions that when he and his colleagues came within four leagues of the bar of Surat, they met with the 'Qzeander', which was one of their fleet anchoring there. It had got a pilot out of a boat of the country, "and left one of our carpenter's mates in hostage for him, whose unwiseleye carryinge some moneys about him, when the moores were from the shippe, they cut his throate and took what he had, as afterwards we were certainly informed."[64]

When Nicholas Withington was in Sind, the Baluchis took a boat in which there were seven Italians and one Portugese fryer. They fought till all of them were slain with the exception of the Portugese. He was taken alive and being very fat, his belly was ripped open by the Baluchi robbers to find out if he was not hiding any gold or jewels there.[65] When Withington went from Ahmadabad to Cambay in 1613, he apprehended on his way a great danger from robbers. At a place named Bareja, the Cambay caravans met on every Tuesday 'for feare of theaves.[66] At one place a man of theirs was lsain an a camel stolen by the thieves. Going further they met a *caravan* from Thatta which had been robbed completely. At the next town, known as Nagar Parker, they met another *caravan,* robbed within two days' journey of Thatta.[67]

When Sir Thomas Roe encamped in Chopra village in November, 1615, he was warned by king's officers against the danger of sleeping outside. There were two hundred thieves in the hills round about. Roe was provided with guard that 'watched all night.'[68]

Thomas Kerridge from Surat informed the English factors at Ahmedabad in a letter of April 10, 1619, that the *rials* they paid on the last bills from Agra, and which were 'beeing dispeeded towards Molies', were stolen by robbers, who had also killed some of the attendants. The loss was upwards of 25,000 *mahmûdies.* The English, however, succeeded in capturing four of the robbers. They 'pitted' three of them 'on so many stakes', and made them pay the penalty with their lives.[69]

An English factor from Masaulipatam wrote, 'My said Bampa was robbed of all, and a peece of hies eare was cut off.'[70]

The Governor of Malwa refused to permit the English *caravan* to depart unless they gave in writing absolving him of all the blame if it were robbed.[71]

An English *caravan* was looted in January, 1619, in the territory of Shah Nawaz Khan, the Khan Khanan's son, between 'Manderbarre and Sundelva. The robders looted 14 'churles' Bayana indigo and killed four or five servants accompanying the carvan. Although the *qâzî* refused to accept the testimony of the camel men', pretending that they were the interested parties, they had lodged the complaint with the Khan Khanan and prayed for compensation and justice. In September 1619, Prince

Shah Jahan ordered the Khan Khanan to compensate the English for the robbery of their indigo.[72]

We learn from a letter of April 11, 1623, from Robert Tottle at Nosari to the English President at Surat that the natives had stolen their butts of *arrack.* They admitted under pressure that they had received two quilts, but denied all knowledge of the chests. Upon their denial the English 'had them whipped tell the skine was of there body', and finding them still obdurate, they sent for their wives and children 'to have them punished to see whether they would acknowledge any thing more.'[73] When they protested their innocence, they were remanded to prison. Robert Tottle again informed the English President in a letter written five days later that it was suspected that the four native peons had emptied one chest of tobacco that had drifted ashore during his absence.[74]

Some time afterwards, a caravan belonging to the East India Company and coming from Ahmedabad, was robbed of three bales, and of a part of the fourth, though they made a stout defence against the robbers.[75]

SHAH JAHAN'S REIGN

Mundy wrote that from Agra to the gates of Ahmedabad was a desert full of thieves. On his way from Surat to Agra, he, along with the caravan, reached a place Viara, which was notorious for its thieves. After a few days they saw the Rajput highwaymen, eleven in number, all on horseback, well armed and provided with guns and swords, lances and arrows. They were robbers in search of a caravan which had gone further into the valley. Nearby lay the bones and skulls of some men, believed to have been killed by these persons. Some days later they arrived at Boadoore. Here they learnt that about 200 horsemen, who, only a short while before, had robbed a whole town, awaited them nearby. On their forward march, their caravan was attacked by a number of thieves. They were successful in carrying away three carts after doing injuries to some of the party.[76]

On their journey from Agra to Cole (Aligarh) Peter Mundy and his party came in December, 1631, to a place called 'Jellesere' (Jelesar). Here they learnt that in the early hours of the morning, certain 'thieves' had carried away two women, four oxen, and six asses that were going towards Agra. This place seemed to them very dangerous on account of robbers.[77]

In August, 1632, they reached a place, Barramal Ka Sarai,

situated between Agra and Patna. One month before a robbery had been committed in the vicinity of 'Ahumolo Sarai'. On inquiry, the goods stolen were discovered in this town. They passed through a little town, 'Roherbuns Ka Sarai'. there they came across a party of men armed with long bows and swords. They were all naked except for a loin-cloth round their waist. These men were called' 'Guares' or 'Rebbells', and forced custom from the travellers, as they did from Mundy's party. On their forward march, they came across more parties of such men as demanded custom from them in an insolent manner.[178]

On his return from Patna to Agra in 1632, Peter Mundy stayed in a *serâi* at Banaras. There some robbers carried away five horses and other goods at night.[79]

At another time Mundy had to go to Agra from Surat. On the way his party came across some robbers in the dark. The robbers aimed shots at them, hit one of the party through the neck to death, stripped him naked and followed others who had taken to their heels. Further, they reached a plain, where a part of a Dutch caravan was assaulted by about sixty robbers, who had carried away some indigo, a few camels laden with goods, and killed one person. On they marched and stayed at a place. There a Koli snatched from a traveller what he had and, when he tried to follow the culprit, the other Koli shot him so hard in the soulder as to make him fall.[80] During their forward march, a number of armed horsemen forced custom from them. Under a tree they found some tombs, all of the same size. They were told that all these belonged to ten Sayyids who had been killed by the Kolis. At another place some 15 thieves set upon their camels grazing in the field. The thieves, when attacked, fled, leaving one behind them. This man, after showing stubborn resistance, surrendered himself. He was brought before the Mughal officer in the city who plainly took his side. At another place they found that the Kolis pillaged the carts of Murari, who formerly was a Government officer at Baroda, and who had much vexed and troubled the Kolis.[81]

In March, 1638, the East India Company complained that a caravan of theirs was looted by the Rajput robbers.[82]

On his return journey to Surat in 1638, the caravan, along which Mandelslo was travelling, was attacked by a band of Rajpt highwaymen. A sharp conflict ensued as a result of which the robbers withdrew. The armed soldiers in the caravan took part in the conflict, as also did Mandelslo and the English merchants with him.[83]

The way from Agra to Thatta in 1639, for a distance of 40 *kos*, was very dangerous owing to a tribe at variance with the Mughals.[84]

The English factor at Broach was expecting a caravan from Ahmedabad in May 1647. He was anxious to make provisions against the highwaymen, who, only a few days before, had looted a caravan nearby.[85]

During the Wars of Succession, when Dara, after his defeat at Samugarh, fled to the Punjab, Manucci also decided to follow him with a party. On the way the traveller lagged behind his companions due to the delay which the cart-driver made in a village. something terrible met his eyes, when his cart entered into a wood. The greater number of the party were heaped together, either wouned or decapitated, and all robbed and ruined. The few who survived had been stripped naked.[86]

AURANGZEB'S REIGN

In a letter to Asad Khan, Aurangzeb recorded that Mu'tamid Khan's *jagir* had been ruined by robbers.[87]

Two Frenchmen who came to visit Aurangzeb's court failed to gain an access thereto. On their way back they were robbed, and one of them was wounded also.[88]

Thevenot who visited India in 1666, found the road from Cambay to Surat dangerous on account of robbers. His friends advised him to take with him a *Châran* along with a woman of his tribe till he was out of danger. The *Chârans* were found all over Gujarat and acted as guards to travellers and goods. If any robber dared to come near, the *Châran* informed him that the traveller was under his charge and in case he (the robber) did any mischief, he would cut his own throat. The woman threatened to cut her own breasts with a razor. The persons of the *Chârans* were held as sacred and it was believed that their blood brought misfortunes on those who caused it to be shed.[89]

Grâsias referred to above, were notorious thieves during Aurangzeb's reign also. While on his way from Cambay to Surat, one *Grâsia* approached Thenenot. His coachman offered him a *pâisa* which the *Grâsia* accepted. Usually they went in troops and one of them being satisfied, others came after upon the same road and wanted satisfaction. His coachman told the traveller that if the least injury was done to him, he would have given the alarm by knocking with his fingers upon his mouth and received prompt assistance from other *Grâsias* in the neighbourhood. Thevenot had to part with half a rupee for another member of the tribe further on the road. The toll 'belongs to the Raja of the country, who is to answer for the Robberies committed within the

Territories.[90]

Mr. Berber, one of the envoys to great Mughal for the concerns of the East Indian Company in France, was robbed of Rs. 31,200 and he demanded this money from the *faujdâr* of Agra. The latter found this astonishing and wrote to the Emperor about the excessive demand made upon him. The envoy warned the *faujdâr* that in case the payment was deferred, there was a likelihood of the demand to be increased as forgotten articles would come to his memory. He also represented his case to the court. The Emperor ordered the *fauzdâr* to pay the envoy Rs. 15,000 by way of compensation. And as he had received physical injuries from the robbers, he was ordered to be paid Rs. 15,000 from the royal treasury.[91] It is interesting to surmise from where the *fauzdâr* could have realised the amount.

It was reported to Aurangzeb on 25th January, 1667, that thefts had ocurred in the city of Shahjahânâbad. Orders were issued to *faujdâr* Fûlad Khân to be very careful.[92]

In Atak, theft had taken place in April, 1667, in the hosue of Tâlib Beg Tehsildar. Orders were sent to Mubarak Khân, *faujdâr* of the place, to investigate and get the property restored to Tâlib Beg.[93]

In June the robbers looted and took away Rs. 25,000. This money was being brought to Gwalior. Letters were sent from the court to different *faujdârs* to exert themselves, chastise the culprits, and get the money back from them.[94]

In July a letter was received from the news-writer of Akbarâbâd about the thefts that had occurred there, the Governor of the province however had written to the contrary. Aurangzeb felt surprised at this and ordered Sayyid Mehdi, the Diwân of the province, to institute an inquiry.[95]

In the same month the relatives of Mohammad Quli Khan were looted of 7,000 *huns* near Akbarâbâd. The *faujdâr* there was ordered to inquire into the robbery and make good the loss.[96]

During the same period the robbers looted merchants of Rs. 16,000 near Nalawari. Abdul 'Aziz han, the *faujdâr* of the area made efforts to find out the clue of the robbers from Nalawari to Faizabad and from there to Panipat and also in the *faujdâri* of Fulad Khan. Hearing this, the Emperor ordered that the *zamindârs* of the area should be sent for and questioned in the royal presence.[97]

On 23rd September a number of Banjârâs petitioned that 200 of their oxen laden with grain had been looted by the robbers near Jaunpur.[98]

In 1688 one Sayyid and twenty Yusafzai Afghans took a house on rent in the capital. The people of the *muhalla* complained to the *kotwâl* that while during the day they kept themselves engaged in gambling, at night they committed theft. They were arrested and put into confinement. On inquiry they confessed that they had committed twenty-four thefts, the proofs of which were also found.[99]

In 1675, a large number of highwaymen, making a force of about 900, plundered a consignment of cloth belonging to the East India Company.[100]

On November 17, 1679, news came from Akbarabâd that the Meo robbers had collected themselves for dacoity near Ferozabad. When the *karorî* and the *amin* of the place prepared themselves to oppose them, they diverted their attention from there and began to loot travellers.[101]

In the same month some persons from the hilly tracts began to loot villages in the *parganâ* of Muradabad. They fled away when Faizullâ Khân, *faujdâr* of Muradabad, collected a force to punish them.[102]

In December, news was received of the occurrence of many thefts in the neighbourhood of Akbarabâd. The Meos committed dacoity in a *serai* where Sheikh Bâzid, the dismissed Bakshi of Orissa, was staying. While on his way to the court, they looted him completely. Moreover, they plundered the treasury of Rohtas and took away 12,000 rupees. The sons of Champat Bundela also committed robberies. The robbers fled away when the Mughal commandant prepared to attack them.[103]

In March, 1680, Sayyid Ibrahim, the *thânedâr* of Sagar, wrote to the Court that a rebel *zamindâr* of the locality had collected a force of 250 persons and committed robberies in the neighbourhood.[104]

It was reported to Aurangzeb on 5th May, 1680, that some gunmen had robbed the fort of Rohtas of a certain quantity of lead. The commandant of the fort took them prisoners and kept them in the fortress. The Emperor ordered that the commandant should realize from the gunmen the price of the lead and then turn them out of the fort.[105]

A letter was written on 14th February, 1681, to Multafat Khan, the *faujdâr* of Akbarâbâd, that frequent reports of thefts had been received from his area. He was forgiven by the Emperor, but was asked to be more careful in the future about thefts.[106] Six days later another robbery took place in the house of a merchant there. Taj Mahammad *Kotwâl* got wounded while fighting with them. The dacoits not only looted the property of the merchant, but killed his seven servants.[107]

News was received on 1st August 1681 by Aurangzeb that Sheikh Abul Makâram, the dismissed *faujdâr* of Mânakpur was deputed by the Governor of Allahabad to Jaunpur after the death of the *faujdâr* of that place. When the Sheikh reached near Jaunpur, the robbers looted him of all his belongings at the time of night.[108]

On 31st August, 1681, a letter was received from Barsar Khan, commandant of Ranthambor, that the rebel Fateh Singh Naroka was indulging in highway robbery. Orders were sent to Sayyid Khwaja Ahmed, *faujdâr* of Shutarpur, and to Rup Singh Hada, *faujdâr* of the other side of the Narbada, to drive away the robber.[109]

On 10th September, 1681, the Emperor ordered on the petitions of Man Singh and Rup Singh Rathor, *faujdârs* of Pur etc., that the Sisodiya Rajputs indulging in highway robbery should be chastised.[110]

During his march from Ajmer to Burhanpur in September 1681, it was reported to Aurangzeb that thefts were taking place in the imperial army. Orders were issued to *faujdârs* and *zamindârs* to guard their frontiers carefully and in case of thefts bear responsibility for the same.[111]

The might of the Mughal armies was required to deal with powerful robbers operating from their strongholds. Among such of them was Gang Singh of Barol who committed highway robbery and spared none. On the written submission from Tej Singh, son of Sher Singh Rathor, Aurangzeb ordered the demolition of the robber fortress. Sa'dulla Khan, son of Mir Bakshi Ruhulla Khan, Sayyad Khwaja Ahmad, *faujdâr* of Sherpur, Daulat Singh, Suraj Mal and others were appointed for the purpose. They were to be assisted by 100 *ahâdis*, 100 matchlockmen, 100 *beldârs,* and 500 horsemen. They were to chastise the robber in case he offered any resistance. At the *Diwân-i-Ghusalkhânâ* of 25th September, 1681, Mir Bakshi Ruhulla Khan submitted that Khanzada had gone along with the force as ordered and that Gang Singh robber had fled away. He further submitted that as the fortress was big and strong, 100 *beldârs* failed to demolish it in one day. the Emperor ordered that 100 extra *beldârs* should be deputed for the purpose.[112]

It was reported to Aurangzeb on 28th September, 1681, that two Mughal servants had looted a few camels laden with goods and killed the camel driver. Sayyad Chand Khan had pursued and captured them. They were ordered to be sent to Ranthambor.[113]

A letter was received on 28th September, 1681, from the commandant of Ranthambor that *parganâ* Alhanbas had become notorious for the nefarious activities of robbers. He suggested the name of a person for the *thânedâri* of the place. Ruhulla Khan was ordered to make inquiries about the rank of the person suggested and report.[114]

On 5th October, 1681, Mir Bakshi Ruhulla Khan submitted at

Kamandgarh a petition of Badi' -uz-Zaman that thieves had entered his house at night and had run away with his belongings leaving him with all but nothing. After five days it was discovered that the theft had taken place with the frontiers of Jagant Singh Hada's *jagir*. The Emperor ordered his *vakil* at the *Diwân-i-Ghusalkhânâ* of 10th October to produce the stolen property of the complainant.[115]

At the *Diwân-i-Adâlat* on 6th October (held at the village of Humayunpur), a communication was received from Rahmat Khan, the Diwan of Prince Shah 'Âlam's *jagir*. It mentioned that Fateh Singh Narokha, Zamindâr of Malpur, in the *jagir* of Prince Mohammad Mu'azzam Shah, raided the village Tomak in shah 'Âlam's *jagir* at night and carried away the belongings of the traders. It was requested to order the *faujdârs* concerned to chastise the culprit. The Emperor ordered that they should write to Asad Khan to institute an inquiry and report. Moreover, the '*Âmils* of Prince Mohammad 'Â'zam's *jagir* were ordered to chastise the said *zamindâr* and see that bad blood was not allowed to be created between the royal princes.[116]

News was received at the *Ghusalkhânâ* court at Burhanpur on 24th November, 1681, that the robbers had broken into the house of Mohammad Mehdi, a *mansabdâr* holding a rank of 500 and Mushriff in charge of the Mecca gifts, had rifled him of all cash and kind, and killed him.[117]

Three days later at the *Ghusalkhânâ* meeting in the same place, the news was received of another dacoity in the house of Sayyad Lutfulla Kolah near Lal Bagh. They had dispossessed him of all his belongings, killed five and wounded eleven servants. Ihtimam Khan *kotwâl* was ordered to pursue the robbers and submit a report.[118]

A letter was received by the Emperor at Burhanpur from Safih Khan, the Governor of Bihar, that robbery was likely to occur in the *serai* of Ranipur in Gaispur *parganâ*. Orders were despatched to the *faujdârs* concerned to remain watchful.[119]

Khan Zaman, the Governor of Burhanpur, wrote to the imperial court in April, 1682, that a number of thieves had committed robbery in the house of Braj Raj merchant there. They wounded him and took away the cash and grain from the house. The Emperor ordered that the Khan should trace the thieves and produce the looted property.[120]

On 26th September, 1682, it was reported from Akbarabad that Kanjhi etc., the servants of the merchants, had come from Shah Jahanabad and stayed near *serâi* Farrukh. There came the robbers, who killed the two servants, looted from them 2,000 *ashrafis* and 25,000 rupees along with their cart. A letter was written under royal orders to Hussain 'Ali to explain why he had failed to strengthen the *thânâ*. No robbery had taken place there before that time. He was ordered to strengthen the *thânâ* and produce the thieves along with the looted property.[121]

On 7th November, a letter was written at the instance of the Emperor to Sayyid Bahâdur, the *zamindâr* and *faujdâr* of Narwar, to explain why so many thefts had taken place in his jurisdiction.[122]

On 20th November report came from Sheogâon that while royal servants had taken oxen belonging to the *topkhânâ* for grazing purposes towards Ankola thânâ, Bhâku Banjârâ attacked them with his men. the robbers killed seven camels, some camelmen and cartsmen, wounded others and then took to flight.[123]

On 2nd January, 1683, letters were issued to 'Âqil Khân, the Governor and to 'Abdullâ Khân, the collector of Jahanabad, under royal orders. It was brought to their notice that many cases of thefts had been reported between Islamâbâd (Mathurâ) and Faridâbâd and that the Muslims there were being put to trouble. They were asked to be careful and the collector was to order the *faujdârs* to be vigilant.[124]

On 14th February, report came that many thefts had been occurring between Shah Jahanabad and the capital.[125]

News was received in the royal court on 7th March that a dacoity had taken place in Burhânpur. The local authorities had asked the *kotwâl* there to produce the thieves or the stolen property. The *kotwâl* replied that he would try to find out the thieves or the stolen property. He succeded in finding out the leader of the gang, Baranga Afghan, in Zainâbâd. He wanted to catch him alive, but in the fight which ensued Baranga got killed and the *kotwâl* and three of his companions got wounded.[126]

Raja Dharam Pal, zamindar of Karoli, in the province of Agra, had been laying waste the villages in *parganâ* Mahauli. He himself was a *mansabdâr* and usurped the *jagirs* of many other *mansabdârs* and refused to come to the court. On 8th January 1684, the Emperor sent a letter to the collector of the district to give him assurances and send him to the Court.[127]

On 21st March came the report of robbery in Akbarâbâd.[128]

A letter was received in the royal court on 17th October, 1684, that a zamindâr of Jahangirâbâd had built a fort in the forest near the town and started commiting robbery in the *parganâ* of Alwar. He had ruined some villages there.[129]

In November of that year, Mubâraz Khan, the *faujdâr* of Mathurâ, who had received his transfer orders, joined a gang of robbers and started helping them in dacoities. This had caused a great panic in the public. A request was made to Aurangzeb that Safi Khan, the revenue *faujdâr*, be ordered to reach there immediately.[130]

As a result of the departure of Mohammad Khalil, *faujdâr* of Narwar, and of the *thanedâr,* for Aurangâbâd, thefts had occurred in Narwar. The Emperor ordered them on 1st January, 1685, to submit explanations to him.[131]

Aurangzeb ordered on 6th January that the twelve brokers arrested on the charge of stealing horses and camels from the royal army and for re-selling them again in the army, should be handed over to Jalâl Chela.[132]

One hundred robbers collected near Himmat Nagar in the District of Akbarâbâd and looted the travellers. Already reports had been received about a number of robberies there. On 8th January, 1685, orders were sent from the imperial court to Safi Khan, the collector, to make proper arrangements and to see that no man was put to trouble.[133]

News was again received of the operations of robbers and highwaymen in the *sarkâr* of Akbarâbâd in the month of January of that year.[134]

A number of dacoits entered the house of Dayâl Zamindâr in Sikandarâbâd, plundered it. wounded the zamindâr, and escaped with the booty. They also attacked Harkishan zamindâr, who had gone there to look after his land and took away his cattle. On 6th February, 1685, orders were despatched to Mohammad Naeem, the Diwân of Shah Jahanâbâd, to ask the *faujdâr* of the place to produce the robbers along with the property that had been looted by them.[135]

In the province of Akbarâbâd, some robbers waylaid a merchant named Jahân, inflicted wounds on his body and forcibly snatched seventy horses from him. Orders were sent to Safi Khan, the Governor of the province, to chastise the culprits.[136]

In the same month, i.e. March, 1685, a few servants of Misri Afghân, while on their way from Shah Jahanâbâd to Garh Muktesar, were set upon by thieves and rifled of all their belongings. On 15 March, orders were issued from the imperial court to 'Âqil Khân, the Governor, to ask the *faujdârs* concerned to produce the thieves along with the stolen property.[137]

Mohammad Afzal, the son of Khushal Jang zamindâr, looted 27,000 rupees from the merchants between Peshawar and Kabul, laid wasted the *serâi* of Khairâbâd, and looted property there. Aurangzeb ordered on 24th July 1685, that the commandant of Aurangâbâd should send to the court Mohammad Ashraf, the second son of Khushal Jang who was already a prisoner of the Mughals.[138]

In Lucknow some thieves killed one Maddâ and wounded four servants at night and fled away with Rs. 2,000. Orders were issued on 16th September to the *faujdâr* of the place to chastise the culprits.[139]

At the same time orders were issued to *Faujdâr* Sher Afghân to produce the thieves who had stolen two horses along with cash and grain from the house of one Ahmad, and who had looted the property of two other merchants, Inâyat and 'Usmân. He was to produce the stolen property also.[140]

Orders were sent on 6th December, 1685, to Rây Râyân to chastise the robbers who had attacked Puran and Nathu Banjârâs carrying grain to Bhelsâ, wounded Nathu and carried away 107 oxen. Moreover, the Rây Râyân was ordered to produce the oxen.[141]

A Mughal caravan under Aghar Khan coming from Kabul was attacked near Agra by the Jât robbers. They seized the cattle and plundered the carts that were in the rear, and carried off some women as prisoners.[142]

Gokul Jât was a merciless and ruthless robber who brought ruin to the *paraganâ* Saidâbâd.[143]

Anand Rai merchant petitioned the Emperor on December 18, 1691, through Fazâil Khan that Alah Dad, *faujdâr* of Ahirwari, had stolen Rs. 16,000 and killed a number of men. It was requested that one mace-bearer be appointed to force the *faujdâr* to return him the money. Aurangzeb ordered on that very day that Sa'âdat Khân should send one mace-bearer to get the money of the merchant restored to him.[144]

A petition on behalf of the inmates of the *serâis* of 'Abdulla Khan and Haidipur was forwarded to the Emperor by *Thânedâr* Bahlad Singh to the effect that robbers had broken into the *serâis,* lighted candles and carried away a box belonging to them.[145]

Sayyid Habibullah of the secret police reported on 30th April, 1693, that Mayora Bâdshâhi in front of the *Thânâ* Burk Kakona in the jurisdiction of Râjâ Kalyân Singh had been killed by the thieves. All the Mayorâs of the *chauki* had come and reported the matter. In this connection, an order had already been issued a day before asking the Râjâ to produce the thieves. Shahâb-ud-din who had gone for investigations, brought the culprits of the said village.[146]

Râjâ Bishan Singh, *faujdâr* of Mathura, wrote to the imperial court in March 1694 that he had killed 300 and captured 700 robbers operating between Agra and Mathura.[147]

A daring case of dacoity was reported on 29th March, 1694, from Agra where the robbers had entered the garden of the new palace, killed the *amîn* of the garden, and removed the silver *kalas* of the palace. It was ordered to write about the affair to the governor concerned (for investigation and report).[148]

Dâmodar and his companion who were in custody, had given a bond in writing that they would stand guarantee against any theft in the imperial army. It was ordered that they should furnish the security of some responsible person and then be released.[149]

It was reported from Bihar that Hamid Khân alias Munshi Ibrâhim, commanant o fthe fortress of Ârâh, had released from custody one Ujjainiya robber. The emperor ordered the dismissal of the commandant.[150]

According to Manucci, when Aurangzeb fell ill in 1694, robbery became rife.[151]

A report came from the province of Ujjain that the rebel 'Umr Afghân had attacked a village in *parganâ* Râmpur and looted the property of Gopâl Singh *zamindâr* at night. Orders were sent to the governor to chastise the robbers and demolish their fort.[152]

It was submitted to Aurangzeb that the main cause of the dearness of grain in the army was robbery on highways.[153]

On 22nd May, 1695, four persons gave a petition that horses and otehr belongings of theirs had been stolen in Gwalior during the tenure of Fidâi Khân *faujdâr*. They had the sealed receipt of the *qâzî* with them. The said *faujdâr* had failed to trace the thieves. Aurangzeb ordered that mace-bearers be appointed to investigate into the matter. In case there was any truth in the allegation, they should make the *faujdâr* compensate the loss of the complainants.[154]

A *harkârâ* made a verbal submission that Sarbâz Khân, *faujdâr* of Bijâpur Konkan, had looted the property of four Dutch merchants amounting to one lac of rupees. Aurangzeb ordered Yar Ali beg to write to the said Khân to present himself at the imperial court.[155]

It was reported to the Emperor on 5th June, 1695, from Karnâtak Bijpâuri that robbers had carried away the belongings of Rahmatullâ and other traders from a village in *parganâ* Bâdâmi and also taken them into custody. The *faujdâr* of the place had failed to chastise the culprits. Orders were given to Himmat Khân to go to the village (and submit a report).[156]

'Abdul Wahâb, Diwân of Bijâpur, submitted that his son, Mir Fakhr-ud-din, had committed theft in his house and carried away everything. It was ordered that he be removed from the army.[157]

On 16th July, 1695, Mirzâ Saf Shikan Khân submitted that out of 120 horses purchased by Mirzâ Beg *mansabdâr* in Kabul and sent for the Emperor, five had been stolen in Ujjain. The Emperor ordered that Sayyid Mohammad should write to the governor to produce the stolen horses or accept responsibility for their cost. A diminution of the rank of Mirzâ Beg was also ordered.[158]

A petition was received from Khawâjâ Musâ, son of Khawâjâ Yaqub, that thieves had broken into his house and made good with everything in cash and kind, and left him in a miserable condition. It was ordered to pay him out of the royal treasury a sum of Rs. 10,000 in cash and grain worth Rs. 3,000. The *kotwâl* was ordered to trace the lost property and restore it to the petitioner.[159]

News came from Ahmadnagar on 22nd January, 1700, that Jâdo Râi *thânedâr* had killed some highway robbers and taken from their possession 1000 gold *muhars* and 500 rupees.[160]

Khawâjâ Mansûr submitted on 11th July, 1700, that thieves had carried away the entire cash and other goods from the house of Jawâhar Mal mason. The deputy *kotwâl* was ordered to investigate and report.[161]

Mohammad Amin, deputy *kotwâl,* was again asked on 12th April, 1701, to produce the entire stolen property in cash and kind that had been stolen from the house of Hakim Mohammad a night before.[162] Mohammad Amin was ordered to investigate into the alleged report of theft in the house of Azhar Khân son of the diseased Anwar Khan.[163] He, again, received orders through 'Arif Khân to trace the thieves who had broken into the house of Siâdat Khân and produce the stolen property.[164]

On 14th February, 1703, a report was received from Balkânûn that Mohammad Shafi', *faujdâr* and commandant of a neighbouring fortress, had kept 50 robber horsemen in the fortress. They carried out robberies in the area of another *faujdâr,* gave four-fifth of the looted property to Mohammad Shafi' and kept one-fifth to themselves. The *faujdâr* concerned had expelled the *harkârâ* and news-writer from his *Jâgîr*. The news-writer was ordered to send a correct report.[165]

On receiving the report on 13th March, 1703, that 'Abbâs Afghân had robbed the imperial post on the other side of the Narbadâ, Aurangzeb remained silent.[166]

When it was brought to his notice on 7th May, 1703, that frequent thefts were occurring in the imperial army, the Emperor ordered Sarbrâh Khân *kotwâl* to arrange for fences.[167]

On 8th June, 1703, Sarbrâh Khân *kotwâl* submitted that three thieves accused of stealing horses from the imperial army, had been captured and brought to the *kotwâlî*. The Emperor ordered that they should be put in prison and chastised.[168]

On 18th December 1703, Sarbrâh Khân *kotwâl* was ordered to get a wall constructed round the imperial army and get the paths round the camp barricaded to prevent camels and oxen of the imperial army from being carried away by thieves.[169]

In Râj Nagar the thieves broke open the house of one Paras Râm, the agent of Râj Singh. The watchman of Râj Singh pursued the thieves, killed three of them and recovered the stolen property.[170]

Some thieves entered the village of Mohan Singh and drove away a number of buffaloes. The villagers chased and killed two of them. The heads of the thieves were presented before the governor who ordered them to be exhibited on the trees.[171]

On 6th March 1704, Aurangzeb ordered that Sarbrâh Khân *kotwâl* should investigate into the cases of thefts alleged to have occurred in the house of Hidâyatullah and pay him the amount of the Rs. 10,000 stolen from his house (in cash and kind).[172]

Letters were also sent to the provincial governors from the parties concerned regarding the occurrences of thefts in their jurisdiction. Such letters are recorded in the provincial news letters, one of which finds mention in the provincial news letters written to the Jaipur Râjâ. The complainant writes that thieves had broken into his house, lighted their candles and removed every thing in the house excepting the clothes on his body.[173]

In 1706, Mân Singh Kumudkar, resident of Othal in the *Sarkâr* of Ujjain, came to the court of Tahawwar Sh'âr 'Ajab Singh *thânedâr* and reported that theft had occurred in his house and thieves had taken away five cows beside other articles. The *thânedâr* replied that he had sent men in different directions in search of the cows. It was learnt from the *chaudharis* and other people of the town that the thieves were living in the village of Nawdâa in the *Jâgîr* of Fâzil Khân. Two horses that had been stolen from Ujjain had also been traced in that very village.[174]

Iskandar Khân, resident of Othal, came before Tahawwar Sh'âr and submitted that the thieves had stolen one sword from his house.

Gopâl *Banjârâ* petitioned that he suspected Bahâr Ganesh, the *muqaddam* of the village Kakroh, to have stolen his horse. Tahawwar Sh'âr 'Ajab singh, *thânedâr* of Othal, took the *muqaddam* into custody and released him on bail. The *muqaddam* paid the price of the horse to the *thânedâr* on the condition that he would get the price from the *Banjârâ* in case the horse was found from somewhere else. In the meanwhile the *thânedâr* was transferred and another, Puran Mal Har Nârâin, came in his place. The *muqaddam* went in search of the horse and learnt that it had been found and the thief arrested by the *hâkim* of the village Tâl. He came back and reported the matter of the *thânedâr* of Othal, who sent a letter to the *hâkim* of Tâl and requested him to send back the thief along with the horse. The *hâkim* replied that he would sent both provided he got the necessary receipt in advance under the seal the *thânedâr* through his trusted man. Then he sent the thief and the horse along with the men who had brought the receipt.The *thânedâr* cast the thief into prison.[175]

Now Bahâr Ganesh *muqaddam* submitted that Gopal *Banjârâ* had wrongly mentioned his name while the horse had been discovered from another village along with the thief. The *Banjârâ* was punished for giving wrong information. He was required to pay ten rupees to the *muqaddam* as the price of the horse which he had already paid to the *thânedâr*. He had to pay Rs. 15/- to the *hâkim* of *parganâ* Tâl. In addition, he had to part with Rs. 15/- for the purchase of cows etc. the *muqaddam* paid one-fourth of Rs. 15 in the Government treasury.[176]

In the same year (1706) Ranjhûr Brâhmin of Othal submitted a detailed list of articles that the thieves had stolen from his house. *Thânedâr* 'Ajab Singh assured him that he had already sent men in all directions in search of the thieves and would bring all the articles from them as soon as their clue was found.[177]

"All the Country between Diu and Dand Point, which is about 30 Leagues along Shore, admits of no Traffick, being inhabited by Freebooters, called Warrels, and often associate with the Sanganians, in exercising Piracies and Depredations."

The Warrels occupy all the Sea-coast as high as Goga, which lies about 12 Leagues within the Gulf of Cambay. and the Coast, from Dand Point to Goga, is very dangerous.

It was perhaps the same Brâhmin (in another place his name is written Rûji) who went to a magician and asked him the name of the person who had committed theft in his house. The magician mentioned the name of a certain cultivator of the town. The Brâhmin mentioned his name to the *thânedâr* who sent for the cultivator and cast him into prison. There he remained for 12 days. Afterwards chief men of the town came and submitted to the *thânedâr* that there was no proof of guilt against him in this connection. On their own suggestion, they were sent to the magician for further inquiry in this connection. He replied that he had named him by mistake and he did not know as to who the thief was. They returned and mentioned the whole fact to the *thânedâr*. He released the cultivator on bail.[178]

MUSLIM LAW

ABOUT THEFT AND ROBBERY

According to Muslim theoretical law, if a man stole out of undoubted custody property worth ten *dirhams,* he incurred the penalty of amputation of hand.[179] No distinction was made between slave and freeman with regard to the punishment of theft.[180] If a group of men committed theft, and every one of them got as his share property worth ten *dirhams* or more, the hands of all of them were to be cut off. They were not liable to amputation, however, if the share of each was less than ten *dirhams.*[181]

The charge of theft was established on the testimony of two witnesses or the confession of the culprit.[182] The *qâzi* was to examine the witnesses as to the manner, time and place of the theft; and when he was satisfied with the answer and the reliability of the witnesses, he was to award the punishment.[183] The thief was to be held in confinement until the witnesses were fully examined.[184] A person who had been robbed could not pardon the thief when sentence had been pronounced against him.[185] In case the witnesses differed, their evidence was not to be accepted.[186]

The owner had the right to slay a thief in self-defence or in an effort to retain his property, when the latter took it out of his safe custody.[187]

If two witnesses withdrew their evidence against a person whose hand had been cut off, and named another as the culprit, their new evidence was not to be accepted and they were required to pay blood money for having caused an innocent person to lose his hand.[188]

No man could suffer punishment unless a certain number of persons gave evidence against him, or unless he himself pleaded guilty.[189]

It It was unlawful to slay a notorious thief if he was not caught red-handed. He was to be arrested and brought before the *qâzî,* who was to imprison him until he repented.[190]

There was no legal punishment for stealing from public treasury. There was to be no amputation for articles such as a cur dog, wood and grass, fish and fowls, garden stuff and fruit on the trees, milk and meat, unreaped grain, fermented liquor, a book, and the door of a mosque.

Amputation was not incurred if a person stole the Holy Qur'ân.[191]

The thief's right hand was to be cut off at the joint of the writst; the stump was kept in hot oil or in fire to stop bleeding. For the second theft, the left foot was to be struck off. For the third, his left hand; for the fourth, his right foot. In case he continued his offence, a magistrate could scourge him or award death punishment on him if he so desired. Punishment could not be inflicted when the weather was too hot or too cold.[192]

ABOUT HIGHWAY ROBBERY

According to Muslim law, highwaymen, who intended to commit highway robbery, but were arrested before they seized any property or caused damage to life, were liable to *ta'zîr* and imprisonment, till they repented. If they robbed and each got property equal to the value of *nisâb* (i.e. ten *dirhams*), their right hands and left feet were to be cut off. In case they committed both robbery and murder, the magistrate could punish them in two ways. He could, if he liked, cut off their right hands and left feet, and then put them to death by the sword or by crucification, or he could kill them at once without inflicting amputation. Their bodies were to be publicly exposed for three days on a cross. If they committed murder and not robbery, they deserved death punishment. This was *hadd* (legal) punishment and the pardoning of the culprits by the heirs of the murdered person carried no weight. If they robbed and wounded, their alternate hands and feet were to be cut off.[193] If ten highwaymen committed both robbery and murder, they all were to be put to death and they incurred the responsibility of the property robbed. Highway robbery was established by confession or if two witnesses bore evidence.[194]

MUGHAL LAW

Making a general observation, Vrinda, a Hindi poet of Akbar's time, has said that punishment should be awarded in accordance with the crime of an offender. A thief accused of stealing some vegetable should be slapped and a stealer of money should be given death punishment.[195]

In 1672, Aurangzeb issued a *farmân* which in some cases supplemented the Muslim theoretical law. In the Muslim law no punishment had been laid down for the theft of articles, the value of which did not reach the *nisâb* (ten *dirhams*). Aurangzeb's *farmân* laid down that if a man stole an article not worth ten *dirhams,* and for which he incurred no *hadd* or legal punishment, he, in the first instance, was to be chastised. In case of the repetition of the crime, he was, after *ta'zîr,* to be kept in prison till he repented. If he committed theft again, he was to be sentenced to life imprisonment or was to be executed. The stolen property was to be restored to the owner, or deposited in the *Bait-ul-mâl.*[196] The accomplice of the thief deserved the same punishment.[197] For cases incurring legal punishment, there was no deviation from the theoretical law. *Hadd* punishment was to be inflicted on a person who committed theft twice. for a third offene, the thief, after *ta'zîr,* was to be kept in prison till he repented. The commission of any further crime made the offender suffer life imprisonment or death punishment.[198]

If a shroud-stealer was arrested, he was, after chastisement, to be released. If, however, he took to it as a profession, the *qâzî* and the court officials could, if they so decided, banish him or cut off his hand. The repetition of the crime condemned him to severe chastisement. But in case he still repeated the offence, he was to suffer life imprisonment.[199] The Fatâwâ-i-'Âlamgiri, on the other hand, is not in favour of the amputation of the hand as far as this crime is concerned.[200]

If a man robbed property of another by setting fire to his house, or by rendering the inmates insensible through the administration of some intoxicants, he was, after severe chastisement, confined till repentance. If he repeated the offence, but showed penitence, he was to be released. In case, however, he still persisted in his crime, he was to be executed.[201]

The habitual malefactors who committed dacoity and did injury to life and property, were to receive death sentence.[202]

A suspected strangler whose case was not legally proved, was to be chastised and imprisoned till repentance. If it was found however, that he was a habitual criminal and thief and the governor and the officers of the court were convinced of this, then he could be executed.[203]

If they arrested a man suspected of theft, robbery, highway robbery or of strangulation, and if the governor and the officers of the court were convinced of the probability of his guilt, then he was imprisoned till he repented. If charged by any one with one of the above offences, he was to be referred to the *qâzî* for trial.[204]

The *Grâsias* and *zamindârs* of Gujarat were often guilty of robbing the people. It was laid down that if the death of such habitual robbers was required in the public interest, they were to be executed, but only after the guilt had been established.[205]

Punishment on a thief was to be inflicted by the *qâzî* in his own presence after the crime had been proved or after the offender had satisfied the conditions necessary for the imposition of *hadd* punishment.[206]

If a thief was captured when theft was rife in the city, he was not to be beheaded or impaled even after proof. It was just possible that that was his first offence.[207]

RECORDED CASES OF PUNISHMENTS IN MUGHAL INDIA

DEATH PUNISHMENTS

It was reported that Jamâl-ud-din, son of Mahmûd Barâh, had resorted to robbery and taken refuge at Pâtan with his uncle, Sayyid Qâsim. The Khân-i-Khânân, in obedience to Akbar's *farmân,* demanded him from Sayyid Qâsim and sent him bound to Lahore. There he was hanged on a stake in the Royal market and was shot at with arrows.[208]

Jahangir ordered a band of one hundred robbers, brought in chains before him, to be carried away for execution and their chief to be torn to pieces by dogs. The prisoners were sent to various corners of the city and executed in the streets. Sir Thomas Roe bears testimony to the fact that the chief was torn to pieces by twelve dogs near his house. He adds, moreover, that the hands and feet of thirteen of his associates were bound together and their necks and heads were cut by sword, 'yet not quite through' and their naked and bloody bodies were left to corrupt in the streets.[209]

On another occasion, Roe saw at a place six 'cosses to Ramsor' the naked bodies of one hundred men, who had been executed on accont of robbery.[210]

Some thieves plundered the public treasury of the *kotwâlî* in 1616. After a few days seven of them were apprehended along with their chief, Nâwal. They received a befitting punishment, which could be nothing but execution. Jahangir ordered their chief to be trampled under the feet of an elephant. The Emperor granted his request to fight the formidable animal. Surprisingly enough Nâwal succeeded in driving back the animal. He was spared his life. He, however, made good his escape, and, when caught again, he was ordered by Jahangir to be hanged by the neck.[211]

According to Manucci, a thief, accused of committing theft in a *serâi*, was awarded capital punishment.[212]

Capital Punishment—Agra to Surat : Feb. 1633. Between Byana and Fatehpur, Mundy saw about 250 to 300 men set on stakes by

Mirza Lashkar, governor there. They were robbers and thieves taken by him.

(Mundy, II, p. 234.)

ff Temple observes that two personages of this name were alive in 1633 : Jan Nisar Khan Yadgar Beg, created Lashkar Khan by Shah Jahan; Mirza Laskri, son of Mukhlis Khan. He could not connect either individual with Bayana.

(Ibid. ff.)

Manucci again records that Aurangzeb, after his coronation ordered the heads of 500 thieves, probably lawfully convicted already, to be cut off. These executions took place in front of the mosque, called Qadma-i-Rasûl.[213]

A gang of robbers waylaid a number of coolies who were carrying the silver cot of Bâkar Khân, a Mughal officer. One of these thieves was arrested and produced before Bâkar Khân. An order was given for the culprit to be trampled under the feet of a furious elephant.[214]

Fidâi Khân, the governor of the Punjab, issued orders for the execution of a powerful and notorious robber, Trika Arâin. He also awarded capital punishment to 15 dacoits, who had robbed a house at midnight. They were executed in front of that very house.[215]

According to Fryer, a gang of about 15 highwaymen was arrested. These men were accused of cunningly making the travellers dismount from their horses, of strangling and robbing them. They used also to lurk in narrow lanes of cities. Aurangzeb sent an express order for their execution. They were condemned to be hanged and delivered to the *kotwâl*, who led them to the execution ground. There was no sign of sorrow manifest on the face of any one of them. Instead, they were signing. They 'were advanced..........half a foot from the ground; and then cutting their legs off that the blood might flow from them, they left them miserable spectacles hanging till they dropped of their own accord.'[216]

The Râjâ of Kâlâbâgh, a tributary to the Mughal, used to rob the caravâns. After his accession to the throne, Aurangzeb ordered the execution of the Râjâ and a number of his associates. He got towers set up near the town on the highway. These towers were pierced all round by several windows where they placed in each one the head of a man. Tavernier while passing by the town in 1655 witnessed these towers.[217]

During his sojourn in India in 1642, the Portugese traveller, Manrique found some roads dangerous even for caravâns.[218] He came across, especially on high roads, columns of stones and lime, in which skulls of malefactors were 'enclosed, as a warning that it was done in the name of justice.[219]

In 1688, one Sayyîd and twenty Yusafzai Afghâns were arrested for alleged gambling in a rented house in the capital and commiting theft at night. They confessed that they had committed twenty-four thefts. The twenty-five Afghans were awarded capital punishment by Aurangzeb.[220]

In 1680, Fûlâd Khân *faujdâr* killed three out of the twenty-four robbers when he led an expedition against them.[221]

Manucci who stayed in India for 34 years, mostly during Aurangzeb's reign, frequently travelled between Agra and Delhi. Every time he found a number of fresh heads on the roadside and many bodies of thieves hanging from the trees as punishment for highway robbery. The passers-by had to hold their noses on account of the odour from the dead bodies.[222]

Manrique also found trees with hanging robbers.[223]

On 26th May, 1695, Aurangzeb ordered the execution of seven Marâthâ robbers.[224]

Dâ'ûd Khan, after mastering the fortress of Vellore in 1703, had all the thieves caught in the army thrown to the crocodiles in the ditch round the fort.[225]

IMPRISONMENT

In 1607 Jahangir encamped at the village Amrohi in the Punjab. In this village and the neighbourhood there were about 8,000 households of Khaturs and Dalzaks, notorious for mischief and oppression and highway robbery. Jahangir ordered that they should capture the headmen of the Khaturs, march all the Dalzaks to Lahore and keep them in prison.[226]

The persons accused of stealing English goods in April, 1623, at Nosâsi, were flogged at the orders of the local officer. On their denial of the crime, they were committed to prison.[227]

On 29th September, 1667, Sayyid Murtazâ Khân informed Aurangzeb that the rebel inhabitants of *paraganâ Nagranu had been imprisoned at the* chabûtrâ of the *kotwâl.* On his suggestion, the Emperor ordered that they be sent to the Fort of Gwalior as prisoners.[228]

Thevenot found Mâlîbâr full of robbers although the magistrates there did their best to root them out. "The truth is", remarks he, "they'll put Man to death for a single loaf of Betli stolen; they tye his hands, and having stretched him out upon his belly, run him through with a Javelin of Areca, then they run him upon his back, and the Javelin being quite through his Body, they fasten it in the ground, and bind the criminal so fast that he cannot stir, but dies in that posture."[228a]

The Sayyid who was the accomplice of the twenty Afghân thieves in 1668, as mentioned above, was sent to the fort of Ranthambor to be kept there as a prisoner.[229]

In June, 1680, Fûlâd Khân, *faujdâr,* led an expedition against and captured forty Meos from the *serâi* of Rûhullâ on a suspicion of robbery and produced them before the *qâzî*. They confessed that they had collected there to commit robbery. The matter was reported to Aurangzeb who ordered their confinement in the fort of Alwar.[230]

On 9th May, 1681, Multafat Khân, the *faujdâr* of Akbarâbâd, captured one of the robbers, who had committed robbery in the village of Birkâ, and put him in prison in the custody of *Daroghâ* of Mahâlât.[231]

TRANSPORTATION AND ENSLAVEMENT

Jahangir sent through Âsaf Khân to Thomas Roe two boys caught on charge of theft, to be sold into slavery. Roe told the *kotwâl* who had been sent to him by Âsaf Khân along with the boys that he was prepared to pay for them on condition that they would be released by him and not kept as prisoners.[232]

According to Manucci, it was the practice of Shahjahan to sentence such criminals as did not deserve death punishment to transportation beyond the Indus, to be sold as slaves.[233]

On October 11, 1692, news was received from Âgra that Amir-ul-umra, Governor of the province, had imprisoned 400 *Mewâtis* at the *chabutra kotwali.* They had given a bond that in case of a theft or robbery in the city they would be held responsible, and suggested the termination of the services of the former foot soldiers. Hearing this, Aurangzeb ordered to inform the Governor to employ the Mewatis himself and also to restore the former foot-soldiers. The suggestion of the Governor was turned down.[233a]

MUTILATION

As mentioned on page 33 above, Jahangir was informed about the theft of some *champâ* tress during his stay in the city of Ahmadâbâd in 1617. A personal inquiry by him established the theft, and, as a consequence thereof, he ordered both the thumbs of the culprit be cut off 'as a warning to others'.[234]

MUTILATION AND RETALIATION

During that very time the *kotwâl* of the city of Ahmadâbâd brought before Jahangir a thief who had committed many thefts before, and was each time punished with the mutilation of a part of his body. Once they cut off his right hand, the second time the thumb of his left hand, the third time his left ear, and fourth time they had hamstrung him and last time they had cut off his nose. Even then he did not stop stealing and entered the house of a grass-seller in order to commit theft. The owner who was awake, succeeded in catching the thief. The latter, however, wounded the grass-cutter several times by his knife and killed him. The relatives of the deseased grass-cutter overpowered the culprit and brought him to the *kotwâl*. Jahangir handed over the thief to them in order to have retaliation on him.[235]

AMPUTATION AND DEATH PUNISHMENT

While Tavernier was in Golconda in September, 1652, he paid a visit to the Prime Minister, Mir Jumla. He found there four prisoners. One of them had been accused of having broken into a house, slain a mother and her three infants. He was condemned to have his hands and feet cut off, and be thrown in a field near the highway. Another was guilty of highway robbery. The Nawâb ordered that his stomach be cut open and he be flung in a drain.[236]

"When a theft is committed at Baghnagar (Golconda), or elsewhere, they punish the thief by cutting off both his hands, which is also the custom in most countries of the Indies."[237]

Thevenot observes with regard to Malabar : "There are many Robbers also in the Country, through the Magistrates, do all they can to root them out. The truth is, They'll put Man to death for a single leaf of Betlie stolen; they tye his hands, and having stretched him out upon his belly, run him through with a Jevelin of *Areca,* then they turn him upon his back, and the Javelin being quite through his Body, they fasten it in the ground and bind the Criminal so fast to it that he cannot stir, but dies in that posture."[238]

Careri who visited the south about 30 years later remarks[239] thus :

"The trial upon suspicion of Theft among them, is by making the Party swim over a River that is full of Crocodiles, and if he gets over safe, he is reputed not Guilty."[240]

In March 1616, Jahangir sent a Mughal on suspicion of felony, to Sir Thomas Roe. In this connection, Roe remarks that "being II loath to execute him, both in regard to his person, the goodliest man I ever saw in India, and that the evidence were not clear, he sent him to me by the officers in irons for a slave, or to dispose of him at my pleasure." This was esteemed a high favour. Roe thanked the king and agreed to use the man as a servant as "in England we had no slaves."

(The Embassy of Sir Thomas Roe p. 132.)

MEASURES AGAINST THE ROBBERS

In addition to the punishments mentioned before, the Mughal Government used to take different measures against the robbers, who also became rebels.

EXPEDITIONS

One such measure was the despatch of expeditions against the robber gangs. These expeditions were commanded by the Emperor himself, by the governor, the *faujdâr* or the *thânedâr*, as the occasion might require. Whenever the Mughal Government learnt that a certain part of the country was being ravaged by robbers or highwaymen, they sent armies to subdue them. In case the robbers were very powerful, large armies were sent against them. The military forces destroyed all their towns, seized their goods, made their wives and children into slaves. Sometimes the heads of these robbers were made into minarets. They were hanged on stakes or by trees, roasted alive or beheaded. Armies were also sent against those who forced custom from travellers. Their towns were burnt, men were massacred, women and children were sold as slaves.[241]

In 1562, Akbar led a small expedition consisting of 200 horsemen and 200 elephants against Athgarha, eight villages, in the *parganâ* of Sâket. These villages were notorious for committing robbery and manslaughter. The immediate cause of attack was the slaughter by them of the son of a Brâhmin named Hâpâ and looting his property. These people fortified themselves in a village called Paronkh and offered a stubborn resistance. Akbar went ahead in person on the elephant Dilsankar and drove the elephant against the gate. The wall broke down and the Emperor entered their dwelling followed by four other elephants. A large number of the people were killed. Many shut themselves into the house.

In obedience to the royal command the house was broken and fire flung in. 'The breath of these ill-fated ones was converted into smoke. Nearly a thousand of them were sent to the abode of annihilation by the fire of the Divine anger.'[242]

Nicholas Withington and his companions found that the commandant of the fort of 'Bollodo' had returned with the heads of 169 Koli robbers.'[243]

In 1695, one Mohammad Diwânậ made disturbance in *parganâ* Samana in *Sarkâr* Sirhand, killed the officiating *faujdâr,* Mir Dost Mohammad, looted the goods and chattels. He also plundered the *parganâ* of Mâler, killed the *shiqdâr* and seized property. A number of persons had collected round him. *Mullâ* Nur-ud-din Ahmad Tarkhan, the *faujdâr* of Samana, on his return to the *parganâ,* went after the rebel with an army, defeated and killed him.[244]

While on his way to Lahore during Jahangir's reign, William Finch (1606-11) had gone some distance from Delhi, when he came across the *Faujdâr* of Delhi along with some two thousand horse and foot. They were in pursuit of robbers, who, following the false report of Jahangir's death, 'were abroad'. The *faujdâr* burnt their towns 'and took them and theirs, whatever he could get'.[245]

When William Hawkins (1608-13) and his companions entered Panipat, they found at 'the entry' a minaret with the heads of some hundred thieves 'newly taken', their bodies set on stakes a mile in length.[246]

Jahangir issued a sanguinary order for the extirpation of the race of the Kolis who were notorious robbers living in the most inaccessible parts of Gujarat. A large number of them were slaughtered and the rest hunted to their mountains and deserts. Withington saw in 1613, 169 heads of such Kilis killed in battle by Nûrullâ Ibrâhim, commander of 'Bollodo'.[247]

In 1623, Jahangir ordered Khân Jahân to lead an expedition of *mansabdârs* against the villagers and cultivators on the other side of the Jumna. These persons, accused of robbery and highway robbery, were ordered to be slaughtered, imprisoned and plundered; their strongholds and forts were to be razed to the ground. Next day the force crossed the Jumna and made an attack on them. After a hot engagement many of them were put to the sword, their womenfolk and children were taken prisoners, and their property was seized.[248]

On 30th October, 1667, orders were issued to Shâistâ Khân, the governor of Bengal, to attack and extirpate the rebel *zamîndârs* of

Assam.[249]

In March, 1680, Aurangzeb ordered Mukarram Khân to lead an expedition against a rebel *zamîndâr,* who, with a force of 250 persons, had been responsible for robberies in the locality of Nagar. Mukarram Khân brought back on the same night (14th March) the heads of a few robbers whom he had killed. He also brought the camels that the robbers had carried away. The Emperor ordered that the camels be entrusted to Ihtimâm Khân *kotwâl* who, after inquiry, was to resore them to their owner.[250]

In June of the same year Fûlâd Khân *faujdâr* led an expedition against the *Meos* who had collected near the *serâi* of Rûhullâ in order to commit robbery. He killed three of them and captured Forty.[251]

In February, 1681, the rebels looted Burhanpur for three days. They besieged the Mughal commandant there. The Diwân of Râjâ Inder Singh fought with the rebels and killed many of them. Aurangzeb sent him orders to despatch their heads to the capital so that a minaret might be made of them.[252]

In December of the same year, Hathi Singh Girâsia, a rebel in the neighbourhood of Ujjain, was attacked by the royal forces and forced to return the looted proeprty.[253]

In February, 1682, Misri and other Mughal servants, while on their way from Bengal to the capital, were attacked by Narind, son of Dîp Chand. They were looted and killed. Orders were issued to *faujdâr* Sayyid Bahâdur to chastise the culprits and produce the looted property.[254]

In April, 1682, Khân Zamân, the governor of Burhanpur, sent a force against the robbers who had committed robbery in the house of Braj Râj merchant.[255]

In May, 1682, some rebels looted a few villages in the *sarkâr* of Shahjahanbad. Shukrullâ Khân, the *faujdâr* of the place, marched against and engaged the rebels and killed many of them.[256]

Aurangzeb ordered on 30th June, 1682, that forty-one horsemen and twenty foot soldiers belonging to Gangâ Râm rebel should all be put to death. They had been captured by Bahroz, son of Murîd Khân, *faujdâr* of Garhi sent to Buzurg Ummed Khân.[257]

The rebel Bhâku *Banjârâ* was attacked by Sardâr Nârâin, the *faujdâr* of Sheogaon in December, 1682. Sardâr Nârâin killed and wounded a large number of the rebels and chased them for seven *kos.*[258]

Akram, the son of the *zamindâr* of Nizamâbâd, collected a number of people around him and went to the villages of Kharli and Sultanpur. The rebels laid waste the villages, took away the cattle and the belongings of the people. Aurangzeb issued orders that Tarbiat Khân, the *faujdâr* of the place should chastise the culprits and get the looted property restored to the owners.[259]

On 17th October, 1684, Aurangzeb ordered that Tarbiat Khân, the *faujdâr* of Jaunpur, Saghîr Andesh Khân, *faujdâr* of Lucknow, Tahawwar Khân, *faujdâr* of Oudh, and Mohammad Khân Bijapuri, *faujdâr* of Bahraich, should pool their resources and kill or chastise the robber *zamîndâr* of Jahangirabad, who had been committing robberies in the *parganâ* of Alwar.[260]

Orders were issued from the royal court to Hanif Khân on 19th January, 1685, to despatch a force to chastise the robbers who were troubling the travellers between Akbarabad and Himmat Nagar.[261]

News was received on 15th April, 1685, by the Emperor of the depredations of Râjâ Râm Jât in the villages of Mathura. In July the rebels were creating trouble in the neighbourhood of Fatehpur itself. They had killed a number of people and taken away the cattle. Orders were issued to the *faujdâr* there to punish the rbels and get the property restored to the owners.[262]

It was reported to Aurangzeb that Gangâ Râm rebel had gone from the province of Bihar and laid waste territory in the neighbourhood of Saharanpur in October, 1685. The Emperor ordered a reduction in the rank of Buzurg Ummed Khân, the collector of Saharanpur, who had failed to prevent the entry of the rebel into his territory.[263] Sayyid Yahiya, the *kotwâl* and *faujdâr* of Shahjahanabad, sent 300 horse to *Thânedâr* Mohammad Sharif who went at night and defeated Gangâ Râm rebel and killed many of his companions.[264]

Durjan had proved very troublesome to the Mughal authorities. He had been indulging in rebellious activities, laying waste villages and looting travellers. Some time he joined Pahâr Singh, another rebel, and created trouble. Orders were issued by the Emperor in October, 1685, to chastise and extirpate the rebels. On 30th October, news was brought to the Emperor that Pahâr Singh along with his son and many followers had been killed by the imperialists in a battle near Ujjain.[265]

On 20th September, 1691, an inhabitant of Mandasor petitioned the Emperor that the rebels of that district had demolished one storey of his house and the mosque belonging to him. He requested that if Kishwar Singh be appointed *zamîndâr* of the district, the situation would improve. His request was granted by the Emperor.[266]

'Azmatullâh, the *kotwâl* of the village Sayyiah, was an accomplice of the Girâsia rebels. In 1705, Tahawwar Dastgâh Udai Singh, *thânedâr* of *parganâ* Bhaurâsâ, district Sârangpur, went to the village concerned along with a band of soldiers and besieged the house of the *kotwâl.* At first the *kotwâl* got ready to give fight to the *thânedâr*, but on second thought, regarding it inadvisable, he surrendered. He was arrested and detained and a guard was placed on his house. The *thânedâr* sent Kesari Singh Râjpût to the capital to intimate the Emperor about the arrest of 'Azmatullâh Khân. After that he took him along with him to the capital, leaving Ânand Râm Râjpût as the assistant Tahawwar Dastagh[267] (*Thânedâr*).

THUGEE AND FORGERY

The cases given below throw an interesting light on the crime of *thugee and forgery* prevalent in Mughal India.

The Hindi poet Banârsi Dâs Jain has recorded in his versified autobiography, *Ardhakathâ,* an interesting case of alleged *thugee.* While on their way to Agra in 1616 A.D. along with his friend, Mahesar,a jeweller of Jaunpur, and seventeen others, they stayed in the village of Korra Gauno near Ghâtampur in a *serâi*. Their two Brâhmin companions went to a *sarrâf* for a change of rupee, purchased provisions for cooking meals, and then went to the house of the Ahîrs. After a short while, the *sarrâf* came to the inn and said that the Brâhmins had given him a counterfeit coin. A quarrel developed and the Brâhmin gave a good thrashing to the *sarrâf.* During this scuffle, the *sarrâf's* brother took out of the purse of the Brâhmins twenty-five rupees and shouted to all the present that they were counterfeit coins. with that money he ran towards his house, exchanged them with counterfeit coins and then went to the *kotwâl* to lodge a complaint that a group of *thugs* had been operating on a large scale. The *kotwâl* went to the *hâkim* who sent along with him his *dîwân* to investigate the case and apprehend the culprits.

The *kotwâl* and the *dîwân* accompainied by a few hundred people of the place went to the inn. Sitting on a cot they sent for the Brâhmins and asked about their bonafides. Then they questioned Mahesar and Banârsi Dâs. The *kotwâl* did not believe the story and ordered them to be bound. The *dîwân,* however, rebuked the *kotwâl* and asked him to postpone the investigation till the morning as it was growing dark. Before retiring, the *kotwâl* ordered a guard to keep an eye on these people and asked them to furnish a surety of some respectable man from one of the three villages of Korra, Ghâtampur and Bâri.

In the morning, they found 19 foot-soldiers arriving with 19 gibbets to hang these alleged thugs with. A few hours later, the *kotwâl* and the *dîwân* also arrived accompanied by the people. The *dîwân* was pleased to learn from Mahesar that he could furnish surety from the village Bâri where his brother, Hari, had been married. The *dîwân* took with him Mahesar to the village on horses and after full satisfaction the *dîwân* returned to the *serâi* and begged forgiveness from Banârsi Dâs who attributed this happening to his past deeds alone.

Next day Banârsi Dâs took six or seven seers of scent to the houses of the *dîwân*, *kotwâl* and of the *hâkim* and requested them to get their money restored from the real *thug*, the *sarrâf*. He was informed that the real culprit had made good his escape and could not be traced despite efforts. They advised him to go back to the inn and distribute *sîrnî* (sweets) by way of thanks-giving.[268]

The servants of 'Abdulla, *mansabdâr* of 150 *zât*, reported to Yâr 'Ali Beg *kotwal* that he had not been paid by his master. The *mansabdâr* produced a deed of discharge to which the seal of the *qâzî* was affixed. When Yâr 'Ali Beg administered the servant a reproof, he replied that the *mansabdâr* was a forger and had in his possession the seals of all the important ministers and grandees. He produced from a bag the seals of Yâr 'Ali Beg, Bahrahmand Khân, Amir Khân, Asad Khân and others. Yâr 'Ali Beg produced the accused before the Emperor in the *diwân-i-'âm*. He ordered that the accused be sent to jail. It was pointed out to the Emperor that the punishment was inadequate and to make it deterrent his hands should be amputated. The Emperor brushed aside the suggestion and ordered that the accused be handed over to the *kotwâl* to be kept in custody and deprived of his *mansab* of 150 *zât*.[269]

Mohammad Bâqar, the provincial *amîn,* sent two forgers to Yâr 'Ali Beg *kotwâl* who reported the matter to the Emperor. One of them was ordered to be handed over to I 'timâd Khân and the other to the *kotwâl* to be kept in custody.[270]

Mahâ Singh and another person were found in the guise of the Chief Secretary. They were deprived of their *mansabs*.[271]

SPECIAL POWERS TO EXECUTIVE OFFICERS

As a second measure against the robbers the executive officers were given special powers to deal with them. Aurangzeb had supplemented the Muslim law by investing his officers with discretionary powers in cases uncovered by the law. He gave the governors and other executive officers the right of keeping in prison notorious offenders even when there were no specific cases against them.[272]

Sometimes the demands of the Muslim law would make it possible for a malefactor to escape lawful conviction. Here Aurangzeb authorized his governors and the officers of the *'adâlat* to step into the breach and avoid 'miscarriage' of justice. They could demand his execution probably when they were convinced of his notoriously evil activities.[273]

RESPONSIBILITY OF OFFICERS

The executive officers had special duties and responsibilities in this connection. Copious references have been given above when the local officers were held responsible for all the thefts and robberies in the localities and were required to produce either the culprits or the stolen property. This must have exercised some restraint on the nefarious activities of the dacoits and made the officers conscious of their duty.

The Governor—The governor was responsible for the robberies committed in his province. In case the offenders were not traced, he was to make up the loss of the plundered person.[274] He would send expeditions against notorious robber gangs to chastise them.

Faujdâr—The *faujdâr* was responsible for all the robberies that occurred in his jurisdiction. He was to guard all the roads and compensate the plundered travellers. He was to traverse the country along with his soldiers and hunt out the robbers.[275]

The *faujdâr* was a police magistrate in charge of a district (*sarkâr*). His functions have been mentioned by Manucci[276] and Ovington.[277]

The *faujdâr* was obliged to 'secure the country about, and to answer for all robberies that are committed there.[278]

It was not uncommon in Mughal India for one and the same person to be appointed *faujdâr* and *kotwâl*. In the 30th year of the reign of Aurangzeb, Sîdî Ibrâhim was appointed *kotwâl* and *faujdâr.*[279] In 1706, Sarbrâh Khân was *kotwâl* and *faujdâr* of the army.[280]

Faujdâri could be enstrusted to a governor also. On 5th January, 1704, Shâistâ Khân, the governor of Malwa, was also appointed the *faujdâr* of Mându by the transfer of Nawâzish Khân.[281]

Kotwâl—The *kotwâl* was answerable for all the robberies committed in the town. The holders of the post, according to Thevenot, were usually very cunning persons and escaped from making payment. An Armenian merchant, robbed of 2,400 sequins at Surat, lodged a complaint but nothing came out of it. The governor of Surat asked the *kotwâl* to compensate the complainant for fear that he might not bring the matter to the notice of the Emperor. The *kotwâl* prevailed upon the governor to allow him to hold a proper inquiry into the charge by putting the Armenian in prison and to torture in order to find out whetehr he had really lost the money and his own men had not stolen it. When the news of this new development was conveyed to the complainant, he decided not to pursue the matter. He rather chose to lose all than to suffer the torments of torture.[282]

"When any one is Robbed, this Officer apprehends all the People of the House both Young and Old where the Robbery hath been committed and causes them to be beaten severely. They are stretched out upon the Belly, and four Men hold him, that is to be punished by Legs and Arms, and two other have each a long Whip. Mundy calls it corulla, 'a whip of twisted cord about a Fathome longe, with a handle about a cubit, from which it goes smaller and smaller to the end'.[282] Some whips had brass rings on them which were very severe and could kill a man. Whip of twisted thongs of Leather made thick and round, wherewith they lash the patient one after another, like Smiths striking on an anvil, till he hath received two or three hundred lashes and be in a gore of Blood. If at first he confesses not the theft, they whip him again next day and so for several days more, until he hath confessed all, or the thing stolen be recovered again; and what is strange, the Cotoual neither searches his House or Goods, but after five or six days, if he do not confess he is dismissed."[284]

Manucci also bears testimony to the *kotwâl's* responsibility for thefts and robberies and describes how the *kotwâl* utilized sweepers who went to clean every house twice daily as his spies.[285]

The *kotwâl,* according to Thevenot, was not only responsible for keeping guard in the city, he was an executive officer as well. He ordered the criminals to be punished in his presence, often in his house, 'either by whipping or cudgeling'. Sometimes the punishment was inflicted in the street at the place of occurrence of the crime.

When he moved into the town, he rode on a horse and was attended by several officers on foot, some of them armed with batons and great whips, others with lances, swords and shields and maces of iron. All had a dagger at their sides.[286]

The *kotwâl* was obliged to go in the streets at night 'to prevent disorder'. If he found any unathorised person moving about in suspicious circumstances, he committed him to prison and administered him whipping. He was accompanied by three sub-ordinates or guards, two of whom beat little drums and the third sounded two or three times a long copper-trumpet and shouted a warning cry, *khabardâr* (be careful). the guards in the neighbouring streets answered with similar cries.[287]

The round was performed three times in the night, at nine o' clock, at midnight and at three o' clock in the morning.[288]

The *kotwâl* was not permitted to interfere in the *Shar'î* matters. It was reported to Aurangzeb from Mathura (renamed by him Islâmâbâd) that Bâzid *kotwâl* attached to the army of Râjâ Bishan Singh, *Faujdâr* of the place, was meddling in the *Shar'î* affairs and paid no heed to the advice of the *qâzî* in this regard. The Chief Bakshi, Bahrahmand Khân, was ordered to write to Râjâ Bishan Singh to transfer the *kotwâl* and appoint another in his place.[289]

From the *Akhbârât* it appears that the post of *Nâib* or Deputy *kotwâl* was quite an important one. Mohammad Amîn, *Nâib-kotwâl* in the royal court in the south was a very important officer. His name occurs frequently in the news letters of 1699, 1700 and 1701 etc. This officer performed not only police but military duties as well. He was continually busy in engagements with the Marathas in addition to his own duties.

PUNISHMENTS OF OFFICERS

In order to compel the executive officers to be diligent in the performance of their duties, the Mughal Emperors as mentioned above held them responsible for thefts and robberies and compelled them either to produce the culprits or to restore the stolen property. The officers who were negligent in their duties were awarded different punishments.

WARNING

Aurangzeb was pained to learn that Feroz Jang, a military commander, had executed a man on the charge of highway robbery without adequate proof. The Emperor feared that he would not be able to support the Khân if the heirs of the slain person refused to accept the price of his blood and demanded retaliation. It was impossible to show mercy in the exercise of penal laws.[290]

COMPENSATION

As mentioned above in invariable cases, the Emperor made the officer concerned compensate the loss of the sufferer. Once he compelled the *faujdâr* of Agra, in whose jurisdiction a French envoy had been plundered and wounded, to pay the Frenchman more than Rs. 15,000 as compenation. Besides, Aurangzeb granted the Frenchman an equal amount from the royal treasury for his injuries.[291]

DISMISSAL

Mubâriz Khân, the *faujdâr* of Mathura, had joined a gang of robbers as a protest against his transfer. Aurangzeb ordered on 1st December, 1684, that Mubâriz Khan should be removed from his post and deprived of his rank and *jâgir*.[292]

Alâh Dâd, the *faujdâr* of Ahirwâri, who was involved in a decoity case, was dismissed from his post on 18th December, 1691.[293]

TRANSFER

Letters were written on 7th November, 1682, under orders of Aurangzeb, to Sayyid Bahâdur, *faujdâr* of Narwar and *zamîndâr* of Karetra, to explain why so many thefts had taken place in his jurisdiction. If he failed to take proper precautions, he was to be punished by transfer.[294]

In the case of Bhâku Banjârâ, who, as mentoned above, had carried away cattle and oxen near Sheogaon in November 1682, it was reported to Aurangzeb that Khandu *Thânedâr* had not chased the dacoits and had thus failed in the performance of his duty. The Emperor ordered that another *thânedâr* should be suggested in his place.[295]

In February, 1683, a report was sent to Aurangzeb that Sayyid Bahâdur, the *Faujdâr* of Narwar, had failed to stop dacoities between the capital and Shahjhanabad. As Bahâr Singh Gaur, the *Faujdâr* of Anuda, was performing his duty diligently, it was recommended that Debi Singh, son of Bahâr Singh, should be appointed *Faujdâr* of Narwar. It was expected that matters would improve that way. The recommendation was accepted by Aurangzeb and Debi Singh was appointed the *Faujdâr* of Narwar.[296]

SERÂIS

In Mughal India there were a large number of *serâis* where travellers stayed at night. Each one of these *serâis* could accommodate

700 to 1000 and even more persons with their horses and camels and carriages. These *serâis* provided security to the travellers against thieves and robbers. Their gates were closed at sunset and opened only in the morning.[297] Earlier, Jahangir had ordered the construction of *serâis* throughout the kingdom at small distances.[298]

WATCHMAN

To prevent robberies in the capital every noble provided watchmen who continually perambulated his particular quarters during the night, crying out *khabrdâr*. There were guards posted round the whole army at every 500 paces who kindled fire and also cried out *khabradâr*. In addition to these precautions, the *kotwâl* sent soldiers in every directon, especially to the *bazârs*, crying out and sounding a trumpet.[299]

During his travels in 1640 A.D., Manrique found these caravanserais in Bengal and Orissa and Bihar. From Patna to Agra and from there to Lahore there existed a network of such caravanserais. They had good, decent and clean rooms with adequate provisions for meals and other comforts for the travellers. They were usually built by wealthy persons as works of piety.[300]

REFERENCES

1. *Encyclopaedia of Islam*IV, p. 173.
2. *Ibid : Fatâwâ-i-Âlamgîrî* II. p. 703; *Dictionary of Islam*, p. 284
3. *Ibid.*
4. *Fatâwâ-i-Âlamgîrî,* II, p. 727.
5. *Ibid.*, p. 728.
6. *Ardhakathâ,* pp. 78, 79.
7. Early Travels in India p. 23.
8. Monserrate's Commentary, p. 13.
9. Akbar Nama, iii, p. 712; Beveridge, iii, 1060-61.
10. *Ibid.*, 1141.
11. Early Travels in India, pp. 113-14.
12. *Ibid.*, p. 136.
13. *Ibid.*, p. 174.
14. *Ibid.*
15. *Ibid.*, p. 206.
16. *Ibid.*, p. 218.
17. *Ibid.*, p. 220.
18. Hindowls Dowson, pp. 103-104.
19. Hindowls Eliot Dowson, p. 172.

20. Eliot and Dowson, VI, p. 495.
21. *Ibid.*, p. 496.
22. The Embassy, p. 480.
23. English Factories, 1622-23, p. 190.
24. *Ibid.*, p. 239.
25. *Ibid.*
25a. Manucci, iv. 116.
26. Tarvernier, i, p. 325.
27. Manrique, ii, p. 188.
28. Eliot & Dowson, VII, pp. 172-73.
29. Eliot & Dowson VII, p. 24; *Eng. Fac.*, 1630-34, p. 122; p. Mundy. II, p. 42, p. 49, pp. 275-76, pp. 339-49; *Journal of Indian History*, 1937, p. 67-68. (Van Twist).
30. Bernier, II, p. 106.
31. Peter Mundy, I, pp. 267-68.
32. Manucci, I, p. 307.
33. *Ibid.*, p. 346.
34. Bernier, Travels in the Mogul Empire (Constable), p. 369.
35. Ovington, pp. 137-38.
36. Orme, p. 142.
37. Manucci, I, p. 67;
    Ibid., II, p. 467.
38. Indian Travels of Careri, p. 216.
39. Indian Travels of Thevenot, p. 57.
40. *Ibid.*, p. 100.
41. *Ibid.*, p. 261.
42. *Letters;* pp. 26-27.
    (Fryer wrote that it was unsafe to be far out from the town at night, unless well-Ivarded. Fryer, p. 252.
43. *Ibid.*, pp. 40-41.
44. *Ibid.*, XL p. 43.
45. Thevenot, III, p. 41., Indian Travels, Thevenot, p. 58. Also see Indian Travels of Careri, p. 216.
46. Manucci, IV, p. 116.
47. Manucci, III, p. 163.
48. Monserrate, p. 13.
49. *Tuzk*, Tr. I, p. 99. Text, I, p. 48-49.
50. *Tuzk*, I Text, p. 49, p. 100.
51. *Early Travels*, pp. 143-44, p. 167.
52. *Ibid.* 198-99.
53. P. Mundy, II, p. 41.
54. *Ibid*, p. 229.
55. Fryer, I, p. 301.
56. Monserrate's Commentary, p. 13.

57. *Early Travels*, p. 210.
58. *Ibid.*
59. *Early Travels*, pp. 213-17.
60. *The Embassy*, p. 339.
61. Ardhakanthâ, pp. 78-79.
62. Badâuni, Text, II, p. 345; Lowe, II, pp. 356-57.
63. Bahâirstân-i-Ghâyabi, I, pp. 281-82.
64. Early Travels, p. 197.
65. *Ibid.*, p. 220.
66. *Ibid.*, p. 206.
67. *Ibid.*, p. 209.
68. The Embassy, p. 67.
69. *English Factories*, 1618-21, p. 91.
70. *Ibid.*, p. 217.
71. *English Factories*, 1618-21, p. 230.
72. *Ibid.* pp. 59-60, p. 81; p. 91; p. 120.
73. *Ibid.*, 1622-23, pp. 219-20.
74. *Ibid.*, pp, 222-23.
75. *Ibid.*, 1624-29. p. 210.
76. Peter Mundy, II, p. 264; p. 40; p. 41; pp. 42-43; pp. 45-46.
77. *Ibid.*, pp. 71-72.
78. *Ibid.*, pp. 109-10; pp. 119-20.
79. *Ibid.* p. 174.
80. Peter Mundy II pp. 253-54; pp. 256-57; p. 263.
81. *Ibid.*, pp. 263-65; pp. 269-70.
82. *English Factories*, 1637-41, p. 61.
83. Mandelslo, pp. 50-51.
84. *English Factories*, 1637-41, p. 137.
85. *Ibid.*, 1646-50, p. 129.
86. *Manucci*, I, p. 308.
87. *Letters*, CXXIV, p. 123.
88. *English Factories*, 1665-67; p. 158; pp. 267-68; Thevenot, III, p. 35.
89. Indian Travels of Thevenot, p. 19.
90. *Ibid.*, p. 20.
91. Indian Travels of Thevenot, p. 50.
92. *Jaipur Akhbârât*, 9th year.
93. *Ibid.*
94. *Ibid.*
95. *Ibid.*
96. *Ibid.*
97. *Jaipur Akhbârât.*
98. *Ibid.*, 10th yar.
99. *Ibid.*
100. *English Factories*, 1670-77, p. 255.

101. Jaipur Akhbârât, *23rd year.*
102. *Ibid.*
103. *Jaipur Akhbârât.*
104. *Ibid.*, 23rd year.
105. *Ibid.*
106. *Ibid.*
107. *Ibid.*, 24th year.
108. Akhbârât-iDarbâr-i-Mu'allâ, 1st August 1681.
109. *Ibid.*, 31st August, 1681
110. Akhbârât-i-Darbâ-i-Mu'llâ, 10th Sepember, 1681
111. *Ibid.*, 16th September, 1681.
112. *Ibid.*, 25th September, 1681.
113. *Ibid.*, 28th September, 1681.
114. *Ibid.*, 26th September, 1681.
115. Akhbârât-i-Dabâ-i-Mu'allâ, 5th Oct., 1681; 10 Oct.
116. *Ibid.*, 6th October, 1681.
117. *Ibid.*, 24th November, 1681.
118. *Ibid.*, 27th November, 1681.
119. *Ibid.*, 21st December, 1681.
120. Jaipur Akhbârât, 25th year.
121. *Ibid.*, 26th year.
122. *Ibid.*
123. *Ibid.*
124. *Ibid.*
125. *Ibid.*
126. Jaipur Akhbârât, 26th year.
127. *Ibid.*
128. *Ibid.*, 26th year.
129. *Ibid.*
130. *Ibid.*
131. *Ibid.*
132. *Ibid.*
133. Jaipur Akhbârât.
134. *Ibid.*, 28th year.
135. *Ibid.*
136. *Ibid.*
137. *Ibid.*
138. *Ibid.*, 29th year.
139. Jaipur Akhbârât.
140. *Ibid.*
141. *Ibid.*, 28th year
142. Eliot & Dowson, vii, p. 343.
143. Ma'âsir-i-Âlamgiri, 62.
144. Jaipur Akhbârât, 35th year.

145. Akhbârât-i-Darbâr-i-Mu'allâ, 24th April, 1693.
146. Jaipur Akhbârât, 38th year.
147. Akhbârât-i-Darbâr-i-Mu'allâ, 29th March, 1694.
148. *Ibid.*, 29th March, 1694.
149. *Ibid.*, 1st Just, 1694.
150. *Ibid.*, 19th July, 1694.
151. Manucci, ii, p. 464.
152. Akhbârât-i-Darbâr-i-Mu'allâ, 16th May, 1695.
153. *Ibid.*, 17th May, 1965.
154. Akhbârât-i-Darbâr-i-Mu'allâ 22nd May, 1695.
155. *Ibid.*, 30th May, 1695.
156. *Ibid.*, 5th June, 1695.
157. *Ibid.*, 9th July, 1695.
158. *Ibid.*, 16th July, 1695.
159. *Ibid.*, 2nd May, 1696.
160. Akhbârât-i-Darbar-i-Mu'allâ, 22nd January, 1700.
161. *Ibid.*, 11th July, 1700.
162. *Ibid.*, 12th April, 1701.
163. *Ibid.*, 23th July, 1701.
164. Akhbâr
ât-i-Darbâr-i-Gîtî Madâr, 16th July, 1702.
165. Akhbârât-i-Darbâr-i-u'allâ, 14th February, 1703.
166. *Ibid.*, 13th March, 1703.
167. *Ibid.*, 7th May, 1703.
168. Akhbârât-i-Darbâr-i-Mu'allâ,' 8th June, 81703.
169. *Ibid.*, 18-12-1703.
170. Akhbârât Op. Cit. Sri Ram sharma, Mughal Government & Administration p. 213.
171. *Ibid.*
172. Akhbârât-i-Darbâr-i-Mu'allâ, 6th March, 1704.
173. Provincial Akhbârât, No. 47 (Jadunath Sarkar Collections).
174. Provincial Akhbârât, No. 47 (Jadunath Sarkar collection).
175. *Ibid.*
176. Jaipur Akhbârât, 49th year.
177. *Ibid.*
178. Jaipur Akhbârât. 49th yar.
179. Fatâwâ-i-Âlamgîrî, ii, p. 703;
Encyclopaedia of Islam, iv, p. 173;
Dictionary of Islam, p. 284;
The Qur'ân prescribed the cutting of the hands of the theives (Qur'ân, 37-38);
Cf. Mughal Administration,4th ed., p. 104.
180. Fatâwâ-i-'Âlamgîrî, ii, p. 704;
Encyclopaedia of Islam, iv, p. 173;

Dictionary of Islam, p. 284.

181. Fatâwâ-i-'Âlamgîrî, ii, p. 705;
Dictionary of Islam, p. 284;
Encyclopaedia of Islam, iv, p. 173.

182. Faṭâwâ-i-'Âlamgîrî, ii, p. 705;
Dictionary of Islam.

183. Fatâwâ-i-'Âlamgîrî, ii, p. 708.

184. *Ibid.*

185. *Ibid.*, ii, p. 709.

186. *Ibid.*

187. *Ibid.*, ii, p. 710.

188. *Ibid.*, p. 711

189. *Ibid.*, pp. 711-13.

190. *Ibid.*

191. *Ibid.*, p. 284; Encyclopaedia of Islam, iv, p. 173;

192. Fatâwâ, ii, 711-13,
Dictionary of Islam, p. 285.
Also see Mughal Administration, (4th ed.) F.N., p. 104.

193. Fatâwâ-i-'Âlamgîrî, ii, 728; Encyclopaedia of Islam; iv, pp. 173-74.

194. Fatâwâ-i-'Âlamgîri, ii, 729.

195. Vrinda-Satsai, 537.

196-200. Sarkar's translation is slightly different from the text. The text reads Hubs-i-Mu'abbad meaning life, and not prolonged imprisonment, as Sir J.N. Sarkar seems to have implied. Again, the text reads Ba Siâsât Ba Qatl Rasânand. It does not mean *siâsat* and execution, as translated by Sarkar, but execution by way of *siâsat,* i.e. punishment.
Mirât-i-Ahmadi, i, p. 278.
Mughal Administration, 4th ed., pp. 109-10.

201. 2 to 6 Mîrât-i-Ahmadi, i, pp. 278-83, Cf. Mughal Administration, 109-115, Fatâwâ-i-'Âlamgiri, ii, 714.

202-7. Mirât-i-Ahmadi, i, pp. 278-83;
Cf. Mughal Administration, p. 109-15; (4th ed.)
Fatâwâ-i-'Âlamgîrî, ii, p. 714.

208. Badâûni, Lowe, ii, pp. 356-67, Text, ii, p. 345.

209. Roe in Kerr's Collection, op. cit, in Eliot & Dowson, VI, p. 506; The Journal of Sir Thomas Roe, p. 201.

210. Eliot & Dowson, VI, p. 510

211. *Ibid.*, pp. 346-47. uzk, Bev., I, pp. 339-40, Text, i, p. 168.

212. Manucci, i, p. 68.

213. *Ibid.*, ii, p. 4.

214. *Ibid.*

215. Peter Mundy, ii, pp. 232-33, Manucci, ii, p. 209.

216. Fryer, p. 244.

217. Manucci, i, p. 58.

218. Manrique, pp. 251-52.
219. *Ibid.*, p. 149.
220. Jaipur Akhbârât, 10th year.
221. *Ibid.*, 27th year.
222. Manucci, i, p. 134.
223. Manrique, ii, p. 149.
224. Akhbârât, 26th May, 1965.
225. *Ibid.*, iii, p. 487.
226. Tuzk, R. & B., I, 100. Text, i, p.49.
227. Eng-Fac, 1622-23. pp. 222-23.
228. Jaipur Akhbârât, 10th year.
229. *Ibid.*
230. Jaipur Akhbârât, 3rd year.
231. *Ibid.*, 24th year.
232. The Embassy, pp. 266-67.
233. Manucci, i. p. 204.
234. Tuzk, Text, I, p. 216; R & B.I, p. 8, 432.
235. Tuzk, Text, I, p. 216; R & B. I, p. 432.
236. Tavernier, I, pp. 292-93.
237. Indian Travels of Thevenot, p. 136.
238. *Ibid.*, p. 125.
239. Indian Travels of Careri, p. 261.
241. Peter Mundy, ii, pp. 73; 90; 110; 110; 185; 234; Letters, xx, pp. 26-27; Manucci. ii p. 451; Thevenot, iii, p. 20; Eliot & Dowson, vii, p. 343; English Factories, 1646-50, p. 129; 1670-77, p. 255; De Leat p. 21, Notes.
242. Akbar Nâmâ, Bev., ii. pp. 251-55; Text, ii, pp. 163-65.
243. Early Travels, p. 209.
244. Akbar Nâmâ, Bev., II, 392-93; 431-35. Text, II, p. 263.
245. Early Travels, pp. 143-44.
246. *Ibid.*, p. 159.
247. Eliot & Dowson, VI, p. 504; Early Travels, p. 209.
248. Tuzk, B. & R., II, pp. 285-86. Text, II, pp. 384-85.
249. Akhbârât, 10th year.
250. Akhbârât, 23rd year.
251. *Ibid.*
252. *Ibid.*
253. Jaipur Akhbârât, 24th year.
254. *Ibid.*
255. *Ibid.*, 25th year.
256. *Ibid.*
257. Jaipur Akhbârât, 25th year.
258. *Ibid.*, 26th year.

259. *Ibid.*, 28th year.
260. *Ibid.*
261. *Ibid.*
262. *Ibid.*, 28th year.
263. *Ibid.*, 29th year, p. 298.
264. Jaipur Akhbârât, p. 333.
265. *Ibid.*, 27th year, pp. 29; 241; 242-43.
266. Akhbârât, 49th year.
267. *Ibid.*
268. *Ardhakathâ* : Banârsi Dâs Jain, pp. 503-44.
269. Akhbârât-i-Darbâr-i-Mu'âllâ, 19th April, 1693.
270. *Ibid.*, 24th June, 1694.
271. *Ibid.*, 31st October, 1703.
272. Mîrât; I, 279-80 cf. Sarkar's Mughal Administration, 4th ed, p. 111.
273. *Ibid.*
274. Manucci; I. 204, Manucci, pp. 461-62; Marshal, p. 39 English Factories, 1637-41, p. 61; 1656-60, 315; 1670-77, 255. Tavernier-I, 47.
275. Thevenot, III, p. 35; English Factories, 1665-67, pp. 267-68.
276. Manucci, II, pp 450-51.
277. Ovington, p. 139.
278. Indian Travels of Thevenot, pp. 28-29.
279. Ma 'âsir-i-'Âlamgîrî, Text, p. 282.
280. Akhbârât-i-Darbâr-i-Mu'allâ, 15th January, 1704.
281. *Ibid.*, 26th November, 1706.
282. Indian Travels of Thevenot, p. 28.
283. Mundy, II, p. 23. See Bernier, p. 228.
284. *Ibid.*
285. Manucci, II, p. 241.
286. Indian Travels of Thevenot, p. 27.
287. *Ibid.*
Also see Ovington, p. 137.
288. Indian Travels of Thevenot, p. 28.
289. Akhbârât-i-Darbâr-i-Mu'allâ, 20th December, 1797.
290. Anecdotes, p. 84.
291. Thevenot, III, p. 35; English Factories, 1665-67, pp. 267-68.
292. Jaipur Akhbârât, 28th year.
293. *Ibid.*, 35th year.
294. *Ibid.*, 26th year.
295. Jaipur Akhbârât 26th year.
296. *Ibid.*, 28th year.
297. Manucci, I, pp. 68-69; p. 164.
298. Tuzk, B. & R. Vol. I, pp. 7-8.
299. Bernier, Travels in the Mughal Empire (Constable), p. 369.
300. Manrique, II, pp. 99; 100; 109; 116; 146; 152; 184; 223; 242; Tavernier (Ball), I, p. 53; Mundy, II, p. 121.

VI
OFFICIAL CORRUPTION

BRIBERY

Bribery was very common during the Mughal rule in India. As the means of communications were undeveloped, it was not easy for the Central Government to remain in close contact with the activities of its officials. Even news-writers, supposed to keep the Central Government informed of the activities of the officials, could fall an easy prey to this vice.[1]

A governor would some time bribe the Emperor to secure his continuance in office.[2]

As even today, the people who were anxious to get their work done in a short time and speedy manner, could afford to pay for it to the persons concerned.

Then there was the system of presents. It was common practice at that time to present gifts to the higher officials or big people whenever visits were paid to them. This practice was prevalent throughout the country and even the Emperor formed no exception. Rather it was regarded as an insult if a person went to the Emperor without a proper present. Even the Princes of the royal blood approached their father with some suitable gift for him. Akbar had issued an order that every person from the lowest to the highest should bring a present when he came to visit him.[3]

The argument was provided in the Hedâyat al-Qawâid. In order to gain favours from the dead saints, people never visited their tombs without handsome offerings of sweets and flowers. How much more are presents necessary fo gaining the favour of living men?[4]

When any one went to Jahangir, he had to offer a present.

The offer or acceptance of the present did not expose its giver or recipient to any odium in society. There are copious references to the

5. Qatl Bi-Sabab.

Qatlul-'Amd or wilful murder arose where the criminal intentionally killed a person with a weapon or something that served for a weapon, such as a club, a sharp stone, or fire. If one committed a wilful murder, one was a sinner and deserved hell; and, secondly, he was liable to retaliation. But retaliation lapsed if the heir or the next of kin either forgave or compounded for the offence. The Muslim Law admitted of no other expiation for wilful murder. The murderer could not benefit by his crime and thus he lost his right of inheritance to the murdered person if such a right otherwise accrued.[4]

With regard to the commission of homicide, Aurangzeb had ordered that when a charge of murder had been proved against any man according to the Holy Law, or was close to certainty, the offender was to be kept in prison and a report of the fact was to be made to the Emperoror.[5]

The following are the cases, available from contemporary records, where the perpetrators of wlful murder were punished in one way or another.

DEATH PUNISHMENTS

SUBHAN QULI VS. ISLÂM KHÂN

Akbar's chief huntsman, Subhân Quli, made an attempt on the life of Islâm Khân, governor of Bengal. He tried to flee, was captured and awarded capital punishment.[6]

ADHAM KHÂN ATKÂ VS. SHAMS-UD-DIN KHAN ATKÂ

Adham Khân Atkâ was very envious of Khan-i-Â'zam, Shamsud-din Mohammad Khân Atkâ, the Prime Minister of India, during Akbar's reign. Both were Akbar's foster brothers. Khân Khânâ Mun'im Khân and Shahâb-ud-din Ahmad were also jealous of the Prime Minister. They abetted and incited Adham Khân against him. On 16th May, 1562, while Mun'im Khân, Shahâb-ud-din Ahmad Khân and Shams-ud-din were sitting in the audience chamber engaged in the business of state, Adham Khân entered in a violent frame of mind with a party of ruffians. Those present in the court rose up to show respect. Shams-ud-din half stood up. Adham Khân clapped his hand to his dagger in a threatening way and cast an angry look upon one of his associates, Khushâm Uzbek. The latter took up the hint, drew his sword, and inflicted a mortal wound in the bosom of the Prime Minister. And, when Shams-ud-din rushed off towards the Emperor's apartments, he received two more sword cuts and fell dead in the courtyard.

This cold-blooded murder of the Prime Minister shocked the Emperor, who, walking from his slumber by the noise, learnt what had happened. Adham Khân, in the meantime, had come to the parapet which surrounded the palace on all sides about the height of a man and a half. The culprit fell at the feet of the Emperor and seized both his hands in a manner that the sword of Akbar fell on the ground. Akbar, however, gave such a fierce blow in his face with his fist that Adham Khân fell senseless. The Emperor ordered Farhat Khân and Sangrâm Hoshnak and others who were standing there to bind the culprit and hurl him headlong from the parapet. This, however, only half-killed him. Akbar ordered them to drag him back by the hair and throw him down more carefully. This broke his neck and knockd out his brains.

Adham Khân undoubtedly deserved capital punishment, yet it was given in a barbarous manner and in a fit of rage.[7]

JUJHÂR KHÂN BAKSHI VS. CHANGEZ KHÂN

Jujhâr Khân Bakshi, one of the great and distinguished officers of Gujarat, slew Changez Khân. The mother of the deceased lodged a complaint with Akbar, who, while on his way to Gujarat in 1573, happened to be at Bharonch. The Emperor ordered a thorough inquiry into the matter. The charge having been proved, and the accused having confessed his guilt, he was awarded capital punishment. He was thrown under the feet of an elephant named Manmil, in the presence of 'high and low.'[8]

WRESTLER VS. KHÂWJÂ 'ÂLAM

the eunuch Khwâjâ 'Âlam was a hard task-master and kept several wrestles under him. He beat one of them with a stick. The wrestler, by way of revenge, killed the eunuch in 1582 with a dagger. The Emperor awarded the murderer capital punishment.[9]

MULLÂ AHMAD VS. MIRZÂ FÛLÂD BEG BARLÂS

Mirzâ Fûlâd Beg Barlâs was a bigoted Sunni and regarded the doctrines of Mullâ Ahmad, a Shiah, with contempt. He was violently opposed to him in matters of religion. On the night of 31st December, 1587, Mirzâ Fûlâd Beg managed to get Mullâ Ahmad out of his house on some pretext. Then, with the help of a companion, he attacked and fatally wounded him in a street of Lahore. Akbar appointed an inquiry committee, consisting of three eminent persons, Abul Fazl, the Khân Khânân, and Âsaf Khân, to investigate and report. They were able to ascertain the truth from Mullâ Ahmad himself who retained some consciousness before he succumbed to injuries. On the submission of the report to the

Emperor, the offenders were awarded capital punishment. The Mirzâ and his companion were bound to the foot of an elephant and dragged through the streets of Lahore, till they gave up the ghost.[10]

A WIDOW'S DAUGHTER VS. MUQARRAB KHÂN'S MAN

In 1610, a widow complained to the Emperor Jahangir that Muqarrab Khân, the Customs-officer of Cambay and Sûrat, had taken her daughter by force to the port of Cambay, kept her in his house and later on declared that she had died a natural death. The Emperor ordered an inquiry as a result of which it was established that one of the attendants of Muqarrab Khân had been guilty of the outrage. He was awarded death punishment by the Emperor. Muqarrab Khan was also punished.[11]

HOSHANG COMMITS MURDER

Hoshang, brother's son of Khan-i-'Âlam, was accused of the commission of an unjust murder. After investigation, Jahangir awarded him capital punishment.[12]

MOTHER VS. PAHÂR

Pahâr, the son of Gaznin Khân, was given the province and fort of Jalaur, the place of his ancestors. He fell upon evil ways and refused to listen to the advice of his own mother. Instead, he got fed up with her advice, and entered his house with some of his companions and killed his mother with his own hands. The matter was reported to Jahangir when he was camping in 1616 in the village of Deh Qâzian in the neighbourhood of Ujjain. The Emperor summoned the murderer into the royal presence and ordered an inquiry. The case was proved against him and he was executed under royal orders.[13]

'ALI NQAI VS. MURÂD

Prince Murâd Baksh, the youngest son of Shahjahan, was guilty, while governor of Gujarat in 1657, of wrongfully killing 'Ali Naqi, his revenue minister and chief counsellor. Four years later, at the instigation of Aurangzeb, the second son of 'Ali Naqi brought a charge against Prince Murâd Baksh. He was sent to the fort of Gwalior where the prince had been kept as a prisoner under orders of Aurangzeb. The *Qâzi* made an inquiry into the charge. The charge having been established, the *Qâzi* suggested to the complainant to accept blood-money. He refused and insisted on retaliation. As a matter of fact, he was demanding this at the Emperor's instance who wanted to get rid of his brother. So on 4th December, 1661, two slaves under the order of the *Qâzi* killed the Prince with two blows of their swords. Khâfi Khân squarely blames Aurangzeb for this.[14]

PORTUGESE VS. HIS WIFE AND DAUGHTER

A Portugese picked a quarrel with his countrymen, and exasperated by their talk, went to his house and killed his wife and daughter. The relations of the woman petitioned the Court for his execution. The Court was prepared to liberate the culprit if he accepted Islam. The Portugese refused to be converted and was consequently executed.[15]

FARJÂM BARLÂS VS. NEPHEW

Farjâm Barlâs, a *faujdâr* in the service of Aurangzeb, broke the marriage bond between his daughter and his sister's son, due to the ill-nature of his sister. The youngman, at the incitement of his mother, killed his uncle in the Diwân-i-'Âm in the presence of all. The case was brought before the Emperor who requested the kinsmen of the murdered person to give up their demand for retaliation. On their refusal to do so, the youngman was awarded capital punishment. He was executed in the presence of all and his body was entrusted to his mother who was waiting at the gate outside the fort.[16]

I'TIMÂD KHÂN VS. MUGHAL SPY

Amir Khân, the governor of Kabul, had arrested some Mughals on charge of espionage. When the matter was reported to the Emperor in 1666, he appointed I'timâd Khân and Mullâ 'Abdul Qawi to investigate into the complaint against them. I'timâd Khân sent for one of the accused. This man entered the audience hall without fetters or shackles or arm. His servant, equipped with arms, was standing outside. The Mughal suddenly left the audience hall, approached his servant, took the sword from him, returned and attacked the Khân with such sudden vehemence that he instantaneously died.[17] The author of Ma'âsir-i-'Âlamgîrî is silent about the fact whether the culprit guilty of double crime was put to death on the spot or after inquiry.

SON OF QÂZI CHAKLÂ HISAR

The son of Qâzi Chaklâ Hisar was accused of committing murder. He was awarded capital punishment and executed on 20th July, 1667.[18]

HARDEV TIWÂRI VS. JEWELLER

On 10th May, 1700, Mohammad Amîn, deputy *kotwâl,* reported to the Emperor at Satârâ a case of cold-blooded murder of a Muslim jeweller by one Hardev Tiwâri. The latter had killed the jeweller who had gone to sell jewels, buried his dead body in his own house and appropriated his valuables. The crime was discovered when after a week his men were found selling in the bazâr two necklaces which were recognized by the heirs of the deceased. The accused Tiwâri was brought to the *chabûtrâ kotwâli*, where, after receiving severe chastisement, he confessed the crime. The dead body and the effects were recovered from his house. Mohammad Amîn submitted that the accused, terrified a the prospects of punishment, was prepared to abjure his faith and embrace Islam. He sought for the emperor's orders.

The Emperor, however, did not accept the offer and rather entrusted the case to the *qâzi* for disposal as he regarded proper. The *qâzi,* in strict accordance with the law, consulted the wishes of the heirs of the deceased. They refused to agree to his release and demanded retaliation. Accordingly, the accused Tiwâri was executed in front of the *Chabûtrâ Kotwâli.*[19]

IMMPRISONMENT

KHWÂJÂ MU'AZZAM VS. WIFE

Khwâjâ Mu'azzam, Akbar's maternal uncle, was notorious for his wicked deeds. One day in 1564, the Khwâja's mother-in-law, Bibi Fâtimâ, complained to Akbar that he was taking her daughter, Zohrâ Âghâ, to his *parganâ* in order to put her to death there. the Emperor soothed and assured her that while going ahunting, he would pay a visit to the Khwâjâ's house and tender him good advice. The Emperor crossed the river by boat and sent two servants to the Khwâjâ's house in order to apprise him of his arrival. Upon this, the Khwâjâ lost his temper, rushed to the female apartments, drew his dagger and killed his wife, Zohrâ Âghâ, when she had just come out from her bath and was dressing herself in the dressing room. Then he threw his sword out of the window to the place where the royal attendants were standing and shouted in a loud voice, 'I have shed her blood, go and tell.' The Emperor felt furious and went into the house. The Khwâjâ was arrested by those standing. When the Emperor enquired from him as to the reason of his wicked deed, he began to utter delirious ravings. They silenced him by blows and kicks. Then they dragged him by the hair and kicking him, brought him to the river, and, under royal orders, dipped him there. He continued his ravings, and they kept on ducking him; but even the strong buffeting of the waves failed to kill the Khwâjâ. The Emperor handed him over to Muqbil Khân to be taken to Gwâlior in order to be imprisoned there. He died of a disordered brain.[20]

KALIYÂN VS. OTHERS

Kaliyan, the son of Râjâ Bikramâjit, was accused of having kept a common Muslim woman with him, and, for fear of being found out, kiiled her fatehr and mother and buried them in his house. The Emperor

Jahangir ordered in 1607 an inquiry against him. After his crime was established, it was ordered that his tongue be cut out and he be imprisoned for life. He was to be fed at the same mess as the dog keepers and sweepers.[21]

BROTHERS VS. MIRZA BADI'-UZ-ZAMÂN

The half-brothers of Mirzâ Badi'-uz-Zamân, the son of Mirzâ Shâh Rukh, the *jâgirdâr* of Patan in Gujarat, murdered Badi'-uz-Zamân one night. The matter was reported to Jahangir in 1623. They were summoned to the royal court; but the mother of the deceased Mirzâ did not demand retaliation. Jahangir ordered the murderers to be kept in prison for the time being and the matter to be taken up again.[22]

(Indian Travels of Thevenot, 97)

In Aurangzeb's time Bengal was regarded as a penal province where officers were transformed as a mark of imperial disfavours. William Finch mentions 3 prisons one which 'Rotas' was in Bengal. (Fister, p. 145)

WÂRRIS MOHAMMAD VS. MULLÂ

Wârris Mohammad Khân, a *mansabdâr* of 900 rank and 500 horse, kept with him by way of giving him protection a certain Mullâ. As the said Mullâ was subject to fits of insanity on occasions, he, at one time, attacked the Khân with a knife and killed him. Before the Khân succumbed to injuries, he gave out that as the Mullâ was not guilty of intentional murder, no body should hold him responsible for it, nor make any claims on him. Aurangzeb was informed of the incident while he was in Ajmer. He ordered on 9th April, 1680, that the Mullâ be kept in prison.[23] Under ordinary circumstances, the Mullâ might have been excused in accordance with the wishes of the victim; but as he was suffering from insanity, he could have proved dangerous to others. Hence, perhaps, this punishment.

The foster-brother of Prince Kâm Baksh bore jealousy towards the Nâzir, Khwâjâ Yâqût, upon whom he made a murderous attack. the Prince tried to shield him. Aurangzeb ordered (1699) that both of them be thrown into prison. He, moreover, deprived the Prince of his rank and occasions, he, at one time, attacked the Khân with a knife and killed him. Before the Khân succumbed to injuries, he gave out that as the Mullâ was not guilty of intentional murder, no body should hold him responsible for it, nor make any claims on him. Aurangzeb was informed of the incident while he was in Ajmer. He ordered on 9th April, 1680, that the Mullâ be kept in prison.[23] Under ordinary circumstances, the Mullâ might have been excused in accordance with the wishes of the victim; but as he was suffering from insanity, he could have proved dangerous to others.

Hence, perhaps, this punishment.

MANIÂ VS. SUNDER

Maniâ was murdered by Sunder and the widow of the deceased lodged a complaint against the accused. He was ordered to be imprisoned.[25]

IMPRISONMENT AND DISMISSAL

It was reported to Aurangzeb at the *Ghusalkhânâ* court at Burhanpur on 13th November, 1681, that Mohammad Sâlih Naqshbandi, holding the rank of 1000 *zât* and 250 *swâr*, had murdered a servant and a mace-bearer in a fit of madness. The Emperor ordered that he be deprived of office and placed in custody.[26]

CUSTODY

On 16th May, 1667, Sayyid Wafâ Mohammad killed the *faujdâr* of Lahore. The governor, Ibrâhim Khân, sent the murderer to the court. He was ordered to be kept in the custody of 'Âbid Khân.[27]

It was submitted to the Emperor on the night of 6th January, 1693, that Muhammad Amin, Mushriff of the First Class Court, had been murdered by his brother. He ordered that the culprit be chastised and entrusted to the custody of the *kotwal.*[28]

'Abul Hasn, accused of murder, was ordered to be handed over to the *kotwâl* on 30th March, 1703.[29]

DISMISSAL

Bijai Singh, holding a rank of 500 *zât* and 300 *swâr* in the army of Prince 'Âzam Shâh, was accused of murder. The Emperor ordered on 21st December, 1681, his removal from service.[30]

Ibrâhim, a *mansabdâr* in the army (under the command of Shahâb-ud-din Khân killed the daughter of a Koli at Nasik. For this offence the Khan had cast him in prison. When the matter was brought to the notice of the Emperor, he ordered the dismissal of the accused.[31]

DIMINUTION OF RANK

WIDOW'S DAUGHTER VS. MUQARRAB KHÂN

In this case as quoted at page 95, the rank of Muqarrab Khân was reduced by one-half.[32]

HARJAS GAUR'S MEN VS. TAHSILDAR'S BROTHER

Parganâ Seomâr in Ranthambor was in the possession of Harjas Gaur and Kesari Singh. The *tahsildar* of the area confiscated the *parganâ*. The men of Harjas Gaur quarrelled with the *tahsildar* and killed on 7th February, 1667, one of his brothers. Aurangzeb punished Harjas Gaur by diminution of his rank.[33]

MUKUND PANDIT VS. GANGÂ RÂM

Mukund Pandit, the *gumâshtâ* of Râjâ Jaswant Singh Bundelâ, murdered one Gangâ Râm, servant of the *faujdâr* of Iraj, and appropriated his property. The Râjâ's rank was reduced by 500.[34]

SHAR'I CASES

The following cases were ordered to be decided in accordance with the *Shar'a*. In such cases choice was allowed to the kinsmen of the murdered person to demand retaliation or blood money or a minor punishment.

LAHORE QÂZI VS. GOVERNOR

Sayyid 'Ali Akbar, *qâzi* of Lahore, was known for his honest intentions, violent temper and arrogant nature. He always refused to kowtow before any one, however highly placed he might have been. The governor and *kotwâl* of Lahore had become wearied of his haughty behaviour and looked forward to an opportunity to seriously punish him and put an end to his life. This they did in 1680 after heaping unheard-of indignities upon him. Amir Qawâmud-din, the governor of Lahore, was particularly responsible for this.

When the matter was brought to the notice of Aurangzeb, he deprived both the governor and the *kotwâl* of their ranks and removed them from service. How the *kotwâl's* life ended at Lahore, is not clear from the Akhbârât. Qawâm-ud-din was called to the royal court at Ajmer where the Emperor entrusted the case to the *qâzi's* court. Now in his turn he became the recipient of daily insults while made to attend the *Shar'î* court. Ultimately the sons of the deceased *qâzi* just refrained from pressing for retaliation. Had they insisted, the ex-governor was surely to suffer death penalty. He, however, did not survive long.[35]

RAGHUNÂTH SINGH VS. GRANDMOTHER AND AUNTS

Raghunâth Singh, the son of Saram Deo Sisodia of Mandalput, was guilty of inflicting wounds on his grandmother and two aunts who had appropriated the property of his deceased father in the village of Koraras, and of killing two persons. Mân Singh, the *faujdâr* of Mandal, sent his men to arrest the accused and then reported the matter to the Emperor. Aurangzeb ordered on 21st December, 1682, that he be sent along with the property to Asad Khân and be punished according to Shar'a.[36]

SHEIKH 'ALÂ-UD-DIN VS. MOTHER-IN-LAW

Sheikh 'Alâ-ud-din, the librarian at Shahjahanabad, sent one night for his mother-in-law to his own house on some pretext, and cut out her tongue, blinded her in one eye and wounded the other. He wound her in a piece of cloth, and asked his enunch Mashûb to throw her in the desert. The *thânedâr* who took the accused into custody and sent the report to 'Âqil Khân, the collector. 'Âqil Khân reported the whole matter to the Emperor at the court. On 21st January, 1685, Aurangzeb sent orders to 'Âqil Khân that the accused be deprived of his mansûb and punished according to Shari'at.[37]

MOHAMMAD RAZÂ VS. MOHAMMAD ZAMÂN

On 4th October, 1691, it was reported to Aurangzeb that Mohammad Razâ and others, nephews of Hakim Mohsan Khân, had killed one Mohammad Zamân by administering arsenic. It was ordered that they be punished according to Sharî'at.[38]

CHATTA VS. PÎR MOHAMMAD

The sons of Chattâ petitioned the *qâzi* that Pir Mohammad had beaten their father to death. The accused was summoned and tried in accordance with the Muslim Law in 1703. When he pleaded not guilty, two witnesses were produced by the plaintiffs. The crime being thus established, the *qâzi* asked the complainants either to demand retaliation or blood-money. They demanded neither. They said that they would be satisfied if two of Pir Mohammad's companions were turned out of the fort. This was acceded to.[39]

CASES WHERE INQUIRY WAS ORDERED BY THE EMPEROR

The following are the cases where the Emperor ordered an inquiry. There is no further reference to the case in the available records. It seems, however, that after the completion of the inquiry, the cases must have been decided in accordance with the Mulim Law.

A SLAVE VS. A BIJÂPURI

A slave who was accused of a crime was imprisoned in Bijâpur. After a time he was excused and released. He, however, had taken the whole thing to heart and wreaked vengeance on a Bijâpuri by putting an end to his life. Aurangzeb ordered on 11th April, 1667, that the report be relied upon if it were confirmed.[40]

A MANSABDÂR VS. A MURDERER

A *mansabdâr* was killed by a certain individual. The Emperor on 13th April, 1667, ordered Fûlâd Khân to make inquiries.[41]

RÂJÂ NARSINGH DÂS VS. HIS DÂWÂN'S SERVANT

Râjâ Narsingh Dâs had killed a servant of his Diwân. According to orders, the 'Âmils produced the Râjâ in the Court. On 13th April, 1667, Aurangzeb ordered Jumdtulmulk to make inquiries.[42]

On 17th October, 1704, Aurangzeb ordered an inquiry into the murder of Abdul Momin Darvesh who was murdered while reading the Qur'ân.[43]

ROYAL PARDON OR SILENCE

MÂHAM ANKÂ VS. TWO MÂLWÂ BEAUTIES

When Akbar was on his way from Sârangur to Agra in 1561, he stayed at Patancor. There Adham Khân intrigued with his mother's servants who waited in the royal harem and spirited away two special beauties from the Emperor's enclosure out of Bâz Bahadur's women. These two ladies had already been exhibited to the Emperor. Learning of this incident, he ordered a search to be made. Mâham Ankâ got afraid of the fact that if they were introduced to the Emperor, it might bring trouble to her son. She, therefore, caused these innocent ladies to be put to death. It was perhaps out of regard for Mâham Ankâ that Akbar overlooked the matter and did not punish the offender.[44]

MUSLIM SOLDIERS VS. CUSTOMS-OFFICER

We learn on the authority of Manucci that a customs-official insisted on seeing the cart in which a soldier's wife was sitting. The soldier repeatedly tried to assure him that the cart contained no tobacco. He put the officer to death when he refused to believe him. Aurangzeb took compassion on the temper of the youngman and granted him pardon.[145]

SUHRÂB VS. AHAD BEG

Suhrâb, the son of Barqandâz Khân, was attached to Bâdshah Quli Khân in the army of Prince Mohammad Akbar. He picked a quarrel with one Ahad Beg on the way and killed him. As a result, he was dismissed from service. Aurangzeb ordered on 27th September, 1680, that one mace-bearer should go to arrest and bring him to the Court. On 16th January, 1681, Lutfulla Khân suggested to the Emperor that it was necessary to inflict death punishment on the accused. Prince Shâh 'Âlam who was present there held a brief for the accused and requested the Emperor that he being a useful man, pardon might be granted him. Aurangzeb pardoned the offence of the accused and ordered that he might be taken back in service.[46]

ESCAPE FROM PUNISHMENT

ABUL FAZL VS. BÎR SINGH DEO

Jahangir himself describes with gusto the heinous deed of getting his father's famous minister Abul Fazl murdered by Bîr Singh Deo who at that time was engaged on a 'plundering expedition'. The murderer was promised favours and considerable rewards if he could kill Abul Fazl on hin way to the court from the Deccan in 1602. Bîr Singh Deo succeeded in his nefarious deed. Jahangir justifies his action, because, according to him, Abul Fazl had been standing between him and his father and had poisoned Akbar's mind against him.

This cold-blooded murder of his favourite minister and the court historian naturally shocked Akbar beyond mention. Orders were issued to inflict punishment on Bîr Singh Deo. Forces were sent against him and they several times attacked his abode and plundered it. The culprit, however, escaped every time. The army of Abdur Rahmân was re-inforced. Râj Singh shot many of his followers and wounded Bîr Singh Deo, but every time he effected his escape. Jahangir, however, thought differently from his father and called Bîr Singh Deo a 'simple-hearted and valorous man'. At the time of his accession, Jahangir rewarded the murderer of his father's minister by promoting him to the rank of 3,000.[47]

SAIF KHÂN'S SOLDIERS VS. HIS DÎWÂN

Saif Khân, the governor of Allahabad, owed to his army three months' salary. When a part of the money came from his *jâgir,* the Khân asked his diwân to distribute salary out of this and give the rest later on. Upon this the soldiers killed the Diwân in 1682 along with 24 of his men, appropriated two lac of rupees and made good their escape.[48]

News was received on 3rd November, 1703, of the murder of a dîwân by the *jam'adâr* of Yâsîn Khan *thânedâr*.[49]

A communication was received on 25th December, 1703, from Ibrâhim Khân, governor of Kashmir, that Râjâ Sa'âdat Yâr Khân, holding the rank of 1000 *zât* and 500 *swâr* had been killed by his own servant.[50]

MURDER CONDONED IN LIEU OF CONVERSION

A scriviner killed his sister and her paramour when he found both of them in the bed together. Woman and eunuch entered into a solemn league to kill the scriviner; but their machinations excited the displeasure of Aurangzeb who considered that the murderer had made a sufficient atonement for his crime by turning *Muselman.*[51]

FINE

MERCHANT VS. WIFE

A rich Muslim merchant slew his wife along with a baby when he found her in bed with her lover. For this crime only a fine was imposed on him.[52]

CASES WHERE NO PUNISHMENT IS MENTIONED

MISRÎ VS. BALRÂM

In 1592, Balrâm, the nephew of Râjâ Bhagwant Dâs, abused Misrî, the elephant driver, in Banâras, while sitting on an elephant. Misri killed him with his dagger.[53]

THIEF VS. KOTWÂL

In 1599, Khairullâ Khân, the *kotwâl* of Lahore, sent for a noted thief from prison in order to examine him in his private room. The thief brought with him his companions, too. They sent out his servants, perhaps on the pretext of supplying information, and killed Malik Khairulla and his son.[54]

ACTUAL AMOUNT OF BLOOD-MONEY

AN ENGLISH MAN VS. PAHALWÂ SAFED'S MEN

The East India Company claimed 560 ¼ Mahmudîs from the Mughal Government for the life of an Englishman who had been killed by the men of *Pahalwân* Safed. This sum was 'according to the rate which we paid in Surat for the like fact done by one of our own people.'[55]

RETALIATION ON THE SPOT

CUSTOMS-OFFICER VS. RÂJPUT SOLDIER

A customs-officer of Surat during Shahjahan's reign excited the fury of a Rârpût soldier by demanding from him custom on some pieces of calico, and abusing him on his refusal to do so. The soldier attacked him fatally, though he himself was hacked to pieces by the attendants.[56]

TWO HINDU RÂJÂS VS. COURT OFFICIAL

Two Hindu Râjâs came to the Court to pay their respects to Emperor Shahjahan. The Grandmaster of the Emperor's house-hold told one of them that he was unaware of the court etiquettes. The Râjâ considered this an insult and slew the official. They were killed on the spot by the attendants.[57]

Khan-i-Dauran was notorious for his harsh nature. His treatment with the people at large was unbecoming. It was perhaps on account of this that his Kashmiri new-Moslem employee murdered him in Lahore in 1645 A.D. Khafi Khan is of the view that the curses of the oppressed people were responsible for his death. There is no mention of any legal action against the accused.

Muntakhib-ul-Lubab, I, Urdu Tr., p. 185.

A PATHÂN VS.SOLDIERS

A tailor in the service of a Pathân was compelled by some soldiers to postpone the Pathân's work and give priority to that of their officer. One of the soldiers grew excited and slew the Pathân's brother. The Pathân got infuriated, killed the members of his own family, and assisted by the tailor, indulged in an open fight with the soldiers and killed many of them. They themselves also received mortal wounds.[58]

A HINDU RÂJÂ VS. AN OFFICIAL

Manucci records the story of a Hindu Râjâ who stabbed a high officer of Shahjahan in the court, and, subsequently was himself cut to pieces.[59]

A RÂJPÛT VS. AN OFFICER

According to Peter Mundy, a *Râjpût,* before he himself was slain, put to death a Mughal officer and some of his companions, when, under the orders of Shahjahan, they tried to demolish a temple.[60]

ACCOMPLICE OF THE MURDERER

MUN'IM KHÂN AND SHAHÂB-UD-DÎN VS. SHAMS-UD-DÎN

Mun'im Khân and Shahâb-ud-din Mohammad Khân, accomplices in the murder of Prime Minister Shams-ud-din, recoiled before the wrath of Akbar and took to flight. Mun'im Khân was arrested in *parganâ* Surat and sent to the Court. The Emperor pardoned both of them.[61]

II. QATL SHIBU'L-'AMD.

When the perpetrator struck a man with something that was neither a weapon nor served as such, the crime was called as qatl shibu'l-'amd. It was held that this was sinful and required expiation. Expiation consisted in freeing a Muslim slave-girl, or in fasting two months succesively. A fine was to be paid with camels only.[62] We do not come across any case under this heading.

III. Qatl U'l-Khatâ or homicide with misadventure was of two kinds : error in intention and error in act. Error in intention was where the mistake occurred with respect to the subject, as where a person aimed an arrow at a man supposing him to be game; or at a Muslim supposing him to be a hostile infidel; error in the act, on the other hand, was where a person shot an arrow at a mark and it hit a man. The homicide with misadventure required expiation and diya; and the slayer was excluded from inheriting the property of the slain.[63]

In 1661 A.D., in the town of Sonpat a group of young boys was busy at the play, 'King and Wazir'. The 'King' ordered that the 'thieves' be beaten. The *'Kotwâl'* gave blows to the 'thieves' so severely that they died on the spot.[64]

IV. Qatl Qâ'im Maqâm'L-Khatâ or homicide of a similar nature by misadventure, was, where a person turning sides in sleep fell upon another so as to kill him by the fall. The same rules applied to it as to homicide by misadventure.[65]

V. Qatl Bi-Sabab or homicide by intermediate cause was where, for example, a man dug a well on the highway or set up a stone and another fell into the well or over the stone, and died. In this case blood-money must be paid.[66]

If a man caused premature birth of a still-born child by striking the belly of a pregnant woman, the offender had to give the woman a slave or a slave girl or a horse worth 500 *dirhams.* If the woman lost her life along with the child, the offender was liable to pay the blood-money for the death of the woman as well. The offence was not regarded as a deliberate murder.[67]

If any one was killed on the false evidence of another, qisâs was not to be executed on the witness. Only diya was to be paid. (Encyclopaedia of Islam, II, p. 825).

If a man built a wall which was not straight and it fell so as to kill somebody or to destroy the property of some one, the owner was to be held responsible.[68]

If the quadruped, on which a person was sitting, trampled another person under foot, the rider was to incur *diya* and expiation and he was to lose his right to inheritance.[69]

If a slave committed an offence which incurred diya, the possessor of the slave was either to lose the slave or give *'arsh.*[70]

A person who killed a slave by misadventure, was to pay the price of the slave.[71]

RETALIATION AND COMPENSATION

RETALIATION (QISAS)

Retaliation was incurred by wilfully killing a person whose blood was under continued protection. In cases of murder a free man was to be slain for a free man and a slave for a slave, a man for a man and a woman for a woman. An infidel was to be slain for the murder of a Muslim, a *zimmi* for a *zimmi* and a Muslim for a *zimmi.* Even if a *zimmi* turned Muslim after putting a *zimmi* to death, he was to be murdered in retaliation. An adult was to be slain for an infant and a sound person for one who was infirm, blind, lame, insane or dismembered. A son was slain for the murder of a father and mother, but a father and mother were not to be slain for the murder of their child. A master was not to be slain for the murder of their child. A master was not to be slain for his slave, and retaliation was not incurred if one of the two partners in a slave killed such a slave. Retaliation was to be executed by the next of the kin with a sword or a sharp weapon like a sword.[72]

There was no retaliation for a man guilty of strangling another person, but if the strangler was a habitual offender, he must be executed.[73] According to a *farmân* of Aurangzeb, a person suspected of this crime was to be kept in prison. In case a specific charge was brought against him, he was to be tried in the court of a *qâzî.*[74]

If a man immersed another person into water from which escape was impossible, retaliation, according to Abu Hanifa was not incurred. His two disciples, however, maintained otherwise.[75] Aurangzeb had ordered that a man who killed another by drowning him into water was to be chastised and imprisoned and *diya* or exculpatory fine was to be charged from him. In case of the repetition of the offence, strict *siâsat* was to be done to him.[76] For striking off hand or foot or tooth of another man, retaliation was incurred.[77]

SUSPECTED POISONING

There was no retaliation for compelling a man to take poison, but *diya* must be paid.[78] We come across a case of suspected poisoning in the *Akhbârât.* It was reported to Aurangzeb on 15th February, 1704, that Mohammad Momin *alias* Shambhunâth Deshmukh of Sultanpur had died. His heirs suspected that he had been poisoned by some one and had also sued that person for murder. It was ordered that the heirs of the deceased should take the case against the accused to the court of law and get it decided in accordance with the Shara'.[79]

In case a man deceitfully killed another by poisoning, he was to be chastised and imprisoned till he repented.[80]

DIYA

Retaliation could be commuted for by a sum of money, called *diya. Diya* could be paid to the heirs of the murdered person in place of retaliation. *Diya* for murder was to be paid for by a hundred camels or a thousand *dînars* or ten thousand *dirhams* according to Abu Hanifa. The same *diya* held good in case of a Muslim, a *zimmi* and a hostile infidel who took refuge in a Muslim country.[81]

Any one who was the rightful heir of the property of the murdered person had the right to demand retaliation. Where there were more than one heir, no one had the right of retaliation unless all heirs agreed. In case of wilful murder the only heir of the murdered person could slay the murderer with sword, whether the *qâzi* ordered it or not. A mad man could kill the slayer of his son in retaliation or compound with him, but he could not excuse him. If the right of retaliaton was shared by a major person and a minor person, the major could exercise it according to Abu Hanifa, but his two disciples disagreed with him.[82] There was difference of opinion as to who would exercise the right of retaliation in case all the heirs of the murdered man were minors. Some viewed that the right would accrue to the Sultân while others held that one or all the heirs should be allowed to grow major. The right of retaliation went to the king and the *qâzî*, if the murdered person was heirless. If a slave, who was the property of two or three persons, was killed, the right of retaliation would belong not to one but to all of them.[83]

Retaliation lapsed if the murderer and the heirs of the murdered person composed among themselves for a certain amount of money. The right agreement should be for an amount less than 100 camels, 1,000 *dînârs,* and 10,000 *dirhams.* There was no retaliation if husband, mother or grandmother of the murdered person forgave the murderer. If one out of the two heirs forgave the murderer, the other would get *diya* from the property of the slayer within three years. If an heir pardoned one out of the two murderers, he could slay the other in retaliation.[84]

There was neither retaliation nor *diya* if a person invited another to kill himself. Retaliation was inflicted if A asked B to kill his (A's) minor son and if a person asked another to kill his brother. In these cases the murderer incurred retaliaton.[85] If a boy lost his life by falling from the root or into water, his parents were to incur expiation in case the boy could not protect himself.[86] If a father caused the death of his son by punishing him for reformation and a husband killed his wife in the same manner, and a teacher his pupil, the father and the husband both incurred expiation and *diya* and the teacher only expiation.[87]

ATTEMPTED SUICIDE

We come across a case of attempted suicide. Kâmgâr Khân tried to commit suicide by inflicting four wounds on his body with *jamdhar.* For this he was removed from his post.[88]

REFERENCES

1. Encyclopaedia of Islam, II, p. 822.
2. *Ibid.,* p. 824.
3. *Ibid.,*
4. Fatâwâ-i-'Âlamgîrî, IV, p. 503;
   Encyclopaedia of Islam, II, p. 823;
   Dictionary of Islam, p. 421.
5. Mîrât-i-Ahmadi, i, p. 282;
   Cf. Mughal Administration, 4th ed., p. 114.
6. Akbar Nâmâ, II, pp. 27-28.
7. Badauni Lowe, II, pp. 49-50 : ext, II, pp. 52-53.
   Tabaqât, De, II. pp. 263, 264, 655; Text, II, pp. 158-59.
   Akbar Nâmâ, Bevertdge, II, pp. 269-73 : Text, II, pp. 158-59.
   Eliot & Dowson, VI, pp. 26-27.
   Farishtâ, III, 334-5. Text, I, p. 377.
   According to Farishtâ, he was murdered while reading the Qur'ân.
   Khâfi Khân, I, pp. 161-62.
8. Akbar Nâmâa, Beveridge, III, p. 46; Text, III, p. 32.
   Badauni, Lowe, II, p. 151; Text, II, p. 147.
   Tabaqât, De, II, p. 389. Text, II, p. 262.

9. Akbar Nâmâ, Beveridge, III, p. 515; Text III, p. 351.
10. Akbar Nâmâ, Beveridge, III, pp. 803-5; Text III, p. 527.
Badauni, Lowe, II, p. 328; p. 376. Text, II, p. 319; pp. 364-65.
11. Tuzk, Beveridge, I, p. 172. Text, I, p. 84.
12. Tuzk, Bev., II, p. 211.
13. Tuzk, R & B., I, p. 353; Text, I. p. 175.
14. Bernier, I, pp. 131-32 : Manucci, I, p. 240; pp. 382-83;
Eliot & Dowson, VII, pp. 131-32; 267-68;
'Âml Salih quoted in Eliot & Dowson's *Shahjahan* published by Susil Gupta Ltd., p. 140.
15. Manucci, II, pp. 425-53.
16. Ma'âsir-i'-'Âlamgîrî, p. 126 (Text).
17. Ma' âsîr-i-'Âlamgîrî, Text, p. 57.
18. Jaipur Akhbârât, 10th year, 20th July, 1667.
19. Akhbârât-i-Darbâr-i-Mu'allâ, 13th May, 1700.
20. Akbarnâmâ, Bev., II, pp. 334-37; Text, pp. 216-19;
Badauni, Lowe, II, p. 71; Text, II, p. 71;
Tabâqât, II. pp. 288-89; Text, II, pp. 175-76.
21. Eliot & Dowson, VI, pp. 314-15;
Tuzk, I, Bev., p. 104; Text, I, p. 51.
22. Tuzk, II, Bev., p. 259; Text, II, p. 368;
Iqbal Nâmâ, p. 140; Text, p. 204.
23. Jaipur Akhbârât, 49th year.
24. Manucci, IV, pp. 253-54;
Ma'âsir-i-'Âlamgîrî, text, pp. 397-400.
25. Jaipur Akhbârât, 46th year.
26. Akhbârât-i-Darbar-i-Mu'allâ, 13th November, 1681.
27. *Ibid.*,10th year.
28. Akhbârât-i-Darbâr-i-Mu'allâ, 6th January, 1693.
29. *Ibid.*, 30th Marth, 1703.
30. *Ibid.*, 21st December, 1681.
31. Jaipur Akhbârât, 25th year.
32. Tuzk, Text, I, p. 84; R & B., I, p. 172.
33. Jaipur Akhbârât, 9th year.
34. *Ibid.*, 25th year.
35. Ma'âsir-i-'Âlamgîrî, Text, p. 188.
36. Jaipur Akhbârât, 26th year.
37. Jaipur Akhbârât, 28t year.
38. *Ibid.*, 4th October, 1691.
39. Akhbârât, 46th year; Cf. Mughal Government & Administration, p. 210.
40. Jaipur Akhbârât, 10th year, 11th April, 1667.
41. *Ibid.*, " 13th April, 1667.
42. *Ibid.*, " 13th April, 1667.

43. Akhbârât-i-Darbâr-i-Mu'allâ, 17th October, 1704.
44. Akbar Nâmâ, Beveridge, II, p. 221. Text, II, p. 143.
45. Manucci, II, p. 175.
46. Jaipur Akhbârât, 24th year.
Eliot & Dowson, VI, pp. 288-89, 442, 106-7, 113-14, Tuzk, I, pp. 24-25, 204-280.
47. Akbar Nâmâ, Bev. III, p. 924; De Laet, pp. 166-68, Tuzk, Text, II, pp. 100-101, 138; Khâfi Khân, I, p. 323.
48. Jaipur Akhbârât, 25th year.
49. Akhbârât-i-Darbâr-i-Mu'allâ, 3rd November, 1703.
50. *Ibid.*, 25th December, 1703.
51. Bernier, I, pp. 146-47.
52. Fryer, I, p. 245.
53. Akbar Nâmâ, Beveridge, III, p. 924, Text, III, p. 605.
54. *Ibid.*, 1135, Text, III, p. 759.
55. English Factories, p. 284.
56. Tavernier, II, pp. 251-52.
57. *Ibid.*, pp. 219-20.
58. Fryer, I, pp. 242-43.
59. Manucci, I, pp. 207-8.
60. Peter Mundy, II, p. 178.
61. Akbar Nâmâ, Bev. II, pp. 269-73; Farishta, II, p. 335; Text, pp. 173-76; Eliot & Dowson, VI, p. 28.
62. Fatâwâ-i-'Âlamgiri, IV, p. 503; Hughes, p. 421; Encyclopaedia, II, p. 824.
63. Fatâwâ-i-'Âlamgîrî, IV, p. 503; Hughes, p. 421; Encyclopaedia, II, p. 324.
64. Ma'asîr-i-'Âlamgîrî p. 39.
65. Fatâwâ-i-'Âlamgîrî, IV, p. 504; Hughes, p. 421; Encyclopaedia II. p. 824.
66. *Ibid.*, Hughes, p. 421; Encyclopaedia of Islam II, p. 824.
67. *Ibid.*, p. 554. Encyclopaedia of Islam, II, p. 825.
68. *Ibid.*, p. 556.
69. *Ibid.*, p. 577.
70. Fatâwâ-i-Âlamgîrî, IV, p. 585.
71. *Ibid.*, p. 620.
72. *Ibid.*, pp. 504-6; Dictionary of Islam, pp. 421; 481.
73. *Ibid.*, pp. 504-6.
74. Mirât, I, p. 279, Mughal Administration 4th ed. p. 111.
75. Fatâwâ, IV, p. 507.
76. Mîrât, I, p. 280; Mughal Administration, 4th ed. pp. 113-14.
77. Dictionary of Islam. p. 481.
78. Fatâwâ-i-'Âlamgîrî, IV, p. 508.
79. Akhbârât-i- Darbâr-i-Mu'allâ, 15th February, 1704.

80. Mîrât, I, p. 280.
81. Fatâwâ-i-'Âlamgîrî, IV, p. 537; Hughes, p. 128.
82. *Ibid.*
83. Fatâwâ-i-'Âlamgîrî, IV, p. 537.
84. *Ibid.*, pp. 531-32. See also Hughes, p. 481.
85. *Ibid.*, p. 546.
86. *Ibid.*, p. 552.
87. *Ibid.*, p. 553.
88. Ma'âsir-i-'Âlamgîrî, p. 192.

V
QATL OR MURDER

In Mughal India *qatl* or murder was looked upon as crime primarily against another person. The right to demand justice lay with the heirs unless the murdered person was heirless. The punishment also depended on the temper of the survivors. It could vary from execution to payment of a varying amount of blood-money. Notice was taken of the circumstances under which the man came to commit the crime and punishment varied accordingly.

In the Qur'ân unlawful slaying is forbidden in a series of verses. In the Qur'ân unlawful slaying is forbidden in a series of verses. The Qur'ân is supplemented by a number of passages from the accounts of the Prophet.[1]

According to Muslim law, *Qatl* or *Jinâyat'l-nafs* is the act of a man where by the life of a fellow human being is brought to a close.[2] It was however qualified by any of the five "legal categories." They were known as *wâjib, mandûb, mubâh,* self-defence, and *makrûh. Wâjib* was the murder that was undertaken out of necessity or duty, such as the killing of the *murtadd* or the apostate. *Mandûb* was a murder that was recommended, e.g., when the *ghâzi* killed his unbelieving kinsmen if they insulted Allâh or His Prophet. *Mubâh* was the permitted *qatl* when the *Imâm* killed the unbelieving prisoners of war. Killing in self-defence was also allowed. The *makrûh* or the disapproved murder was that when the *ghâzi* killed his unbelieving kinsmen without their having insulted Allâh or His Prophet. It was illegal and therefore forbidden, ***harâm.***[3]

Homicide of which Muslim Law takes cognizance is of five kinds :

1. Qatul-'Amd;
2. Qatl Shibu'l-'amd;
3. Qatlu'l-Khatâ;
4. Qatl Qâ'im Maqâm'l-Khatâ;

system of gifts by the foreign travellers. Even official records have made no secret of the fact.

Through the mediation of Nûr Jahân, Jalâ'ir Khân was appointed the governor of Orissâ on a promise of a *peshkash* of three lacs of rupees from his income. Mirzâ Ahmad Beg, a relation of the Begum, and a nephew of the Bengal governor, Ibrâhim Khân, represented to her and got the appointment transferred in his favour. Jalâ'ir Khân whose appointment had been cancelled, demanded the return of the money paid by him. For this he had to undergo many troubles. It was with some difficulty that he could save his *mansab* and *jâgîr*.[5]

Mirzâ Nathan presented to the Bengal governor, Ibrahim Khân Fateh-Jang, a number of elephants, 100 small and big boats and other gifts. The Khân became highly pleased and recommended to the 'Sublime Court' and particularly to Nûr Jahân Begum his promotion in rank and title. Moreover, it became 'incumbent' upon Mirzâ Nathan to send suitable gifts as *peshkash* to the Court to Nûr Jahân, I'timâd-ud-daulâ and other nobles. Mirzâ Nathan collected all the rare gifts from his house and obtained others on credit and sent these in charge of Hâtim Khân and Gopâl Dâs to the Court. These included one suitable elephant for the Emperor and one female elephant for Nûr Jahân. The total value of these gifts was Rs. 40,000.[6]

Ibrâhim Khân, the governor of Bengal (1617-23), offered the office of the Sardâr of the Sylhat territory, after the death of Sheikh Suleiman, *thânedar,* to Mirzâ Nathan, on payment of an imperial *peshkash* of Rs. 2,000.[7]

Mirzâ Nathan returned from Hâjo without permission of the governor, Ibrâhîm Khân. Mukhlis Khân Dîwân calmed the furious governor and brought about a reconciliation between the two. Next day when the Dîwân came to the house of Mirzî Nathan to console him, the Mirzâ presented him with nine costly horses, a hundred *thâns* of rare cloth of Bengal, one mound of high class *agar* (aloe-wood), and Rs. 5,000 in cash. Mukhlis Khân accepted only the *agar* and one horse.[8]

Tahawwar Sha'âr Ajaib Singh, *thanedâr* of Othal in the *sarkâr* of Ujjain, accepted in 1706 one rupee by way of thanks when he released the two wives of one Mohan. They had quarrelled with one another and had been kept in custody by him.[9]

In the same year *Tahawwar Dastgâh* Udai singh, *thanedâr* of *parganâ* Bhaurasâ in the *sarkâr* of Sârangpur, went to the village of Sahiya in connection with a serious complaint against the *kotwâl* there. The *muqaddams* of the village came and each presented one rupee by way of present. Moreover, he enjoyed a feast there along with his soldiers.[10]

Similarly, *Rif'at Panâh* Banârsi Dâs, *mutsaddi* of the *jâgîr* of *Nawâb* Nawâzish Khân, who visited the town of Othal, was presented one rupee each by the *qânûngos* and *chaudharis* in 1706.[11]

There was no normal code to guide the conduct of the government officials in those days and the general conditions of the times did not warrant such a code. The officers as a rule did not feel any sense of responsibility towards the people in this connection. Mostly they lived fast and were always badly in need of money. Moreover, particularly because of the system of presents, it had not been possible for a strong public opinion in the country to develop against the prevalent vice of bribery.

Hâji Ibrâhim Sirhindi was accused in 1584 of accepting illegal gratifications. He was dismissed and confined in the fortress of Ranthmbor.[12]

Daulat Khân, entitled Nazîr-ud-daulâ, the head eunuch in Akbar's reign, had, according to Jahangir, no equal in the 'receipt of bribes'. He left ten *krors* of *ashrafis* and jewels worth three *krors*. All the money was appropriated by the Emperor.[13]

We learn from the letters written by the English factors to the East India Company that quite often they had to bribe the officials before they could get their goods released.

Sir Thomas Roe records with satisfaction that in November, 1616, he was successful in recovering all the money that had been taken by the Mughal officials from the servants of the Company before his time.[14]

During the governorship in Bengal of Ibrâhim Khân, one *Sheikh* Ibrâhim Karori misappropriated seven lac of rupees and rebelled. He offered bribe to another imperial officer who accepted it. Moreover, he bribed twenty-five imperial horsemen.[15]

There is a reference to the corruption by governors and other officials in a letter of 18th February, 1620, written by Thomas Kerridge to the Company. He complains that from "the king to the lowest" there was great corruption.[16]

Prior to this, an English caravan was detained at Burhanpur by the Mughal authorities on the complaint of a Portugese that some Englishmen owed him some silver etc. The Surat factors wrote to James at Burhanpur to spend, if necessary, any reasonable amount in bribes. The caravan was released later on by the orders of Prince Khurram.[17]

A letter of 28th March, 1620, has given details about the amounts of bribe to be paid to the governor of Gujarât, the customs-officer of Surat and the broker there. In lieu of these bribes the English would have their coral released and gain the liberty to buy and sell at their discretion.[18]

The customs-officer, however, broke the pledge, and, in spite of the bribes, fined both the broker and the *shroff* for buying and selling with the English.[19]

During a consultation held in Surat by President Kerridge and others on 20th February, 1621, they decided the amounts of bribe to be paid to different persons serving in the Customs Department there. It was resolved to offer cloth worth 600 *mahmûdis* to the Customer, of half the value to the Chief Writer, and to distribute 200 *mahmûdis* among other officials. Earlier, they had settled with the Customer to offer him a scarf worth 25 *mahmûdis,* but he, instead, took one worth 47 *mahmûdis.* They agreed to this on the understanding that the expected caravan from Mându would be permitted to come in without further bribes to him or other officers.[20]

On 10th April, 1621, Thomas Kerridge wrote to the Company that there was such a tough opposition in Surat at the arrival of their coral there, that he had to pay Customs-Officer a large sum of money in bribe.[21]

Some time they bribed the Customs-Officers of Surat to help them recover their debt from some Indian merchant as a letter of September 1621 shows.[22] They complain in another letter that on their refusal to give the Customs-Officer a certain quantity of cloth, he 'stop the current of your business[23]......'

A letter of 23rd August, 1623, records that Nicholas Bangham, an English factor, had to pay a bribe of Rs. 30 to the Diwân and his subordinates before he could be permitted to depart from Broach.[24]

In a letter of 26th October, 1623 Hopkins wrote from Surat to President Rastell to send them grapewine as Safi Khan had demanded it twice.

Mirzâ Ghiâs Beg, the father of Nûr Jahân, was notorious for taking bribes.[26]

Âqâ Taqi, the chief officer of Qulîj Khân, the *sardâr* of Hanjo in Bengal, had misappropriated all the revenues of the dismissed *sardâr.* Qulij Khan imprisoned his clerks and took his family as hostages to his next officer, Mirzâ Nathan.[27]

When Shahryar shut himself up in the fort of Lahore after the defeat of his forces by the imperialists under Dâwar Baksh and Âsaf

Khân late in 1627, his officers accepted bribes and admitted the imperialists into the fort.[28].

Khan Jahan Lodi, the governor of the Deccan, in the beginning of Shahjahan's reign, had accepted a bribe of three lacs of rupees from the Nizâm-u-mulk and surrendered to him the territory of Bâlâghât.[29]

Manrique found that in the reign of Shahjahan, the Catholics had managed to control trade in India by bribing the 'governor', i.e. the customs-officer of Surat and his chief officials.[30]

When Shahjahan rewarded a musician with Rs. 1,000 the latter burst into tears and disclosed that he would have to part with money to the gate-keepers of the palace by way of bribery. This clever representation of the case made the Emperor laugh. He ordered the twenty-five gate-keepers then on duty to receive one thousand stripes each by way of punishment.[31]

Wazîr Khân, a noble at Shahjahan's court, took huge bribes, some time amounting to Rs. 30,000 a day. According to Mandelslo, the merchants at Ahmadabad, had to pay no customs on the export or import of goods. They paid, however, fifteen pence per wagon to the *kotwâl* of the place. Thevenot discovered at the Surat customs-house that every way-farer had to pay about 18 pence to the waiter as a tip.[32]

In March 1628 the English and the Dutch got into trouble with the Mughal authorities for buying and transporting salt-petre without the permission of the government. Two of the English factors, Clement and Bangham, were kept prisoners in the castle for a night and day. They were released when they gave bribe and present to an officer, Razâ Bahâdur.[33]

On their way from Surat to Agra in November 1630, Peter Mundy, accompanied by the caravan, came to a place called 'Barnolee'. He was asked there to pay Rs. 20 as custom. He evaded the payment by giving one *mahmûdi* to the peons as bribe.[34] Two years later, Peter Mundy bribed the *faujdâr* of Banaras and got released his cart which had been confiscated for *begâr*.[35]

In August 1636, John Drake was at the royal camp on the *Narbadâ*. He experienced much trouble in procuring a *farmân* from the Emperor as every one demanded bribe from him. Khusrow Beg would accept nothing less than Rs. 500/-. Drake gave him a gold chain and Rs. 100.[36]

Methwold and the Council warned the English factors at Ahmadabad in March 1638 not to give further bribes to Saif Khân.[37]

During Aurangzeb's viceroyalty in the Deccan (1636-44), his

representative Bandâ Rizai embezzled money and amassed a good fortune. He was recalled and imprisoned.[38]

Complaints were made to Shahjahan against Mohammad Sa'id *kotwâl* who did not decide cases in a just manner and took bribe. He was ordered to be bitten by a cobra in the presence of the king.[39]

As salt-petre was a prohibited commodity, it had become a practice to pay some quantity of it to the officer concerned. In March 1654, the English at Surat were sure that the salt-petre at Ahmadabad would not be released without a heavy bribe to the customs-officer.[49] In December 1654, a quantity of salt-petre belonging to the English was stopped at Râjmahal. The English factors there opined that to secure its release and for future negotiations it would be necessary to bribe the governor and other officers. They were of the opinion that in such matters they should follow the example of the Dutch and pay annual presents.[41]

'Inâyat Khân, the commandant of Surat, used to draw from the treasury the pay of 50 soldiers but had for long appropriated the money without maintaining a proper force.

The rich people, to avoid Shivaji's attack, bribed 'Inâyat and found shelter in the fort.[42]

Towards the close of 1669, the Dutch in Bengal captured salt-petre belonging to the English. The latter complained to the Mughal authorities who instituted a sort of inquiry. It was considered that the presents sent by the Dutch to Shâistâ Khân would stifle all further inquiry.[43]

Even the princes of royal blood and ministers of state were not above the vice of corruption.

We are informed by Manucci that a few days before his departure for the Deccan for the conquest of the territories of Golcunda, Prince Dârâ had deprived him by bribery of the eighty European artillerymen in his (Mir Jumla's) service.[44]

After Dârâ's defeat and Aurangzeb's entry into Agra, Aurangzeb communicated with the artillerymen under an Englishman, Rubern Smith, who were in the fort under Shahjahan. After accepting bribe from Aurangzeb, they escaped by descending the walls with the help of ropes.[45]

Manucci has narrated the story of an Armenian, Khwâjâ Safar, who took from the Surat merchants cloth worth Rs. 15,000, loaded it from there, then declared himself bankrupt. They took him to the court where the judge delivered the judgment in his favour as he had already won him over by giving him a bribe of Rs. 5,000.[6]

Jâ'far Khân Wazîr (1664-70) was notorious for taking bribes.[47]

Sometimes the people of a certain locality refused to put up with the excesses of an oppressive executive official or a corrupt judge. They wrote to the court demanding his replacement. During his stay at Burhanpur in November, 1681, the citizens made a complaint to the Emperor against *qâzi* Mohammad Rashîd. They accused him of having accepted illegal gratifications and delivering unjust and wrong judgments, and of causing unnecessary inconvenience to the public at large. Aurangzeb decreed that Ihtimâm Khân should arrest the said *qâzi* and send him to *qâzi* Sheikh-ul-Islam who was to institute legal proceedings against him.[48]

In a letter written to Aurangzeb on 26th October 1692, the news-writers of Berar were accused of accepting bribes from the *gumâshtâs* of the *jâgirdârs* and of their failure to report against their excessive oppressions of the *ryots* there. Orders were sent from the Emperor's court warning the news-writers against this wrong practice. They were asked to send factual reports.[49] The guilty ones were ordered to be transferred.

During the last days of Aurangzeb's reign, it had become a common practice for officers in distant provinces to bribe the powerful persons at the court and do things in their own manner.[50]

A Bengali Muslim in the party of Manrique was accused of killing two peacocks. He was got released by the Portugese traveller by paying valuable presents to the wife of the *qâzi.*[51]

The paucity of the recorded cases might make one believe that bribery was very infrequent in Mughal India. It is necessary, however, to remember that these cases show the general prevalence of bribery among the public servants at that time. The convention of offering presents had its evil effects. Every one expected similar presents from those below in rank. The result was that bribery in itself was not considered a crime, though a complaint could be made against an officer who was suspected of having been bribed into giving an unjust decision in a particular case. This is further proved by the fact that the Fatâwâ-i-'Âlamgiri does not seem to say a word about bribery as a crime. All the foreign travellers including Palsaert have complained about the greedy nature of the Mughal officials. His invective even goes against the governors who accepted bribes from thieves and remained inactive, for 'avarice dominates manly honour'.[52]

EMBEZZLEMENT

The contemporary records do not contain adequate information regarding peculation as a crime. We learn that whenever a case of embezzlement was brought to the notice of the Emperor, he ordered inquiries to be made. The lack of sufficient material does not help us to form an opinion about the punishment of this form of offence. Aurangzeb had ordered that an official, on a charge of embezzlement, was to be dismissed from his post or imprisoned, but he was not to be fined.[53]

Khwâjâ Shah Mansûr, 'an adept at the mysteries of accounts', was an accountant in the Perfumery Department. Later on, he joined the service of Mun'im Khân. After the Khan's death, Râjâ Todar Mal 'on account of question about accounts', imprisoned him in 1576 and put chains on his body. Not only was he pardoned by the Emperor, but promoted to the exalted post of Vazir.[54]

In 1580, 'Alâ-ud-dîn Yazdi, the Dîwân of Gujarat, was suspected of embezzlement. The governor of the province Mirzâ 'Azîz Kokaltâsh, handed the Diwân over to his servant, Tâlib, to be kept as a prisoner. Tâlib, however, exceeded the limits of his powers, and wrongfully killed 'Ala-ud-dîn Yazdi. Fcr this offence, the Mirza ordered the execution of Tâlib.[55]

Roshan Beg, a collector of exchequer lands in Bengal, embezzled money and fled to Kabul some time before the Bengal revolt in 1580. Later on, he received capital punishment but on a different charge of rebellion.[56]

The son of *qâzi* Jalâl Multâni, the *qâzi* of the army, was accused of having embezzled treasury money. *Qâzi* Jalâl himself had forged in a *farmân* a draft of one lac of *tankâs* and had drawn it from the treasury for his own use. Khwâjâ Fatehullâh Shîrâzi was his accomplice in this act. Both qâzi Jalâl Multâni and the Khwâjâ were exiled to Mecca in 1582. The *qâzi* Jalâl Multâni and the Khwâjâ were exiled to Mecca in 1582. The *qâzi* died in Mecca.[57] There is no mention of the punishment that was meted out to the son of the *qâzi*.

I'timâd-ud-daulâ was accused by his Hindu sevant, Uttam Chand, of having embezzled Rs. 5,000. The Emperor ordered him to be handed over to Dayânat Khân who was to keep him in custody.[58]

Shahjahan came to know that the wife of Khalil Ullâh Khân wore shoes worth three millions of rupees. He took this as a sign of the vast wealth of the noble, a greater part of which he must have got by 'theft', meaning thereby perhaps embezzlement. Khalil Ullâ was required to render his accounts in detail so that it might be found out how he had come by that money.[59]

The officials, we learn, availed themselves of every opportunity to embezzle the government collections.[60] Manucci complains that it was always their habit to keep three-fourth for themselves and pay one-fourth to the State.[61]

It was reported by the people of Karnal on 16th December, 1666, that the *qâzi* of the place had appropriated public money. Aurangzeb ordered that he be entrusted to 'Âqil Khan.[162]

Aurangzeb learnt that the treasurer and district officer of Lauli collected about Rs. 16,000 annually as toll on merchants and travellers and sent only about Rs. 2,000 to the royal treasury. The Emperor ordered prince Â'zam to make inquiries.[63]

It came to the knowledge of Aurangzeb that Amir Habîb Ullâh of Jaunpur, the *amîn* of the toll tax on non-Muslims, had admitted to have appropriated from the imperial treasury a sum of Rs. 40,000. The Amir was detained by 'Inayat Ullâh Khân who had appointed strict collectors to exact money from him. The Emperor forgave the *amîn* as he had spent all the money for charitable purposes.[64]

Bahâdur Khân, the governor of the Deccan, was accused of embezzlement. Orders for his dismissal and for the confiscation of his property were issued. Later on he was forgiven. 'Abdullâ Khân, the Bakshi there, was dismissed on the ground of making wrong entries of the collections.[65]

Aurangzeb came to know that Tarbiat Khân, who had got money for distribution among the soldiers of the fortresses, kept it for his own private use. Â'zam was ordered to make inquiries and take suitable action.[66]

Muttalib Khan, *dâroghâ* of the mace-bearers, made a sub-mission through Mihr Yâr 'Ali to the effect that Banwâri had a claim of 1.50 lacs of rupees against Mohammad 'Evaz, the dismissed *mutasaddi* of Surat. Banwâri had also brought to his notice that the same official had misappropriated 9 lacs of rupees there. He was prepared to furnish a proof of This from the account books of the local money-lenders (*Sâhûkârs*). In the petition, the *dâroghâ* had requested the Emperor to appoint two mace-bearers as *sazâwals*.

The Emperor conceded his request and ordered the appointment of Siddiq Beg and Mohammad Sa'id for the purpose.[67]

REFERENCES

1. Manucci, II, pp. 451-52
2. English Factories, 1630-34, p. 193; Tavernier, I, p. 17.
3. Badâûni, Lowe, II. p. 332. Text, II, p. 322.
4. Hedâyat-al-Qawâid, pp. 27-32; Âîin, II, pp. 37-40. Mughal Administration, 4th ed. p. 50.
5. Bahâristân-i-Ghâybi, II, p. 634.
6. *Ibid.*, II, p. 629.
7. *Ibid.*, II,.p. 633.
8. Bahâristan-i-Ghâyhi II, p. 501.
9. Jaipur Akhbârât, 49th year;
10. *Ibid.*
11. *Ibid.*
12. Mîrat, op. cit Saran; Prov. Govt. pp. 368-69.
13. Eliot & Dowson, VI, pp. 496-97, Price's Memoirs, p. 34.
14. The Embassy, p. 290.
15. Bahâristân-i-Ghâybi, ii, pp. 443, 448, 461.
16. English Factories, 1618-21, p. 183.
17. *Ibid.*, p. 118.
18. *Ibid.*, p. 187.
19. *Ibid.*, p. 189.
20. English Factories, p. 232.
21. *Ibid.*, p. 249.
22. *Ibid.*, p. 270.
23. *Ibid.*, p. 282-83.
24. *Ibid.*, 122-23.
25. *Ibid.*, p. 292.
26. Eliot & Dowson, Tatima-i-Jahangiri, VI, p. 397.
27. Bahâristân, II, p. 663.
28. Beni Prasad : History of Jahangir IV, p. 371.
29. Banarsi Prasad, History of Shahjahan.
30. Manrique, I, pp. 48-49.
31. Manucci, I, p. 189.
32. *Ibid.*, p. 207.
33. English Factories, 1624-29, p. 270.
34. Peter Mundy, ii, p. 40.
35. *Ibid.*, p. 122.
36. English Factories, 1634-36, p. 28.
37. *Ibid.*, p. 280.
38. History of Shahjahan by B.P. Sexena.
39. Manucci, i, p. 17.
40. English Factories, 1651-54. p. 251.
41. *Ibid.*, pp. 303-4.

42. Short History of Aurangzeb.
43. English Factories, 1667-70, p. 160;
Bernier, I, pp. 269-70;
Fryer. I, p. 244;
Manucci, II, p. 115.
44. Manucci, i, p. 226.
45. *Ibid.*, p. 293.
46. A Pepys of Mogul India, p. 115.
47. Manucci. II, p. 345.
48. Akhbârât-i-Darbâr-i-Mu'allâ, 16 November, 1681.
49. Akhbârât-i-Darbâr-i-Mu'allâ, 26 October, 1692.
50. Manucci, ii, p. 100.
51. Manrique, II, pp. 105-15.
52. Jahangir's India B. Pelsaert, p. 59.
53. Âina-i-Gujarat, I, pp. 77-78.
54. Akbar Nâmâ. Text, III, p. 193; Bev., III, p. 273.
55. *Ibid.*, Text III 266; Bev., III, p. 387.
56. *Ibid.*, Text, III, p. 292; Bev., III, p. 341.
57. Akbar Nâmâ, Beveridge, III, pp 554-55; Badâûni, Lowe, II, p. 323.
Akbar Nâmâ, Text, III, pp. 377-78; Badâûnî, Text, II, p. 313.
58. De Laet, p. 178.
59. Manucci, I, p. 193.
60. *Ibid.*, II, p. 315: English Factories, 1670-77, p. 267; Letters CXLI, p. 137.
61. Manucci, II, p. 291.
62. Jaipur Akhbârât, 16th December, p. 1666.
63. Letters, LI, p. 52.
64. Anecdotes, pp. 96-97.
65. Ma'âsîr-î-'Âlamgîrî, p. 116.
66. Letters, CXLIV, pp. 139-40.
67. Akhbârât-i-Darbâr-i-Mu'allâ, 30th September, 1704.

VII
ABUSE OF AUTHORITY BY PUBLIC SERVANTS

There are many references by the contemporary authorities to the tyranny exercised on the people by the governors and *faujdârs,* customs and revenue officials. The peasants had to suffer at the hands of the greedy officials and soldiers. The former extorted money out of them and the latter marched through their fields and damaged their crops. The artisans worked under hard conditions and were molested by the customs and other officers. The Mughal Emperors did not usually ignore the offences of the officers, whether ministers or governors, and awarded suitable punishment to the guilty in accordance with the nature of the crime. The punishment varied from fine and imprisonment to dismissal and death.

COMPLAINTS AGAINST THE GOVERNORS

Banârsi Dâs, *jauhari* of Jaunpur and a contemporary of Akbar and Jahangir, has given an account of the oppressions committed by the Hâkim of Jaunpur, Qulîch Khân, on the diamond dealers of the city in 1595 A.D. When they failed to provide him with the required 'big article', he, one morning in that year, ordered the arrest of all the *jauharis* there. Like thieves they were brought in his presence and mercilessly flogged with 'thorny' whips. They were let off in a half-dead conditon. Terrified at this treatment, they left the city and fled to different places. Banârsi's own father Kharag Sen *jauhari,* left Jaunpur with his entire family, crossed the Ganges and came to Shahzâdpur in the west. From there they wandered to Allahabad, Fatehpur and other places. They did not return home for full four years. Such was the terror of the name of Qulîch Khân. Kharg Sen's own and other *jauhari* families returned to Jaunpur in 1599 A.D. only when they learnt that the tyrant had gone to

Agra.[1]

Orme remarked about the 'unhappy' system of oppression that prevailed throughout India from the highest to the lowest scale.[2]

Bernier felt pity for the poor lot of the Mughal subjects. They groaned under the tyrannies of the provincial governors, possessing boundless authority. The people suffered less under governors of some standing than under those, who, indigent and greedy, first took charge of their provinces. The tyranny was somewhat mitigated by the apprehension that if too much oppressed, the people would abandon the country.[3] –

The same traveller again complains of the absence of a higher authority before whom an injured tradesman, peasant or artisan, could pour out his complaints against the tyrannies of 'merciless oppressors'.[4] The Mughal subjects could hope for no redress against the cruelties of the provincial governors, however grievous their injuries might have been.[5]

The people felt compelled to labour for fear of the cudgel and the whip. Compelled to despair by this cruel treatment, they thought of flight or revolt but were prevented from this step due to the presence of military force.[6]

For a peasant or an artisan it was not easy to travel a long distance to file an appeal in the imperial court. The obstacles that lay before him were almost insurmountable. How could he defray the expenses of a long journey? Was not there lurking in his mind the constant fear of the highwaymen who waited for every opportunity to waylay and murder a traveller? Then there was the danger of falling into the hands of the governor's men. His difficulties did not abate even if he managed to approach the royal court. He would find his oppresor's friends busy in distorting the truth, and misrepresenting the whole affair to the Emperor. And there was a likelihood of the case being reverted to the local court at the commands of the Emperor.[7] These difficulties, however, were peculiar not to Mughal India, but were characteristic of the times. Bernier levels the entire blame for all failure in agriculture, industry, and social welfare in India during the Mughal rule to the tyranny of the governors.[8]

Our authorities fail to inform us of any case of complaint against the governors during Akbar's time.

On the death in 1614 of Mirzâ Gâzi Tarkhân, the governor of Thattâ, Rustam Khân was appointed in his place. He committed such oppression on the people that they complained against his wickedness to Jahangir.[9]

Islâm Khân, governor of Bengal, confiscated the *jâgîr* of Tuqmâq Khan, son of Maqbûl, as he was accused of enslaving the people by force and violence. It was restored, however, at the intercession of Ghiyâs Khân.[10]

During Qâsim Khân's governorship of Bengal, Mohammad Zamân, *karori* of Kuntâghât was accused of oppressing the *ryots* and seizing their beautiful boys and girls. He died of witchcraft. He was replaced as *Mustâjir* by Salîm Beg Khâksâr. There were complaints against him also by the people. In his place was sent Mirzâ Momin Marvi as *Karori* and *Faujdâr.* He returned as a result of serious illness and then a *zunnârdâr* (Brâhmin) Râjâ Râm was sent as the *Mustâjir*.[11]

There were charges of extortion against Akram Khân who was in charge of the affairs at Jahângîrâbâd or Gilhanay. His rivals collected reports against him and decided to send these to the royal court. Mirzâ Nathan proved the falsity of some of the charges and thus stopped the report from being sent.[12]

One day when the *Dîwân* of Bengal, Mirzâ Husain Beg, was present in the governor's court, an altercation took place between his men and the *kotwâl.* Qâsim Khân governor's men were killed and wounded. When some men were sent to bring the sons of the *Diwân,* they offered a vigorous resistance. A large crowd gathered and broke the gates of the building with the aid of elephants. One officer of the governor whose accounts of treasureship had been hindered by Husain eg, threw all the account books of the *Diwân* into a well. The two sons of the *Diwân* were caught and with their hands tied behind their backs, they were brought to Qâsim Khân bare-headed and bare-footed. The governor grew furious and ordered them to be handed over to those persons whose brother had been killed by them in battle, so that they might be killed in the square of the city market. They were scourged and then taken to the market square. When the executioner took out his naked sword to do his job, two officers, Mubâriz Khân and Mîrak Bahâdur Jalâ'ir approached the governor with the request to cancel his orders for the execution of the young brothers. Their plea was that fault lay on both the sides and there was looting and killing by the other party as well, and that the death punishment for such a crime was not justified. They recommended that the case should be referred to the Emperor. The Khân agreed and ordered the two brothers to be carried from the market place and confined in the prison along with their father. He released them after *six pahars* when the two Khâns had signed a memorandum that the two brothers and their father were guilty. He ordered the confiscation of all the property of the *Dîwân.*

The two Khâns did not feel satisfied with this mode of treatment and left for their respective *thânâs*.

This incident caused a predicament for the provincial newswriter, Khawâjâ Yaghmâ, particularly after the governor had secured the *tazkirâ* (memorandum) from the two Khâns. He was well aware of the fact that Qâsim Khân had secured the frontiers in such a manner that not 'even a bird' could fly from this side to northern India. The astute news-writer thought of a device. He asked his two grooms to be dressed like *jogîs* (mendicants) and sent them with the report of the whole incident to Ani Râi Singh-Dalan at the Court. The Râjâ took them to the *jharokâ* (salutation window) where Jahangir was witnessing the elephant fight and presented the two in the same dress along with the report to the Emperor.

The Emperor issued a peremptory *farmân* for Qâsim Khan. He ordered that a great noble of the imperial Court would be sent to Bengal for an investigation into the matter. Taking in view the services of the Chishti family, the Emperor refrained from ruining the career of Qâsim Khân. He was, however, ordered to pacify by all possible means Hussain Beg and his sons, obtain a letter of satisfaction from them and send it along with the special envoy Sa'âdat Khân *alias* Mirzâ Lûtî. Failing this the governor was to face diverse punishments. In accordance with the custom, Qâsim Khân received Sa'âdat Khân with the greatest humility and respect.

After having known the contents of the royal *farmân,* the governor returned all the goods and property of Mirzâ Hussain, gave him and his sons one lac of rupees, assigned them a *jâgîr* in the *parganâ* of Mahadpur Bhagwân, and took a deed of agreement and satisfaction from the Mirzâ and his sons. After this was done, Sa'âdat Khân returned to the imperial court to report the matter to the Emperor.

There had been other reports from the *Dîwân* and the *Bakshi* of the province about the improper behaviour of the governor towards the imperial officers. The Emperor sent a special officer Ibrâhim Kalâl, entitled Ihtimâm Khân, who was the superintendent of the Court of Justice. Reaching Dâcâ, he gave verbal admonition to Qâsim Khân, the governor, and to the *Diwân* and the *Bakshi* and news-writer and returned to the capital.

He conveyed to the Bakshi the displeasure of the Emperor at his failure to report the matter to the imperial court and asked him to be careful in the future.[13]

In 1615 A.D. Jahangir appointed Âghâ Nûr as the governor of Jaunpur. The very news spread terror among the populace and the people began to flee their houses and went to different directions. Banârsi Dâs and his poet friend Narottam Dâs came from Ayodhyâ to Jaunpur to learn that Âghâ Nûr had perpetrated tyrannies on the people between Banaras and Jaunpur and given thrashing to them. He had arrested all the jewellers and *jauharis, sarrâfs* and their agents, flogged some, enchained others. Terrified at the news, Banârasi and Narottam left the city, crossed the river on a ghanai (made by joining the overturned heads of two pitchers and tying them with bamboos) and fled to the jungles. There they lived for full forty days. They returned only after they had learnt that the tyrant had returned to Agra although having taken with him a few rich *jauhris* after giving them furious beating.[14]

Manucci complains against the tyrannies prepetrated by the provincial governors.[15]

The merchants of Gujarat complained against the exactions of the *Dîwân,* Hâfiz Mohammad Nâsir. An enquiry was ordered. Th report was found to be authentic. The offender was awarded life imprisonment and was confined in Patna.[16]

Complaints were received that Fidâi Khân, the governor of Bengal, oppressed the people. Shahjahan took action against him and removed him from power. On his representation that the reports were untrue and not liable to be proved, he was restored to his post.[17]

Â'zam Khân, the governor of Gujarat in about 1639, although judicious and a man of understanding, was so rigorous that his government was inclined somewhat towards cruelty. He put to death some dancing girls who had refused to come to his place in obedience to his summons.[18]

The English factors complained of the 'unheered of tiranie' and oppressions of the 'villaine' governor of Surat in 1647-48. He oppressed the innocent and the poor. Whole towns of the miserably poor people were depopulated by him on the pretext of their harbouring rogues and thieves.[19]

'Izzak Khân, the governor of Sind, had great weakness for women and tried all methods, fair or foul, to procure a beautiful girl that came within his knowledge.[20]

Prince Murâd Baksh, while governor of Gujarat, during the last years of Shahjahan's reign, oppressed the *Banjârâs* to such an extent that they gave up their trade in saltpetre.[21]

The news-writer of Lahore wrote to Aurangzeb about the oppression which the governor, Khân Jahân Bahâdur, committed at the time of his return.[22]

Aurangzeb brought to the notice of Â'zam the cruelties of an officer appointed by the Prince. The subjects under him were bewailing and lamenting.[23]

In another letter to the same Prince, the Emperor protested against the appointment by him of a Superintendent of Police at Ahmedabad. He had been exercising tyranny on the people.[24]

In yet another letter Aurangzeb complained against the failure of Prince Â'zam to punish the tyrants in his province.[25]

It was submitted to Aurangzeb that Ibrâhim Khân, the governor of Lahore, had oppressed the Qâzi of Kâshmir. He was punished with diminution of one thousand horse.[26]

"The Omrâhs and Nawâbs appointed to govern the provinces oppress the people in the most miserable manner imaginable."[27]

GRIEVANCES OF THE RYOTS

The shortness and uncertainty of the term of a governor forced him at times to exercise oppression on the *ryots*. He tried to exact land revenue in advance by frequent resort to force. When the wretched peasant failed to pay, their wives and children were made into slaves. Unable to put up with this kind of treatment, the villagers fled from their homes and left the villages completely ruined.[28]

The agriculturist suffered hardship at the time of payment of land revenue. Whenever he failed to give ready money, he suffered disgrace and torment. A good deal of thrashing and forcible infliction of hunger and thirst made the villagers part with only paltry sums of money. It was surprising how this treatment often did not cause their death. They were bound to a tree and even whipped mercilessly. Some times the whips made 'wheels' on their bodies and 'broke their skins.'[29]

Whenever the cases of tyranny came to the knowledge of the Mughal Emperor, he did not fail to take speedy action.

Khân-i-Daurân was notorious for his harsh nature. His treatment of the people at large was unbecoming. It was perhaps on account of this behaviour that his Kâshmîrî non-Muslim employees murdered him in Lahore in 1645 A.D. Khâfi Khân is of the view that the curses of the oppressed people were responsible for his death.[30]

In Aurangâbâd the men of Brahm Dev Sisodia cut down the crops of the peasants in 1666 for the use of their horses. On receipt of the news, Aurangzeb ordered a diminution in their ranks.[31]

The heirs of Mardam Bandi petitioned Aurangzeb on 19th May, 1681, that Shahâb-ud-din Khân had laid waste their village Rai'ti and captured the men and cattle of the village. They had committed no fault and had been wrongly captured and sent to the court. They termed it as a clear case of oppression. Aurangzeb ordered that the matter be decided in accordance with the *Shar'a.*[32]

The contents of Muhtashim Khân's letter were read out to the Emperor in the Court on 6th September, 1681. He had complained that Sa'âdat Khân, *zamndâr* of Fatehpur, was indulging in a policy of oppression and the *ryots* were feeling distressed. His brother 'Abdul Dânam had gone to the extent of killing eight employees of the *qânûngo* of Fatehpur. The Emperor was requested to issue a warning to the *zamindâr* against the repetition of such offences. The Emperor decreed that orders be issued to him for the chastisement of the culprits. He further remarked that the offenders, whoever they might be, must be punished.[33]

On 26th October, 1692, Qâzi Khwâjâ 'Abdullâ submitted that Mîrak Husain, deputy *dîwân* of Berar province, had made a written complaint against the *gumâshtâs* of the *jâgîrdârs* there. They were accused of having exercised excessive oppression upon the *ryots.* The news-writers had accepted illegal gratification from them and therefore refrained from reporting against them.

Aurangzeb asked Bahrhamand Khân to write to Mîrak Husain in this connection. He was to warn the news-writers and ask them to submit factual reports. In case he found them guilty, he was to transfer them under intimation to the Emperor.[34]

Kohammad Mâh, the *qâzî* of Cambay, sent a report to the imperial court that the people there, no longer able to put up with the oppressive activities of Rustam Jang, *mutasaddi,* had migrated to Ahmedabad. The Emperor ordered that I'timad Khân, *dîwân* of the province, and Mohammad Momin should be asked to investigate into the allegations and submit a detailed report.[35]

The same *mutassaddi* sent a report to the Emperor against a local merchant, Mohammad Hasan, for his maltreatment of the people in Cambay. Mohammad Ghâlib mace-bearer was ordered to fetch the trader to the royal presence.[36]

On 4th January, 1693, Aurangzeb ordered the dismissal of Mohammad Hayât, the commandant of Gooty. It was complained that he used to come out of the fort and persecute the people.[37]

On 12th January, 1693, Aurangzeb received a report against Amar *Jamâ'dâr,* employee of Râjâ Kishan Singh, *zamîndâr* of Chândâ, who was attached to the army of Mu'iz-ud-din at Chûrâgarh. He was charged with having looted a number of villages. Maqsûd Beg, *faujdâr*-commandant of Mohammadâbâd or Badr, had failed to chastise him. It was ordered by the Emperor to write a letter to Maqsûd Beg askings him to put the culprit to death and inform the Râjâ.[38]

A report was received on 31st October, 1693, that in Karnâtak Bijâpuri, the *Desmukh,* in collaboration with the *faujdâr*-commandant of a certain fortress, had imposed a charge of two rupees on every inhabitant of the place as a result of which people had been deserting their homes. Bahrahmand Khân was ordered to write to the *dîwân* of the place to warn the alleged offenders against charging money from and committing oppression on the people.[39]

Sheikh Hâmid, commandant of Mâlâpur, was alleged to have sent foot-soldiers and horsemen in the *jâgir* of Mohammad 'Abbâs, posted in the army of Qâsim Khân Bîjâpuri in Karnâtak Bijâpuri. These soldiers persecuted the peole and rendered them miserable. The Emperor ordered the Chief Bakshi Bahrahmand Khân to write to Sheikh Hâmid to desist from such objectionable activities.[40]

The people of Ghâzipur *thânâ* put up a complaint against the persecutions of Mohammad Bâqi Afghân. The Emperor ordered that they should be asked to address themselves to the *faujdâr* of their area.[41] A similar order for bringing the case of oppression against Daulat Singh to the notice of the *faujdâr* was issued again in the same month.[42]

On 11th July, 1694, Aurangzeb ordered to bring to his presence the *gumâshtâ* of Râjâ Sâhû against whom cmplaints of the persecution of the *ryots* were received.[43]

Mahâ Singh who was posted at Jodhpur, was dismissed from his assignment. He came to Toda Bhîm, turned his brother out of his *jâgir* and took it under his possession. He arrested one money-lender, seized from him Rs. 5,000 and after a few days put him to death. The Emperor ordered that they should write to the *nâzir* of the place and appoint two mace-bearers to bring Mahâ Singh and Anûu Singh to the court.[44]

Mohammad Hasan merchant put up a complaint that Mu'azzam Khân had taken from him forcibly 3 horses costing Rs. 2,000 and paid him only Rs. 1,000. Aurangzeb ordered that Yâr 'Ali should see that the balance was paid to the complainant by the respondent.[45]

A number of traders put up a petition that the grain taken from them during the hunting expedition of Prince Mohammad Bedâr Bakhat, had not been paid for. It was ordered that 'Abdul Khair should send the traders to the *Dîwân-i-Shikâr* for the necessary payment to the complainants.[46]

The secret news-writer of Berâr province wrote to the court that the *thânedârs* appointed by the governor were molesting the people and the governor did not pay heed to their complaint. Bahrahmand Khân was ordered to bring this fact to the notice of the governor.[47]

Dîwân 'Abdul ~Alîm, the royal *tan bakshi,* was accused of oppressive activities, and the deputy *kotwâl* had been ordered to arrest him. When his men reached there, the *tan bakshi* showed readiness to offer fight and refused to see reason. Mukhtâr Khân, *Mir-i-Âtish,* and Muttalib Khân were ordered to go there with artillery and bring him on the path of reason, and, in case they remained adamant, to chastise them. After the *'adâlat* was over, it was submitted to the Emperor on behalf of Hamîdullâ Khân *kotwâl* that Mukhtâr Khân and Muttalib Khân had already been ordered to go for the chastisement of Prince Mu'iz-ud-din's men. The Emperor decreed that in that case Hamîdullâ Khân alone should be sent for the purpose.[48]

A woman filed a petition that the *gumâshtâ* of Râjâ Kishan Singh, *zamîdâr* of Chândâ, had imprisoned her son by way of persecution. A letter was ordered to be written to the *tahsildâr* there to send the said *gumâshtâ* to the court.[49]

A letter was despatched in 1695 from the Court to the Râjâ of Jaipur. His attention was drawn to the fact that a number of peasants as Keso, Lâl Chand, Dâne, Chûrâman, Dûrgâ, Dayâ Ram, Murlî, Dhanpâl and Bhâgîrat of village Jagnerabe, belonging to the crown lands had been taken into custody by his men. The Râjâ was asked to see that these people were set free and warn his employees against tyrannizing over the *rytos* in the crownlands.[50]

A despatch from 'Âmil Faqîr of *parganâ* Jalalpur *alias* Lonkheri revealed that some Râjputs residing there had been persecuting the local people in a variety of ways and were responsible in laying waste a number of villages. One of them had asserted that he was under the Râjâ of Jaipur implying thereby that he did not care for the authority of the Mughal Emperor.

The above facts were brought to the notice of the Râjâ in a letter sent from the Court. He was instructed to appoint a man with a view to expelling these Rârputs from the *paragnâ* so that the *ryots* there could live in peace.[51]

Bashârat Khân, the *dîwân* of Berar province, complained in writing to the Emperor against the tyrannical behaviour of Mohammad Sa'eed *dâroghâ* in charge of the supply of grain there. Orders were issued for his transfer and appointment of another person in his place.[52]

Yâsîn Khân, *thânedâr* of Karrâbâd, submitted that Mohammad Wazir, *thânedâr* of Bahmanwârâ, was guilty of oppression upon the people. He recommended the removal of Mohammad Wazîr and appointment of Mohammad Hussain, son of Sayyid Ibrâhîm. The Emperor approved of this and ordered at the same time diminution in the rank of Mohammad Wazîr.[53]

The *gumâshtâs* of Prince Mohammad Mu'azzam Bahâdur Shâh were accused of molesting Maulvi 'Abdullâ of Siâlkot. The Emperor ordered that Mun'im Khân should send a letter under his own seal to the *gumâshtâs* through Lutfullâ Beg mace-bearer.[54].

Faqîr Mohammad, holding a rank of 500 *zât* and 100 *swâr*, and posted in the army of 'Umadtulmulk Khân Feroz Jang, had gone to Haidrâbâd province and there forcibly married a girl. He was punished with diminution of rank by 100 *zât* and 20 *swar.*[55]

On 12th August, 1704, the petition of Mirzâ Safavi Khân was placed before the Emperor. He had submitted that property worth 4 lacs of rupees in his ship in the sea near Surat had been carried away by the Europeans during the tenure of Mohammad 'Ivaz *alias* Ikhtiâr Khân, the dismissed *mutasaddi* of Surat. 'Ivaz Khân had seized the property from them and taken it into his possession. On the request of the applicant, 'Inâyat-ullah khân was asked to get the property restored to the owner without delay. We learn from the newsletter of 30th August 1704 that he was taken into custody and then imprisoned at the court of the *dîwân*. He could not be presented before the Emperor on account of ill-health. He was ordered to go to the house of Amîr Khân and give a written bond.[56]

Report came from Saharanpur on 29th August 1704 that Bahâr Safshikan Khan, the dismissed *zamîndâr* of Lakhi Jungle, had gone to the village of Sultânpur in *parganâ* Badhanâ and was exercising tyranny on the people there. Mace-bearers were sent to the place for *sazawali* and to fetch him from there.[57]

COMPLAINTS AGAINST FAUJDARS

When the *ryots* could no longer bear the excessive acts of oppression on the part of the *faujdârs,* they rose in rebellion, and, as a result, suffered penalty.[58]

Even the foreign travellers were not spared. Peter Mundy had to bribe off the *faujdâr* of Banaras when all his carts were confiscated in September, 1632, under the orders of that official. The carts were required for transportation of the family and household staff of Qalij

Khân, the former governor of Allahabad.[59]

A Hindu merchant petitoned the Emperor on 20th January, 1667, that Mohammad Khân *faujdâr* had seized from him a large amount of money. Aurangzeb ordered that mace-bearers be sent with him in order to bring the erring *faujdâr* to the royal presence.[60]

A report was received from Bengal that Muzaffar Khân, son of Nâsir Khân, *faujdâr* of Makhsûdâbâd, was exercising tyranny upon the *ryots.*[61]

Complaint was received against Latif, *faujdâr*-commandant of Bijâgarh (holding a rank of 500 *zât* and 300 *swâr*) to the effect that he had usurped a horse from 'Abdul Ghani and other merchants by way of *râhdârî.* His rank was reduced by 100.[62]

The *ryots* of the *parganâ* of Dahokâsâl sent a petition to Aurangzeb against the tyranny perpetrated by Shamsuddin, *faujdâr* of the place. Orders for his replacement were issued.[63]

On a complaint received from the *ryots* and *qânûngos* of the *parganâ* Marha orders were issued for the transfer of the *faujdâr* and appointment of another.[64]

A petition was received from Safshikan, *jâgîrdâr* Aurangabâd, that as a result of the tyranny exercised by Bahâdur Khân *faujdâr, ryots* were taking to flight. A letter was ordered to be addressed to the governor to stop the recurrence of such incidents.[65]

The people of *parganâ* Ambâh Bânûr made a complaint against the oppressive policy of 'Azizullâh, *faujdâr* of the place. The Emperor ordered the report about the rank held by him.[66]

'Abdul Razzâq, *faujdâr*-commandant of Bâdâmi fortress was alleged to have forcibly removed and taken into his possession all the belongings from the house of 'Abdl Rasûl, *zamindâr* of the place. Hearing the complaint, Aurangzeb ordered that one mace-bearer be despatched to make him return all the articles usurped in this objectionable manner.[67]

The *vakil* of Mohan Singh commandant wrote to the Court that the son of 'Abdullâh Khân, *faujdâr* of Ajmer, had gone to the *jâgir* of his client, shown high-handedness and forcibly seized money. He had requested the Emperor for a mace-bearer who should get the money restored to his client. The Emperor ordered that he should be asked to write to the governor of Agra about this case.[68]

DAMAGE TO CROPS

Another serious complaint of the agriculturist was that irreparable damage was done to his crops during the march of imperial armies. When the soldiers passed through the villages, they plundered every thing they could lay had on-food, supplies, grass, straw and even cattle. In order to produce fuel they would go to the extent of burning houses of the poor peasants. As if this was not enough, they imposed *begâr* on and forced to carry their baggage.[69]

The Mughal Emperors being keenly interested in the welfare of the agriculturists, took particular care against any damage to them by imperial officers. Special steps were taken to protect the crops during the march of imperial armies. Inspectors were appointed for the measurement of damaged crops and for payment of the loss sustained.

"To guard against damage to standing crops in times of warfare", during the reign of Akbar, "a special staff was recruited for the purpose of assessing such damage and paying the cultivators its assessed value.[70]

The system introduced by Akbar continued throughout the Mughal period.

When during the Spring of 1609, Jahangir left for hunting, he writes : "As the Rabi Fasl had arrived, for fear of any damage should happen to the cultivation of the *ryots* from the passage of the army, and notwithstanding that I had appointed a Qûr Yasâwal with the band of *ahâdîs* for the purpose of guarding the fields, I ordered certain men to see what damage had been done to the crops from stage to stage and pay compensation to the *ryots*."[71]

Prior to his journey to Kâshmir in 1632, Shahjahan issued orders for the protection of crops. The punishment fixed for the cutting of one ear of corn was amputation of hand and payment of double the price of the damage to the cultivator. In case, however, the march of the army through the fields could not be helped in view of the narrow paths, inspectors were appointed for the assessment and payment of the actual damage suffered by them.[72]

The same practice was continued by Aurangzeb. He had a regular department whose duty it was to find out the extent of damage to the standing crops and pay compensation to the suffering cultivators. In the Jaipur Newsletters we come across two kinds of officers in this department. One was *amîn* and the other was *dâroghâ*. On 17th November, 1701, Ziâ Ullâh was appointed *dârogha* and Khwâjâ Mohammad Shâh, *amîn* of the right wing of the army and Sheikh Hidâya Keesh and Ghulâm Mohammad were appointed respectively *dârogha* and *amîn* of the right wing.[73]

Râm Singh, son of Ratan Singh Râthor, *faujdâr* of Jalaur, complained to Rûhullâ Khân at the imperial Court on 5th May 1681, that the movements of the rebel and the royal armies during the war had laid waste the country-side and ruined a large number of village in his *faujdâri.*[74]

On 31st August, 1681, Asad Khân submitted that he had received information from the *gumâshtâ* of Rao Anurudh Singh that the crops in Bundi had been ruined due to the movement of troops and the uprooted *ryots* were finding it difficult to resettle in their homes. the Emperor ordered inquiries to be made to find out if there could be any alternate route for the troops.[75]

During his march from Ajmer to Burhanpur, it was brought to the notice of Aurangzeb on 12th September, 1681, that an extensive damage had been done to the standing crops. He ordered that 'Abul Qâsim, *Khush Manzil*, should be asked to pay the entire amount of damage to the cultivators concerned.[76]

Yâr 'Ali *Dâroghâ* in charge of the protection of crops, brought to Aurangzeb's notice on 16th September the complaints of the *ryots* about the destruction of crops as a result of the march of the royal army. The Emperor ordered that the complainants be paid Rs. 1,000/- out of the crownlands.[77]

On 21st September, the Emperor asked Bahrahmand Khân to find out the extent of the damage to crops suffered by the cultivators on account of the marching of the imperial camp that day. The superintendent of Artillery was ordered to remain behind and report names of the *dâroghâ* in charge of the protection of the crops and of the artillerymen posted for the purpose.[78]

The Emperor told Prince Shah 'Âlam on 26th October that there was an extensive damage to the crops as a result of the march of his army. He was asked to pay compensation to the cultivators right from the start of the march of his army from Ajmer.[7]

A representation of the *zamindârs* of Thânâ Mor and Rahmatpur etc. was submitted to the Emperor on 26th November 1699. They had offered to pay Rs. 10,000 by way of present to the Emperor in case their crops were spared from damage and destruction[80] (due to the movement of troops.)

Aurangzeb during his march in the south, told Tarbiat Khân, *Mîr-i-Âtish,* on 17th November, 1701, that extensive damage had been caused to the crops as a result of the movement of the army.[81]

A report came to the Emperor that the soldiers were cutting the standing crops and exercising tyranny on the *ryots.* It was ordered that Hamid-ud-din Khân Bahâdur be posted in the rear of the army and

Tarbiat Khân Bahâdur should be transferred from there and be put in charge of the protection of crops.[82]

OPPRESSIONS BY TAX-COLLECTORS

The Mughal Emperors never failed to issue orders for the abolition of various duties termed as *abwâbs* or illegal cesses. Akbar was the first Emperor who abolished these exactions.[83]

Jahangir abolished *tamghâ* and *mîrbahari* and other illegal cesses which the *jâgirdârs* used to harge forcibly from the people.[84]

By a *farmân* issued on 20th November, 1665, Aurangzeb declared a number of duties as illega. The *Mîrât* has given a detailed list of such duties.[85]

Khâfi Khân is of the view that the taxes abolished by Aurangzeb by his *farmân* amounted to crores of rupees.[86] He, however, feels sceptical of the efficacy of the *farmân.* He does not conceal his feelings about Aurangzeb's orders which usually remained uncomplied with. Not that this great Emperor failed in taking prompt action against the culprits. He took steps in meting out proper punishments to the guilty officers. He ordered their dismissal or diminution in their ranks. He sent mace-bearers for the punishment of the erring *zamindârs.* These mace-bearers did stop the officials concerned from collecting the illegal taxes. This was only for a few days after which they were bribed off. The *jâgirdârs* who had been punished for these illegal taxes, usually succeeded in getting the diminution in their ranks restored with the help of some patron at the court and the *vakîls* whom they had to pay. Thus the remission of majority of cesses failed of implementation. Khâfi Khân regarded the *râhdâri* tax as the most obnoxious of taxes. It had been charged by the *faujdârs* and *jagirdârs* with utmost severity from the traders, needy and distressed travellers, and continued to be levied with the same rigour in the whole of Mughal India. Khâfi Khân further remarks that when the *zamindârs* were convinced that they were to be answerable before none, they began to levy this tax in their own areas with greater severity than in the *khâlsâ* lands. The result was that the prices of articles invariably got doubled by the time they were to be answerable before none, they began to levy this tax in their own areas with greater severity than in the *khâlsâ* lands. The result was that the prices of articles invariably got doubled by the time they reached their destination. He laments that there was always trouble on the highways, in public places and on thorough-fares; the life of the people using them was at the mercy of the *zamindârs* and *jâgirdârs*. Thousands of travellers lost their lives in the tumults and wranglings in those place. He felt so distressed at the whole situation that he seemed to have lost faith in Aurangzeb's sense of justice and good administration and pinned his hope in the justice of God. The tyranny from which people were suffering could be removed only if He sent a just and strong ruler capable of meting out condign punishments to these evil-doers.[87]

John Francis Careri, the Italian traveller, who visited India in 1695, remarks :

"After Aurangzeb had prescribed himself this sort of Life (vegetarianism), he ceased to be Bloody as before, and on the contrary became so mild, that the Governors and *Omrahs* did not pay him the Duty the ought; knowing his Mercy would never suffer him to punish them. Thus the Poor were oppressed by the great without knowing who to have recourse to[88]....."

The Jaipur new-letters corroborate the statement of Khâfi Khân. The Provincial News-letters are replete with the complaints sent by the Centre to the Jaipur Râjâ regarding the charging of illegal cesses by the *thânedârs* and *zamindârs* from the crownlands inspite of orders to the contrary. Some of these cases are quoted below.

We learn from one of these letters that Hâji 'Ali Dost, *jâgirdâr* of some village in *parganâ* Sa'dâbâd, had complained against the *thânedâr* of the place who charged from them illegal cesses. The letter from the Court advised the Râjâ to pull up the *thânedâr* and the *peshkârs* and warn them against molestation of the people in his *jâgîr*.[89]

In another letter the attention of the Râjâ was drawn to the complaints of one Harkishan, a wine merchant. The man had purchased goods worth Rs. 449, to be taken to Daryâpur and paid the due taxes to the tax-collectors at Shâhganj and obtained their receipt. Even then Kosal *thânedâr* of *parganâ* Sa'dabâd confiscated three oxen and all the goods along with four of his men whom he took into custody. The Râjâ was asked to issue prohibitory orders to the *thânedâr* concerned who was to restore the goods, explain his conduct and promise not to repeat the offence. A mild advice was tendered to the Râjâ that such acts were not conducive to the prosecution of trade, were bound seriously to affect the imperial revenue and bring bad name to him.[90]

In yet another letter of May 1695 from the Court to the Râjâ, his attention was drawn to the activities of the same *thânedâr*. This time he collected illegal taxes from the village Kajrole out of which he kept to himself Rs. 600 as cess of guns and *foujdâri* and deposited the balance in the treasury only after heated arguments. The letter ended with the remarks that the same *thânedâr* was in the habit of receiving money from other villages as well in the same (tyrrannical) manner.[91]

Jahân and Khwâjâ Ahmed and other traders had written to the imperial court that they were bringing 300 camels from the province of Multan. When they came to Islâmâbâd (Mathura), Râjâ Bishan Singh's men seized from them Rs. 3,300 and at the Chambal ferry at Dholpur. They charged from them toll tax. A letter was addressed from the Court to the Râjâ to see that there was no recurrence of such offences in the future.[92]

Besides these cases recorded in the Provincial News-letters, there are a few others mentioned in the *Akhbârât.*

Amârat Khân, *faujdâr*-commandant of Ahmadnagar, was alleged to have charged from the people Rs. 5/- per ox as tax. When the Emperor learnt of this, he ordered a letter to be issued to the said Khân to desist from charging this forbidden cess and in case of repetition of the offence to face royal censure.[93]

Sharif Khân, *karori* of Ganj, submitted that the *faujdârs* had forcibly charged tax from the *Banjârâs* who were bringing corn for the Emperor from the side of Haidrabad. They refused to accept the royal *farmân* of tax-exemption in their case. The Emperor ordered that Nâzim Beg, mace-bearer, should be deputed with the *Banjârâs* and the entire amount seized from them as toll tax was to be got restored to them. The *faujdârs* were to be forbidden from charging this tax in the future.[94]

Orders were despatched to the *faujdârs* of Etâwâ and those in the neighbourhood of Agra to see that the *thânedârs* did not levy the *râhdâri* tax on the traders. They had to issue similar orders to their *gumâshtâs* and warn them that non-compliance with these orders would be detrimental to their interests.[95]

The Emperor told Kalim-ud-din *faujdâr* of Jâler, that he had received complaints against his *gumâshtâ* Khudâ Quli for charging *râhdâri* from traders and travellers. The *faujdâr* was asked to give him proper chastisement on receipt of further complaints of this sort.[96]

The *vakil* of the Jaipur Râjâ posted at the court at Agra sent him a letter on 3rd June, 1695. He mentioned therein that the *kahârs* who had brought melons from Shahjahanabad for the governor of Agra had been forced by the employees of the *faujdârs* under his Exalted Highness to pay *râhdâri* at every *chowki.* They should have at least spared the articles of the *Nawâb* (governor) who had brought this to the notice of the *vakil.*[97]

Aurangzeb ordered on 15th June, 1695, a letter to be written to the *faujdâr*-commandant of Karnool asking him to prevent the *kotwâl* there from levying the forbidden tax of one rupee from the widows.[98]

Persons engaged in the sale of leather goods lodged a complaint in the *'adâlat* that Sarbrâh Khân *kotwâl's* men were charging from them illegal tax on leather goods. They requested the Emperor for the exemption of this duty.[99]

OPPRESSIONS AGAINST ARTISANS

We are asked to believe that an artisan laboured under severe restraints. If a noble required his services, he sent for him. The poor fellow had no alternative but to work for the 'unfeeling lord'. the remuneration was paid not according to the value of the former's work, but in accordance with the caprice of the latter.[100] It was not surprising if some time the artisan got nothing whatever in return for his labour.[101] According to Bernier, the long and terrible whip, hanging at the door of every noble, was a source of constant terror to him. He was extremely lucky if he did not receive this in 'part payment.'[102] The governor's men were a sort of perpetual drain on his meagre income. They exacted fees from him under the pretence of pressing him from his daily work into gaining the service of their master.[103] A craftsman saw no advantage in gaining distinction; for having acquired a little more money than his fellow workers he might be compelled to part with it.[104]

In 1636, the governor of Gujarat required cloth for his servants. He asked the weavers' brokers at Baroda to sell the cloth to him at his own price. At their refusal to comply with his order, he cast them into prison. The weavers, however showed a grim resolve and left the city in a body. They did not return unless assured by the governor of a better treatment in the future.[105]

A tailor in the service of a Pathân was seized by some servants of a governor for their master's service. As the Pathân rushed to the help of the tailor, a soldier put to death the brother of the Pathân. This developed into a fight in which both the parties sustained heavy losses.[106]

COMPLAINTS OF THE MERCHANTS

Almost all the European travellers who visited India during the reign of the Mughals, are one in their condemnation of the tyrannical rule of many a provincial governor and other high officers. Their complaints were manifold—

1. The Emperor would open their chest and boxes and keep whatever he liked for himself.
2. Their goods were seized by the governors or other high officers on the pretext of presenting them to the Emperor.
3. The provincial governors demanded money from the merchants.
4. Their articles were searched at the customs houses.
5. Their articles were seized by the officers and arbitrary prices were offered to them.
6. Some time they were not allowed to leave the port without permission of the authorities.
7. Tolls were demanded from them.
8. There were some minor complaints.

Some of these complaints may be true; but a close analysis of the accounts shows that the foreign merchants were also in many cases at fault. It was the usual practice for the customs-officials to search all the boxes and packages at the port and it was the usual practice of the merchants, as at present, to avoid the payment of customs. They tried to smuggle in commodities or to pay less custom than required. A thorough search of the articles took long time and the merchants felt that their patience was taxed. The rightful measures taken by the authorities to stop the unauthorised inland trade carried on by the foreign travellers was taken by them as iniquitous. Then there was the practice of presents. It is a ridiculous statement that the Mughal Emperors or the Princes of the royal blood were anxious to take articles from the foreign merchants without making any payment. Money was never the consideration with the Mughals. They only liked the curios, and made their own selection. It may be that their orders regarding the payment of a certain article were not alwas carried out by the officials resulting in the complaints by the merchants. So far as the seizure of the articles at arbitrary prices was concerned, we are to remember one thing. It seems it was always a tendency of the merchants to expect and demand a much higher price for an article than it was justified for them to charge. The government would at such times intervene and fix prices for articles. This caused resentment among the merchants who were bent upon reaping larger profits. If a foreign merchant had to suffer for non-payment of toll at certain places, he had only to blame himself for this. There was another significant point to remember. The Mughal authorities did not always like the movement of the European merchants in India. The former often suffered heavy losses on account of the piratical activities on the seas, and the pirates, almost all of them, belonged to European nations. The foreign merchant companies in India encouraged their sea captains to loot Indian ships laden with merchandise and imprison the crew. To this they resorted sometime, no doubt, to get their demands (which were not always just and fair) accepted and their grievances redressed. In the absence of an effective and efficient navy the only possible check on the nefarious activities of the foreign culprits was to put pressure on their fellow countrymen in India. The spirit of obstinacy exhibited by the latter was bound to inflame the already excited feelings of the Mughal authorities who had to be harsh on the foreign factors. Hence the clamour of high-handed treatment of the Mughal provincial governors.

It may be that in certain cases their complaints were genuine. Some governors and high officers may have been guilty of demanding and accepting bribes from the merchants. But were those merchants and the merchant companies not equally guilty in this respect? The offer of bribe is no less a crime than its acceptance. And in many cases do we come across instructions issued by higher authorities to the English factors to bribe the governors and high officers for various favours. We come across frequent references to the fact that whenever the English merchants found some difficulties in the way of their trade, they thought of resorting to force on the high seas in order to intimidate the Indian authorities. That is never the way of peaceful merchants living in foreign lands.

Manucci complains that the customs-officers exercised much severity upon travellers and deprived them of the money they found upon them. They felt no mercy for the poor, and, when they found no money with them, they seized from them their shirts, coats and sheets. Manucci, however, makes an extreme statement which is difficult to believe that after rifling the travellers of all their possessions, the customs-officers would put them to death.[107]

Complaints were received by Jahangir against the 'tyrannical injustice' done by Muqarrab Khân, the customs-officer of Surat. Hawkins had complained against Muqarrab Khân's seizure of his goods and non-payment of the price. Jahangir sent for the officer and ordered the attachment of his goods.[108]

The Englis factors at Burhanpur told Afzal Khân, the *Dîwân* of Prince Shahjahan, that they had undergone 'insufferable injuries' at the hands of the Prince's servants and officers in Surat. They had suffered from 'other the king and Princes subjects elsewhere : That wee weare not only abused in our persons, dispoyled of our goods, but debarred of our trade, which hath been and now is graunted us by their sundry firmaens extant'. They told him that though they had tried to get their grievances redressed, they had failed in their efforts. Rather more sufferings were heaped on them. They wrote to the English President and Council at Surat : 'We...must be playne and give them to understand that wee intend to right our wrongs by our own force, seeing we cannot finde justice by the Prince, to whom we are dayly sutors......'.[109]

"The Banyans are tyrannised over by the Magolls and they cleave to the strongest, who is a mischievous, malicious devil, would have me daily to sallam and acknowledge him, and this five months privately understand hath hindered the sale both of ours and the Dutches' goods, will buy them himself at his own price, and etail it at his pleasure. He expresseth not this, yet his actions declare his intents, and all men fear to meddle with our commodities, whereof before his coming we sold good quantities."

Latters Received IV, 351

An un Schhumber failed to bribe and presents from in Eng., he perrfosily opposed tham. When they passed in the sheets, 'beggars rail in in-sufferable manner, set in purpose, in order to provoke them to some mischief & subsequently to implicate them in same cases.

Ibid. P. 352.

Sir Thomas Roe complained that Emperor Jahangir caused his chests to be privately brought to him and opened, but finding nothing of his liking, he returned all.[110]

In 1614, Sir Robert Shirley was abused at Laribunder and when he went to Thatta, he was used very unkindly by Mirzâ Rustam, the governor of Sind. The latter took away his jewels and other things of his choice on the pretext that they were to be sent to the Emperor.[111]

Roe complained that Prince Khurram had intercepted the presents and goods on their way up, to satisfy his own 'base and greedy inclinations.'[112]

Peter Mundy grumbled against the 'bad' governor of Bihar whose cruel nature was a great impediment in the way of the prosecution of trade by the English in India. The same traveller complained about the tyranny of the governor of Ahmadabad who exacted a sum of Rs. 4,000/- from the East India Company.[113]

In March, 1636, the governor of Gujarat forced the Dutch to pay Rs. 5000. His covetousness made him an object of general hatred there.[114]

The English complained that the customs-officer of Surat in 1648 ruined the trade of the place by oppressing and 'robbing' men of all sorts.

The 'villaine' either seized the goods of the traders or shared the profits of whatever was brought and sold.[115]

Again, in 1669, there is mention of the gross injustice done by the customs-officer of Surat. He placed many obstacles in the way of the English trade and was always actuated by the feelings of price and self-interest. They had to offer him many presents as was done by the French and the Dutch.[116]

Aungier was forbidden by the customs-officer of Surat in 1672 to depart for Bombay. The latter demanded from him a 'round sum of money.' The Council was determined not to yield on this point. This enraged the customs-officer who sent a strong force of horse and foot to take possession of the factory house and the neighbourhood. The English endured all the violence perpetrated by the guard and handed over at the demand of the customs-officer all the arms and trumpet of the factory. They remained adamant and showed no inclination to part with the money. The customs-officer, however, persisted in his demands and did not withdraw his orders unless he had forced from the Company's Indian broker Rs. 500/- threatening to size his estate, house, wife and children in case of non-compliance with his demand.[117]

At one time Roe was upset because Prince Khurram ordered his goods to be sealed. He had done so because his officers had not received custom on them and he desired to get them opened in his own presence. On the complaint of Roe to Jahangir, Prince Khurram undertook to pay for every thing that had been taken by him from the Ambassador by force.[118]

Then there were complaint about the seizure ot goods and the payment of indifferent and arbitrary prices for them.

William Hawkins, while in Surat in 1608, was 'misused' by Muqarrab Khân, the customs-officer of Surat and Cambay. He took possession of his goods, and kept what he liked for himself 'giving me such a price as his own barbarous conscience afforded'. For three months he was kept on empty promises. In the meantime he came to Hawkin's house three times, 'sweeping me cleane of all things that were good.'[118]

When Hawkins met Jahangir at Agra, he made a sweet present to him and lodged a complaint against Muqarrab Khân. Jahangir told him that he had already received reports against that officer and assured him that he would 'remedie all'. When, again, there was complaint by Hawkins, the Emperor angrily ordered Abul Hasn, his 'chiefe vazir', to see the debt discharged. Thus Hawkins received from Abul Hasn the sum that Muqarrab Khân had taken from him.[120]

In 1623, the customs-officer of Surat appropriated two chests and three bales of tobacco belonging to the East India Company.[121]

The Council at Surat advised Bangham in March, 1633, to sell cloth at Burhanpur to Mahâbat Khân at any price he thought proper. He was asked not to hazard controversy with that noble about it lest he should force from them the 'whole complement'.[122]

In April 1633 the English at Surat feared that the customs-officer there would buy the lead at his own price. It was bound to remain there unsold if the price were not accepted.[123]

Towards the end of the same year, the Mughal officers at Biana seized saltpetre from the English and offered only half the English price for it.[124]

In 1650, Shahjahan got displeased with Mu'iz-ul-mulk, the customs-officer of Surat, as he had done injustice to the merchants. The governor of Gujarat seized all the saltpetre provided by the English at Ahmedabad and one consigment of theirs from Agra.[125] In about 1655, the servants of the East India Company at Patna and Rajmahal were arrested and their privilges were violated.[126] The English factor at Agra wrote in the same year that he could not let the saltpetre remain there for long. There was every likelihood of its being confiscated by the ministers, as it had been done previously.[127]

We hear about the 'yadd' government of Ṭhatta in June 1656. The real authority there rested with the wife of the governor. She did much wrong to the traders by taking away their goods from them and paying not even half the market price for it.[128]

There was yet another complaint. The English were not authorized to leave the port without the permission of the authorities.

In the month of November, 1619, Ishâq Beg, the customs-officer of Surat, tried to induce the English to retain part of their fleet that as going to sail for England. He wanted their help against a probable attack of some Mâlâbâr junks. Soon after some of the young factors returning home late were set upon by a number of persons sent by the customs-officer.[129]

They beat and wounded them along with a poor messenger. The English shot five times into the air; but one shot of theirs wounded one of the Indians in the neck. The wounded man was taken to the customs-officer and the report was spread that he was dead. When Ishâq Beg sent for them to answer for this, they refused to go without a pledge of safety. The supply of meat and drink was refused to the English and their servants were cast into prison. At a conference arranged later on, Ishâq

Beg abused and threatened the English. The English factors petitioned Afzal Khân, the *Dîwân* of Prince Khurram, Jamshed Beg, the new customs-officer, and Prince Khurram himself against the maltreatment meted out to them by Ishâq Beg and demanded redress.[80]

The English at Surat complained that they dared not dispose of their ships according to their wishes or for fear of making the 'rogue' customs-officer angry.[131] Some years later in 1636, they complained again that their president was not allowed to go on board the 'Discovery'. Orders against him were withdrawn only when they learnt that the native ships would also be detained in consequence.[132] In 1639, their President was again not permitted to repair on board.[133] In 1651, the customs-officers of the same place forbade the freighting of the English ships bound for Gambroon unless the vessels of the Mughal Emperor were laden.[134] A year before, the customs-officer of Surat had not permitted the English to finish a small vessel which they had begun and only half finished.[135]

The English complained that some time they were not allowed to march from a city in India without permission. On learning that Nicholas Bangham, the English factor, had lef Broach without his permission, Khân-i-Â'zam sent the *kotwâl* to his house. When the *kotwâl* did not find him there, he punished the two servants left by Bangham. They received one hundred stripes each. The porters of the city gates were also whipped for permitting him to depart.[136]

PUNISHMENTS

Our authorities inform us that the Mughal Emperors did not fail to take suitable action against any officer whenever oppressions of any kind were brought to their notice.[137] Punishments varied according to the nature of the offence. The governors of the provinces were warned not to be negligent in taking measures against tyrannous officers. With regard to cases of a less serious nature, only reproof would do. Complaints were inquired into and suitable punishments were awarded.[138] Diminution of rank, dismissal, imprisonment and execution could be the various punishments. We learn that even the common people were not slow to assert and exercise their rights. They would submit a petition to the Imperial Court against the appointment of a governor who had earned notoriety somewhere else.[139] They tried all sorts of measures in acquainting the Emperor with their grievances.[140] In case their efforts did not meet with success, they took resort to tricks and apprised the Emperor of the real situation and got the officer punished.[141]

While Akbar was on his way to Ajmer in 1562, the keeper of the imperial leapords 'waxed proud' and forcibly took off and appropriated a man's pairs of shoes. When the cries of the lamenting owner reached Akbar's ears, he discovered the truth, called the wrong-doer into royal presence and ordered his feet to be cut off. It was rather a harsh punishment, although Abul Fazl has tried to justify it.[142]

When Akbar was at Dhâr (Malwa) in 1564, a woman complained to him that an officer by the name of Mohammad Hussain, had committed various acts of tyranny against her minor daughter and plundered her house. Akbar ordered that he be seized and punished. Abul Fazl does not mention the punishment, but it appears from the nature of the crime and the tone of his writing that the offender was perhaps awarded capital punishment.[143]

An order was promulgated by Akbar in 1582, on the suggestion of Râjâ Todar Mal, to stop the tyranny of the collectors. The excess rent that they charged from the cultivators, was to be regarded as part of the collections.[144]

Another order was issued in the same year to protect the peasantry from the oppression of the malefactors. The commander, the fief-holder and the collector were to get together against those who dwelled in ravines, and taking advantage of the ruggedness of their country, extended the arm of oppression to the peasantry. They were ordered first to admonish such persons, and in case that proved ineffectual, to chastise and punish them. If the soldiers were injured in these operations, the culprits were to be fined.[145]

Râjâ Todar Mal complained to Akbar in 1580 that at a time when imperial armies were engaged in the difficult task of crushing rebellion, Khwâjâ Shâh Mansûr was pressing for demands and causing oppression. The Khwâjâ was dismissed from his high post and given over to Shâh Quli Khân Mahram as a prisoner. Sometime afterwards, however, he was released and re-instated as *vazir.*[146]

Constant complaints of the tyranny and oppression on the part of Hâji Ibrâhim Sirhandi, the *Sadr* of Gujarat, reached Akbar's ears. He was ordered to be arrested and imprisoned in the fortress of Ranthambor where he died in 1586.[147]

On his way to Kâshmir in 1589, Akbar arrived at Gunâchor in Jullundur *Sarkâr*. There it was reported to him that Allâh Vardi, the agent of Sâdiq, and *shiqdâr* of Tibâ Hânû and Raiz had been oppressing the weak. 'Azdu-d-daulâ, Shâh Beg and Qâsim Beg were ordered to sit in judgement on him. As he was found guilty, he was awarded capital punishment.[148]

It was reported to Akbar in 1595 that some persons exacted tolls at ferries. An order was issued to punish the offenders.[149]

A favourite servant of Râi Singh was accused of oppressing the people. When Akbar asked for explanation, the Amir concealed the matter and reported that the said servant had fled. The Râjâ was excluded from performing *kornish*[150] (1596).

Sheikh Sultân, a learned man of Thânesar, was appointed *karori* there. He exercised tyranny upon the people and satisfied his old grudges. When Akbar arrived there on his way back from the Punjab in 1598, the matter was reported to him. The Emperor ordered an enquiry as a result of which the Sheikh was ordered to be hanged.[151]

Next year in 1599, Khwâjâ Malik 'Ali, Bakhshi of the camp, was censured for tyranny and removed from his post. Later on, when he showed repentance, he was forgiven and taken back into service.[152]

While Viceroy of Allahabad, Jahangir inflicted most cruel punishments on his three servants who had absconded. One of them was flayed alive, the other was castrated and the third was beaten to death. Akbar could have come in person to Allahabad and punished the Prince but for the serious illness of his mother. Later on when the Prince came to the capital to mourn the death of the Queen Mother, the Emperor had him arrested and conveyed to the female apartment. There he was to be supplied no wine and had to remain in a closet. This was a very harsh punishment for him, and, only at the intercession of the royal ladies was he released after ten days.[153]

Jahangir ordered that government officers and the *jâgirdârs* should not forcibly seize the lands of the subjects and cultivate them for their own benefit.[154]

It was reported to Jahangir that the eunuchs of Sa'eed Khân oppressed the poor and tyrannized over the weak. When Sa'eed Khân was appointed governor of the Punjab in 1605, Jahangir sent him a message that he would not put up with the oppressions of great or small; and if any cases of cruelty or harshness of his relations reached the Emperor, Sa'eed Khân would receive punishment. According to some accounts the Khân gave a bond that if his people were found to be oppressive, he would forfeit his head.[155]

It was reported to Jahangir in 1605 that two persons, Râjû and Ambâ had been making their livelihood by practising oppressions and tyranny. The Emperor awarded Râjû death punishment and on Ambâ he levied a fine of Rs. 15,000/-.[156]

When in 1608, Jahangir was informed for the second time the Murtazâ Khân, the governor of Gujarat, had faield to restrain his relations from committing oppressions of the people, he ordered his transfer and appointed another governor in his place.[57]

In 1614, the people of Thatta complained against the tyranny of the newly-appointed governor, Rustam Khân. The Emperor Jahangir sent one of his servants to bring him to the Court. He was handed over to Anirâi Singh-Dalan who was to inquire into the complaints against him. If found guilty he was to receive prompt punishment as a warning to others.[158]

It was reported to Jahangir in 1618 that the brothers and sons-in-law of Jahangir Quli Khân, the governor of Bihar, were exercising tyranny on the people. Orders were issued for the dismissal of Jahangir Quli Khân and the appointment in his place of Muqarrab Khân.[159]

Shahjahan was informed in 1639 of the excesses of the customs-officer of Surat. Virji Vohrâ, a leading merchant of the place, had suffered much at his hands. The offender was called to the Court to answer in person. Mu'iz-ul-mulk was sent to make an inquiry on the spot and collect full information regarding the grievances of the people. As a result of the inquiry, the said officer was removed from his post,[160] and Mu'iz-ul-mulk was appointed in his place.[161] In 1650, Mu'iz-l-mulk got into difficulty. He was accused of causing injury to the merchants in Surat and of ruining some villages near that city. Shahjahan at first ordered diminution of his rank and then his dismissal from service.[162]

Nâsir Khân, the governor of Gujarat previous to Murâd, became notorious for his cruelties. The merchants of Ahmedabad complained against him to Shahjahan. An inquiry was ordered as a result of which Nâsir Khân was sent away as a prisoner to the fortress of Rohtâsgarh to sigh away his days there. His property was confiscated.[163]

Aurangzeb's strong sense of justice revolted whenever he came to know of any sort of oppression perpetrated by any officer. He would issue commands to the governors to punish the guilty without delay after making full inquirites.[164]

When Prince Mohammad Â'zam inflicted death punishment on an oppressive official, Aurangzeb administered him a mild reproof for his unpardonable haste.[165]

When reports about the oppressions of Kartib Khân, the customs-officer of Surat, reached royal ears, Aurangzeb summoned him to the Court. Before, however, he could reach the there he was ordered by the

Emperor to swallow poison.[166]

In 1677, the merchants of Surat grew discontented with Ghiâs-ud-din Khân, the customs-officer of the place. Headed by Mirzâ Mu'azzam, they lodged a complaint against him with Mohammad Amin Khân, the governor of Gujarat, and then with the Emperor. As a result of this, Ghiâs-ud-din was dismissed.[167]

REFERENCES

1. Ardhakathâ, pp. 110-115; 127; 14; 148.
2. Orme, pp. 450-51.
3. Bernier, I, pp. 261-62.
4. *Ibid.,* p. 253-54.
5. *Ibid.*, pp. 261-62.
6. Bernier (Constable); p. 230.
7. Bernier, I, pp. 266-68.
8. Bernier, I, pp. 255-56.
9. Tuzk-i-Jahângîrî. R. & B., I. pp. 262-63; Text, I, Iqbâlnâmâ, pp. 31-52.pp. 129-30. Text, p. 75.
10. Bahâristân, I. p. 11.
11. *Ibid.*, p. 274.
12. *Ibid.*, pp. 275-76.
13. Bahâristân, I—pp. 282-87; 308-10.
14. Ardha-kathâ, pp. 461-62, 465-73.
15. Manucci, II, p. 432; IV, p. 437.
16. *Ibid.*, I, p. 198.
17. Ma'âsir-u-Umarâ, p. 563.
18. Mandelslo, pp. 38-40.
19. English Factories, 1646-50, pp. 27-28; 18.
20. Manucci, II, pp. 219-20.
21. English Factories, 1655-60, pp. 312-13.
22. Ancedotes, pp. 86-87.
23. Letters, XIV pp. 19-20.
24. *Ibid.*, XXIII, pp. 29-30.
25. *Ibid.*, pp. 40-41.
26. Jaipur Akhbârât, 16th Oct., 1685.
27. Indian Travels of Careri, p. 236.
28. Manrique, I, pp. 53754;
    Tavernier, I, pp; 53-54;
    Manucci, II, pp. 450-51;
    Bernier, I, pp, 230; 243; 255;
    English Factories, 1646-50, pp. 334-35.
29. Manrique, I, pp. 53-54.

30. Muntakhib-ul-Lûbâb, Urdu Tr., p. 185.
31. Jaipur Akhbârât, 4th Oct., 1666.
32. Akhbârât-i-Darbar-i-Mu'allâ, 19.5.1681.
33. *Ibid.*, 6.9.1681.
34. Akhbârât-i-Dârbâr-i-Mu'allâ. 26th Oct., 1692.
35. *Ibid.* 21.11.1692.
36. *Ibid.* 24.12.1692.
37. Akhbârât-i-Darbâr-i-Mu'allâ, 4th Jan., 1693.
38. *Ibid.* 12th Jan., 1693.
39. *Ibid.* 31st Oct., 1693.
40. Akhbârât-i-Darbâr-i-Mu'allâ, 17th March, 1694.
41. Akhbârât-i-Darbâr-i-Mu'allâ, 1.7.1694.
42. *Ibid.* 19.7.1694.
43. *Ibid.* 11.7.1694.
44. *Ibid.* 27.8.169
45. Akhbârât-i-Darbâr-i-Mu'allâ, 9.9.1694.
46. *Ibid.* 10.9.1694.
47. Akhbârât-i-Darbar-i-Mu'allâ, 23.9.1694.
48. Akhbârât-i-Darbar-i-Mu'allâ, 17.12.1694.
49. *Ibid.* 12/13.4.1695.
50. *Ibid.*
51. Akhbârât (Provincial), No. 48.
52. Akhbârât-i-Darbâr-i-Mu'allâ.
53. *Ibid.*, 9.5.1703.
54. *Ibid.*, 13.9.1703.
55. *Ibid.*, 19.9.1705.
56. Akhbârât-i-Darbâr-i-Mu'allâ, 19/30.8.1704.
57. Akhbârât-i-Darbâr-i-Mu'allâ, 29.8.1704.
58. Manucci, II, pp. 450-51.
Ibid., IV, p. 439.
59. Peter Mundy, II, p. 122.
60. Jaipur Akhbârât, 20.1.1667.
61. Akhbârât-i-Darbâr-i-Mu'allâ, 17.6.1694.
62. *Ibid.*, 25.6.1694.
63. Akhbârât-i-Darbâr-i-Mu'allâ, 8.9.1694.
64. *Ibid.*, 20.9.1694.
65. *Ibid.*, 1.6.1695.
66. *Ibid.*, 19.3.1696.
67. *Ibid.*, 26.3.1696.
68. Akhbârât-i-Darbâr-i-Mu'allâ, 20.12.1699.
69. Manucci, II, p. 451.
70. Mughal Government and Administration, p. 84.
71. Tuzk-i-Jahângîrî, Rogers & Beveridge, Vol. I, p. 163.
72 Muntakhib-ul-Lubâb, I, Urdu Tr., pp. 91-92.

93. Akhbârât-i-Darbâr-i-Mu'allâ, 17.11.1701.
74. Jaipur Akhbârât 5.5.181.
75. Akhbârât-i-Darbâr-i-Mu'allâ, 31.8.1681.
76. *Ibid.*, 12.9.1681.
77. *Ibid.*, 16.9.1681.
78. *Ibid.*, 21.9.1681.
79. Akhbârât-i-Darbâr-i-Mu'allâ, 26.10.1681.
80. Akhbârât-i-Darbâr-i-Mu'allâ, 26.11.1699.
81. *Ibid.*, 17th Nov., 1701.
82. *Ibid.*, 6.3.1704.
83. Âîn. II, pp. 72-73.
84. Eliot, vi, p. 493;
Mîrât-i-Ahmadi, I, p. 78;
Tuzk, R. & B. I, p. 7.
85. Mîrât, I, pp. 260-63; 287.
86. Mauntakhib-ul-Lubâb, II, p. 87-89.
87. Muntakhib-ul-Lubâb, II, pp. 88-89.
88. Indian Travels of Careri, p. 236.
89. Akhbârât, (Provincial), No. 48.
90. *Ibid.*
91. News-letters (Provincial), No. 48.
92. News-letters (Provincial), No. 48.
93. Akhbârât-i-Darbâr-i-Mu'allâ, 10th Oct., 1692.
94. Akhbârât-i-Darbâr-i-Mu'allâ, 17.7.1694.
95. *Ibid.*
96. Newsletters (Provincial), No. 48.
91. Akhbârât-i-Darbâr-i-Mu'allâ, 3.6.1695.
98. Akhbârât-i-Darbâr-i-Mu'allâ, 15.6.1695.
99. *Ibid.*, 16.1.1703.
100. Bernier, I, pp. 257-58; 291; Orme, p. 405.
101. Fryer, I, pp. 242-43.
102. Bernier, I, p. 257-58; 291.
103. Fryer, I, pp. 242-43.
104. Orme, p. 405.
105. English Factories. 1634-36, p. 290.
106. Fryer, I, p. 242-43.
107. Manucci, IV, pp. 116-17.
108. Early Travels in India, William Hawkins (1608-13).
109. English Factories, 1612-21 pp. 374-75.
110. Roe in Kerr's Collection op. cit, Eliot & Dowson. Vol. VI, pp. 498-99.
111. Nicholas Withington in Early Travels, pp. 212.
112. Kerr's Collection, op. cit. Eliot & Dowson, VI, pp. 498-99.
113. Peter Mundy. II, p. 300.

114. English Factories, 1634-36, p. 244.
115. *Ibid.*, 1646-50, p. 47.
116. English Factories, 1668-69, p. 181.
117. *Ibid.*, 1670-77, p. 143.
118. Roe in Kerr's Collection, Cf. Eliot & Dowson. VI, pp. 498-99.
119. Early Travels, pp. 75-76.
120. Early Travels, pp. 7576.
121. English Factories, 1622-23 p. 258.
122. *Ibid.*, 1630-34, p. 285.
123. English Factories, 1634-36, p. 244.
124. *Ibid.*, 1646-50; p. 225.
125. *Ibid.*, pp. 334-35.
126. *Ibid.*, 1651-54, p. 224.
127. English Factories, 1655-60, p. 51.
128. English Factories, 1655-60, pp. 63-64.
129. *Ibid.*, p. 79.
130. English Factories, 1618-21, pp. 145-49; p. 167.
131. *Ibid.*, 1630-33. p. 288.
132. English Factories, 1634-36; p. 189.
133. English Factories, 1639-41, p. 128.
134. *Ibid.*, 1651-54, p. 71.
135. *Ibid.*, 1655-60, p. 143.
136. Ovington, p. 120.
137. Manucci, I, pp. 198-99.
138. *Ibid.*
139. English Factories, 1618-21; 1622-23; 1624-29.
140. *Ibid.*
141. Akbar Nâmâ, Beveridge, II, 242. Text, II, p. 156.
142. *Ibid.*, 1622-23, p. 258.
143. Akbar Nâmâ, Beveridge, II, pp. 346-50. Text, II, pp. 226-29.
144. *Ibid.*, III, p. 562. Text, III, 382.
145. *Ibid.*, 563-64. Text, III, pp. 382-83.
146. Akbar Nâmâ, 461-62; 480. Text; III, 316; 328. Badâûni, Lowe, II, pp. 295-96 Text, II, pp. 287-88.
147. Akbar Nâmâ, III, Bev, p. 606. Text, III, pp. 408-9.
148. Akbar Nâmâ, Bev., III, 818. Text, III, p. 328.
149. *Ibid.*, p. 1029. Text, III, p. 670.
150. *Ibid.*, p. 1068.
151. *Ibid.*, p. 1118, Iqbâ Nâmâ, p. 104;
Ibid., Text, III, 748.
152. *Ibid.*, p. 1176; Text, III, 785.
153. Akbar Nâmâ, (Supplement), 1242-43; p. 1248. Text, III, pp. 829-30; 833.
154. Eliot & Dowson, VI, p. 511-12.

155. Tuzk, Beveridge, I, p. 13; Price's Memoris, p. 16; Ma'âsir, II, 405. Tuzk, Text, I, p. 7.
156. Tuzk, Bev., I, p. 73. Text, p. 35.
157. *Ibid.*, p. 153. Text, I, p. 74.
158. Tuzk, 262-63, Iqbâl Nâmâ, pp. 51-52. Text, 75; Tuzk, Text, I, 129-30.
159. *Ibid.*, II, pp. 37-38;
Tuzk, Text, II, p. 246.
160. English Factories, 1637-41, pp. 108-10.
161. *Ibid.*, 1642-45, p. 23.
162. *Ibid.*, 1646-50, pp. 334-33.
163. Manucci, I, pp. 198-99.
164. Letters, XIV; pp. 19-20; XXIII, pp. 29-30; XXXVII, pp. 40-41.
165. *Ibid.*, XXVI, p. 48.
166. Manucci, II, p. 259.
167. English Factories, 1670-77, p. 283.

VIII
RELIGIOUS CRIMES

Akbar secularized the Muslim state and in doing so he destroyed many of the religious crimes. Jahangir brought about some modification this system. Shahjahan, however, introduced several changes making many acts criminal again. Aurangzeb tried to govern entirely in accordance with the advice of the theologians and restored the entire Muslim penal code in the religious sphere.

We shall take up the subject under the following sub-heads:—

1. Drinking And Sale of Liquor.
2. Gambling.
3. Prostitution.
4. Fallacious Writings.
5. Blasphemy.
6. Heresy.
7. Marriages.
8. Slaughter Of Animals.
9. Conversions From Islam.
10. Sati.
11. Forbidden Hindu Practices.

DRINKING AND SALE OF LIQUOR

Drinking of wine is forbidden in the Qur'ân. In case a Muslim takes liquor and is seized while his breath yet smells of wine, or is brought before the *qâzi* while intoxicated, and two witnesses give evidence that he had taken wine, scourging is to be inflicted. The punishment is eighty lashes for a free man and forty lashes for a slave.[1] According to Mâ'alim-Al-Qarbâ the punishment was forty stripes for a free man and twenty stripes for a slave.[2] Before awarding the punishment it was necessary to establish the offence. If a man smelled of wine and did not confess his guilt, or two witnesses did not give evidence, he was not to be punished.[3]

The Muslim law provides no penalty for the sale of wine. Aurangzeb, however, supplemented the Muslim law by providing penalty for this offence. For the first offence a wine-seller was to be severely whipped. The repetition of the offence condemned him, after the chastisement, to imprisonment till he repented. Severe whipping was to be inflicted on a distiller in the service of a wine merchant and the merchant was to be reprimanded.[4]

Despite the ban by Islâmic law, drinking sems to have been a common feature in Mughal India. The kings and the nobility formed no exception. While encamping outside the fortress of Surat in 1573 A.D., Akbar at a pleasure party of select companions enjoyed the European wine brought in vessels by the Portugese of Daman and the coast. Distinguished officers like Khân-i-Â'zam, Muzaffar Khân and Lashkar Khân became unconscious from the excessive use of alchohol.[5]

All the four Mughal emperors, however, took steps to bring the consumption of wine under control. Akbar issued an ordinance in 1593 that wine could be taken on medical grounds and on the advice of the physician alone. He did not prohibit the drinking of wine as such, but laid down that severe punishment would be meted out to those who indulged in excessive 'drinking carousals and disorderly conduct'. In order to control the vice, Akbar ordered a wine shop to be set up near the palace. The Porter's wife was placed in charge of the shop. She belonged by birth to a class of wine-dealers.[6]

Jahangir in the first year of his reign forbade drinking, manufacture and sale of every sort of intoxicating liquor.[7] In 1609, he stopped the use of *bhang* and *bûjâ* (rice spirit) as these were injurious to health. Their sale in the market was forbidden.[8] *Arack* was a kind of wine distilled during Jahangir's time.[9]

According to Badâûni, Akbar failed in his prohibition policy. Jahangir's efforts in this direction remained futile. He himself was a confirmed drinker, and took as many as twenty cups of double-distilled liquor in the early years of his reign. He reduced this quantity to five or six cups only after a period of seven years.[10]

We learn on the authority of Sir Thomas Roe, the English Ambassador at Jahangir's court, that drunkenness was a 'common and glorious vice' in the country.[11] In a letter of 25th January, 1616, to the East India Company, he has recorded that Jahangir and the Prince were extremely fond and enamoured of the English red wine. He was of the view that as the Emperor had solicited for more, 'four or five cases of that wine would be more welcome than the richest jewell in Cheapsyde.'[12] During a visit to the royal *durbâr* some time later, Roe inquired of the Emperor through the medium of 'Âsaf Khân if he should send him some English red wine which was getting hard. Jahangir accepted the offer and the blessed thing was then sent to the *ghuslkhânâ.*[13]

The high nobility was no less fond of liquor than the Emperor. They had a special preference for the English wine. The English Ambassador often supplied them the stuff that he got from England, particularly the red wine. He did so naturally to grind his own axe and secure favours. It served as a good lever to expedite his work. On 14th July, 1616, he sent 'Âsaf Khân a bottle of liquor 'putting him in mÿnd to dispatch the sealing of our priviledges'. In his turn the minister promised to do the needful with expedition.[14]

Jahangir would feel delighted to offer the English Ambassador wine in the *durbâr.* On 2nd September, 1616, he sent for Roe at night when the latter was 'abedd', and offered him in the *durbâr* mixed wine in a cup of gold. The Englishman found it much stronger than any liquor he had tasted so far and sneezed. This excited Jahangir's laughter who ordered for him raisins, almonds and sliced lemons, which were offered him in a plate of gold.[15]

During Jahangir's time, wine-drinking had rather become too common.

In the third week of March, 1617, Jahangir organized a wine party where he entertained 'servants who were engaged in waiting on me.'[16]

In the same year Mahâ Singh, a high official, and grandson of Râjâ Mân Singh, died of excessive wine-drinking at Bâlâpur in the province of Berâr.[17]

Dayânat Khân, Bakshi of Ahâdis, and one of the intimate attendants of Jahangir, died of the after-effect of wine-drinking in 1618 A.D.[18]

Khân Jahân Lodi, whom Jahangir called his *'farzand'* or son, had become 'ill from the madness of wine'. The vice rather threatened his life and he was obligHed to reform his habit and did not drink afterwards.[19]

Next year, in 1621 A.D., took place the death of Râjâ Bhâo Singh, the son of Râjâ Mân Singh, from over-drinking.[20]

During the time of Jahangir there was a regular wine-cellar which was in the charge of an officer.[21]

Jahangir has refferred to the use of a special drink, known as

Âcchi in Pakli. It was prepared from bread and rice. 'Its intoxicating effects are aphrodisiac, but its taste is harsh'. They mixed it with *bhang* and that increased its intoxicating power.[22]

Although wine-drinking was a common vice, yet none dared enter the royal presence in a state of drunkenness. None could come near the Emperor if he smelt of wine.[23] William Hawkins, an addict to the vice, offended against the regulation. He was publicly insulted by Jahangir and forbidden to sit in the place meant for him near the Emperor.[24] It was stirctly forbidden for any person to enter the *ghûsalkhânâ* even if he smelt of liquor. the 'porters smell his breath, and, if he have but tasted wine, is not suffered to come in; and, if the reason be known of his absence, he shall with difficulty skape the whip; for, if the king once take the offence, the father will not speake for sonne'.[25]

On 24th October, 1616, Jahangir entertained the Persian Ambassador to a grand feast at Hâfiz Jamâl, the delightful garden resort in the neighbourhood of Ajmer. The Emperor drank to excess and so also the majority of the nobles present there. Next day, some one in the court brought this fact to the notice of the Emperor, who, considering it an offence, 'and not remembering his own command,' meted out harsh punishments to those guilty of wine-drinking. Some were heavily fined, others received as many as 130 stripes each causing four wounds at one stroke, resulting in grievous injury to many and death to one.[26]

On 18th January, 1618, Thomas Roe received a letter from Surat to the effect that Thomes Spragge and Howard, the English employees of the East India Company at Burhanpur, had been imprisoned; their house and goods were confiscated and their lives were in danger. They were guilty of having drunk in the company of the *kotwâl* whose one servant had died of excessive drinking. The *kotwâl* had extricated himself from the predicament on some false excuse.[27]

In the sixth year of his reign, Shahjahan issued an order prohibiting the sale, public or private, of wine. In the previous reign, the law had confined itself only to public sales. Now it was extended to the private sales as well. The Christians, however, formed an exception and retained the right of manufacturing drinks for their own use.[28] The Mughal royal Princes often drank to excess. Shujâ' was one.[29] Dârâ formed no exception, although he showed moderation.[30] Princess Jahânârâ was exceedingly fond of wine imported from Perisa, Kabul and Kâshmir. The best liquor she got distilled in her own palace.[31]

Sebastien Manrique who visited India during Shahjahan's reign did not find in Bengal any vineyards and hence no grape wine in the country excepting that imported by the Portugese from Portugal.[32]

The Indians, however, made a fermented liquor from rice which was very potent. *Jagrâ* made from sugar was a more viscous liquor.[33]

The popular liquor in Surat in 1689 was the *Shîrâz* wine and 'Arack Punch.' These two varieties were frequently used by the English factors residing there. European wines and the English beers were most coveted and desirable liquors. Although they sold at exorbitant rates, they were 'purchased and drunk with pleasure.[34]

Careri who visited India six year later than Ovington found the south Indians drinking the juice of the herb known as *bhang.*[35]

Opium, taken from *post,* was a bitter black extract used by the 'orientals to assist in the gratification of lust and lewdness, by increasing their sexual power.' The *post* was well mixed up in water and then taken. 'The drinking of this extremely increases sexual power, but at the same time destroys natural strength.[36]

Aurangzeb made strict rules against the manufacture, use and sale of wine. It was prohibited to use wines brought from Persia or any other place. Restraint was placed on the use and sale of beverages like *bhang,* toddy and opium.[37] To stop the sale of wine and other beverages, orders for the closure of wine shops were issued. The Christians, however, were allowed to prepare spirits for their own consumption. They could use strong drugs according to their religious practices. Aurangzeb ordered all the Christians, with the exception of physicians and surgeons, to leave the imperial capital. They were to remove themselves to a place at a distance of one league from the city. There they could prepare and drink wine, but were not permitted to sell it.[38]

Aurangzeb was anxious to make his prohibition scheme a real success. For this he made several provisions. The Chief Muhtasib and the large body of subordinate censors under his were required to explain to the people the harm done by the use of intoxicants. If they found arguments of no avail, they could use force. In that case the censors could break the pots and pans in which these beverages and liquor were found.[39] They were required to prohibit the use of wine even in the camps of the *mansabdârs.*[40] The *bâzârs* where these *mansabdârs* purchased wine, were to be abolished. To guard against the Christians selling wine, sentinels were kept over them.[41] By a royal order the provincial governors were required to render all possible assistance to the censors. Books. such as the Diwâ-i-Hâfiz, serving as incentives to the use of wine, were prescribed in the schools.[42]

All these precautions, however, were not destined to guarantee success. Innumerable references to the infringement of these rules have come down to us. If we believe Manucci's statement, every person in the kingdom, with the only exception of Aurangzeb himself, was addicted to the use of wine. Although, according to the Muslim law, non-Muslims were not to be punished for taking intoxicating liquors, Aurangzeb had extended the law to them also. The Christians who formed an exception, were permitted the use, though not the sale, of wine. they, however, frequently infringed the law and engaged themselves in the sale of prohibited spirits. They knew that it was easy for them to make money by supplying wine to those who could not do without it. For this they resorted to numberless expedients and sold it on the sly.[48] The *Muhtasib* had to face practical difficulties in the performance of his duties, as the opposition came from the ministers themselves who 'loved to be drunk.'[44]

When Prince Shâh 'Âlam was in Kabul, an army general complained against the misbehaviour of a commander of 500 horse. The Prince had just finished off several bottles of the Kabul wine, and, in this condition of drunkenness, issued an order for the punishment of the said commander. He, however, had to repent later on.[45]

Shâh 'Âlam's sons were also addicted to the vice. Once Manucci sent a bottle of wine to Sultân Mu'iz-ud-din. A spy reported the whole affair to Aurangzeb. The Prince extricated himself from a difficult situation on the plea that the wine was to be used as a medicine for a sick lady.[46]

Like all other Princes, Sultân Mohammad Â'zam also took wine secretly. The reports about his misbehaviour reached Aurangzeb, who, out of affection for the Prince, usually overlooked them.[47]

The news-writers of the province of Gujarat informed the Emperor that Mohammad Amîn Khân, the governor, held the court while in his cups. The Emperor considered it scandalous.[48]

Manucci narrates the story of twelve officials who emptied cups of wine and enjoyed the company of women in the Dilkushâ garden at Lahore.[49]

Aurangzeb got enraged to learn that a reporter, Hidâya Keesh by name, had the temerity to adopt an insulting behaviour towards a deceased saint. He had gone to his tomb in a state of intoxication. He was ordered to be brought in chains to the Emperor's presence.[50]

Complaints reached the Emperor about some *mansabdârs* who violated the prohibition rules by the purchase and use of wine.[51]

Some time reports would disturb the royal mind about a whole army exceeding the bounds of decency by indulging in wine.[52]

Different types of punishment were inflicted if a person infringed the rules. The police raided his house and put fetters on him. With the still hung round his neck and receiving constant showers of blows on the way he was brought before the *kotwâl*. He was hurled into prison where he had to remain for many months. He was released after he had received a good deal of thrashing and paid a heavy fine.[53]

For the offence, a *mansabdâr* could be transferred or degraded.[54] Some *mansabdârs* who were charged with the offence of purchasing wine from the *Bâzâr-i-Mansbdârân*, were ordered to remove their tents to the neighbourhood of the imperial *bâzâr*.[55]

Aurangzeb got enraged at the door-keepers of the apartment of a concubine. They were guilty of allowing wine to pass into her room. They were ordered to be bastinadoed.[56]

Prince Â'zam, when charged at a time with the offence of drinking wine, was locked up and remained in prison for a year.[57]

On 12th November, 1679, it was learnt from a report of the secret police that Zâbitâ Khân commandant was indulging in the use of liquor. 'Abdul Wasî' was ordered to inquire and report.[58]

On 28th October, 1692, Sheikh Nur-ul-Haq *Muhtasib* brought to the notice of the Emperor that Mukhtâr Khân, *Mîr-i-Âtish,* had drunk and gambled in the house of Bali Ram. Soldiers had been sent to stop him from this practice. He was punished with diminution of rank. He was, moreover, forbidden to attend the *dîwân-i-khâs*.[59]

A report was received from Shahjahanabad that Ratan Râme[60] posted to the army of Râjâ Bishan Singh, came and indulged in wine drinking and other forbidden practices. His *jâgir* was transferred.[61]

On 14th March 1694, a report from Îraj in the province of Agra revealed that there was excessive use and sale of wine in Orchhâ, which was Râjâ Uday Singh's home town. The Emperor ordered that they should take a bond from the *vakîl* of the Râjâ against the use and sale of wine and other forbidden articles.[62]

On 14th July, 1695, news was again received from Shahjahanabad that Fatehullâ son of Farzullâh prepared wine in his own house and drank it to excess. He was deprived of his *mansab* of 250 *zât* and 80 *swâr*.[63]

'Abdul Karîm, grandson of the late Islâm Khân was accused of drinking wine and oppressing people and of indulging in other objectionable habits. He held the rank of 900 *zât* and 900 *swâr*. A reduction in his rank was ordered by 400 *zât* and 200 *swâr*.[64]

On 7th August, 1701, Khwâjâ Mas'ûd complained to the Emperor against Abul Hasn, the son of the late Amîr Khân. The Khwâjâ had gone to the village of Pachkânu to look after the gardens there. Abul Hasn who had also gone there in the company of 50 persons, started indulging in drinking wine. He also got the trees in the garden uprooted by his elephant. When the imperial servants tried to stop him from such activities, he attacked them and engaged in fight as a result of which four or five persons received injuries and one lost his life. Abul Hasn held the rank of 700 *zât* and 200 *swâr*. The Emperor reduced it by 200 *zât* and 100 *swâr*. Moreover, he and his brothers were farbidden to attend the *dîwân-î-khâs.*[65]

Ten days later another complaint was lodged, this time by Yâr 'Ali Beg *kotwâl,* against two other sons of the late Amîr Khân, Mohammad Ishâq and Mohammad 'Ali. These two had gone towards Shahjahanabad and on the way started indulging in wine and troubling the people. Both of them were deprived of their *mansab,* though an annuity was fixed separately for both fo them.[66]

A report came from Bengal on 9th June, 1702, that Mân Singh and other officers were found drinking liquor and other intoxicants in the *bâzâr* of Dâcâ. The other officers were Gazanfar 'Ali Bakshi, Mohammad 'Azîm, Ni'mat-ullâh, *dârroghâ* artillery, and Rahmat Khân. The ranks of all these officers were reduced.[67]

News came on 1st December, 1703, from Odni that Mohammad Ghyâs and Pîr Mohammad Hazâr Zubân posted in the fort, drank wine, went to the house of Mîr 'Abdullâ, *dârroghâ* artillery of the fort, and started throwing stones. The complainant had to stand guard with his sword assisted by a few servants. The Emperor ordered that the guilty persons should be asked to pay a fine to the tune of two months' salary.[60]

GAMBLING

During the reign of Akbar, gambling was much prevalent in India. Akbar never tried to abolish the practice, but he brought it under state control.[69] On the other hand, Jahangir ordered the complete abolition of gambling in the state.[70] Aurangzeb ordered that if after proper inquiries, a charge of gambling was proved against a person, he was to be chastised. In case he took it as a profession, he was, after proper chastisement, to be imprisoned, till he repented. If he still repeated the crime, he was to be given life imprisonment The property thus obtained, was to be restored to the owner or to be kept in trust.[91]

Aurangzeb was aggrieved to learn that the son of the Superintendent of the Palace of Mohammad Â'zam had taken to gambling. The Prince was reprimanded for showing indifference and carelessness. The Emperor ordered him to appoint news-writers to give correct information.[72]

The *khufia-navîs* posted in the Deccan wrote to the Emperor that Khânjahân Bahâdur and Rustam Khân used to gamble between themselves and Rustam Khân had lost to Khânjâhân a few thousand rupees. As the former had no cash to pay, the latter sent his *'âmils* to Rustam Khân's *jâgir* to attach it as a result of which he got distressed and fled away. Hearing this, the Emperor ordered on 15th December, 1681, to write to Kâmyâb Khâ, Bakshi of the Deccan, that he had failed to send the account of these happenings. He was punished with the diminution of his rank by 500.[73]

PROSTITUTION

Like drinking and gambling, Akbar tried to control the vice of prostitution also. Badâûnî informs us that the prostitutes of the imperial dominions had gathered in the capital in such swarms as to defy counting or numbering. Akbar set apart separate quarters for them outside the city, called *Shaitânpurâ.* A staff of officers consisting of a Keeper, a Deputy and a Secretary, was appointed there. Any one who wanted to associate himself with these people or to take them home, had to give his name or address. According to Badâûnî, prostitution could not be controlled despite many rules and regulations. Akbar would sometime call some of the prostitutes into his presence and ask the name of officers who had visited them. Many a time a number of imperial officers were reprimanded and imprisoned in this connection.[14] Aurangzeb proclaimed an ordinance that prostitutes and dancing girls should either marry or leave the kingdom.[75] In 1665, he issued orders for the suppression of prostitution.[76] These orders do not seem to have served their purpose as in 1679 Ovington found in Surat a large number of prostitutes and dancing girls.[77]

FALLACIOUS WRITINGS

It was considered a crime to indulge in any sort of fallacious writing. Qâzi Mîr, who had been the chief minister and chancelor of Shâh 'Âlam, and was renowned for learning, wrote a book with pro-Christian views. Aurangzeb took serious exception to it. The Chief Qâzi, however did not see eye to eye with the Emperor on this point and refused to pronounce death sentence on him. He was imprisoned in Asîrgarh fort and later on executed. Yet another person was executed for a similar offence.[78]

BLASPHEMY

The literal meaning of blasphemy is to hide (the truth). 'It included a denial of any of the essential principles of Islam. A Muslim convicted of this crime was sentenced to death in Muslim countries.[79]

In Mughal India, particularly in the reign of Shajahan and Aurangzeb, the punishment was extended to non-Muslims as well. During Shahjahan's reign a Hindu who was charged with the offence of using disrespectful language towards the Qur'ân, was awarded death punishment. Another Hindu, alleged to have uttered abusive words about the Prophet, also received capital punishment.[80]

During Aurangzeb's reign, a man charged with this crime, could receive any serious, including death, punishment.[81] Sometime a Muslim could intimidate and silence a Hindu merchant that in case the latter persisted in his demands of debt, he would level the charge of blasphemy against him. If the merchant refused to be cowed down and to forego his debt, the other fellow could charge him with the crime, and the *qâzî* could force him to be circumcised and converted.[82]

Hussain Malik, a Shia', earned death punishment for using disrespectful language towards the Companions of the Prophet.[83]

Dîwân Mohammad Tâhir was beheaded for uttering abusive words about the first three Caliphs.[84]

'Ali Sirhindî, when asked to give up the habit of drinking, gave out that he stod on an equal footing with the angles in this respect. He was executed for using such a language.[85]

The son of a learned man of Siâlkot forsook his father's house and took the garb of an ascetic to preach the gospel of Christ, and started attacking the Qur'ân. He reached Ahmedabad in 1699 and started discussions with the *qâzî* of the place. He extolled the Christian Gospels and decried what the Prophet had enjoined. The *qâzi* grew furious and gave the young man a good thrashing. He, however, refused to be intimidated and continued his attacks. He was ordered to be thrown into prison. For full forty days questions were put to him followed by bright promises and honeyed words. Adamant as he remained thrashing was administered to him almost every day. In the end he was beheaded.[86]

HERESY

Heresy was also considered a crime. It was reported to Jahangir that soon after his accession, Sheikh Ibrâhim had set himself up as a religious leader in the *pargânâ* of Lahore. A large number of Aghâns had gathered round him as his followers. He was ordered to be brought before the Emperor. As he could not satisfy him, he was entrusted to Parvez to be imprisoned in the fortress of Chunâr.[87]

Jahangir ordered Qâzi Nûrullâh to be flogged to death on the charge of being an effective Shi'a writer.[88]

Jahangir learnt that Kaukab, son of Qamar Khân, had become intimate with a Sanyâsin and had made his cousins, 'Abdul Latîf and Sharîf, 'partners' in that sin. Kaukab and Sharif were ordered to be flogged and imprisoned and 'Abdul Latif received one hundred lashes in the presence of the Emperor.[89]

During Shahjahan's reign, reign, when Aurangzeb was the Viceroy of Gujarat, one Sayyid Râju was accused of giving expression to heretical views. He was ordered to be expelled from Ahmedabad. Officers were sent to hasten his departure. As he offered opposition, he was subsequently killed.[90]

A person who instigated others to innovations in religion, was an enemy of orthodox Islam. Aurangzeb ordered that if in the teachings of such a man there was the possibility of the spread of heresy, he was to suffer capital punishment.[91]

Dârâ, in reality the political opponent of Aurangzeb, was executed on the excuse that he held heretical views. He considered the Vedas as the revealed books, had translated the Upanishads, adopted the Hindu epithet for God i.e. Prabhu, and had abandoned the Muslim religious obligation such as prayer and fasting as imposed by Islam.[92]

Aurangzeb became angry with an illiterate *dervesh* who spoke against charity. He wrote to Asad Khân to demand from the *faqîr* an explanation for his conduct. In case he failed to furnish a satisfactory reply, he was to receive the punishment due to a heretic.[93]

On 16th November, 1692, a report was received from Râmgarh to the effect that Maqsûd Beg, commandant of the fort, had fallen ill. He was told that in the fortress there lived a demon; if he sent to the evil spirit in the fortress two jars of wine, two buffaloes, and betel leaves he would be cured of illness. Accordingly, he started sending to the fortress for the evil spirit the said provisions. The Emperor Aurangzeb ordered to write to him to discontinue this practice in the future.[94]

In July, 1694, a *faqîr* was accused of having called himself God. He was taken before *Qâzî* 'Abdullâ who sent him on to the *muftî*. The *faqîr* repeated the statement in his presence also. When questioned whether he was a follower of Mohammad who was the messenger of God, the *faqîr* replied that he himself was God and that Mohammad was his follower. The *muftî* gave the verdict of guilty deserving capital punishment. Upon this, the Emperor held, *'adâlat* when the night had passed four *gharîs* and ordered that the *faqîr* be awarded death punishment. Accordingly, he was executed by the executioners.[95]

Sarmad, the famous *Sûfî faqîr*, was asked through the Chief *qâzî* the reason of his nudity. His answer offended the *qîzî*. He was ordered to present himself at the royal court and there repeat the whole of the Muslim creed. In his reply he denied the existence of God and declared that beyond that he knew nothing. For this offence, he was awarded capital punishment.[96]

Zaki, a saint of Lahore, was awarded death punishment for his heretical opinions.[97]

MARRIAGES

Akbar promulgated orders regarding marriages as well. In 1583, it was laid down that no one was to marry one's cousin or near relation. The marriageable age of boys was fixed at sixteen and that of the girls at fourteen.

Five years later it was laid down that a man was not to have more than one legal wife, unless he was childless. Widows were permitted to re-marry.

Still seven years afterwards in 1595, Akbar issued an order that if a woman was older than her husband by twelve years, he should leave her.

No son or daughter of the common people was to be married unless they had gone to the office of the Chief of the Police, and had been seen by his agents and correct age of both the parties was investigated.

These orders regulating marriage were not in accordance with the Isamic law. It does not seem that any effort was made to enforce them seriously. Nor do we come across any punishment meted out to those who infringed them.

If a young woman were found running about the lanes and *bâzârs* of the town unveiled, or if a woman were deceitful and quarrelled with her husband, she was to go to the quarters of the prostitutes.[98]

SLAUGHTER OF ANIMALS

In 1584, Akbar issued orders against the use of animal flesh. It was prohibited to slaughter animals on the first day of the week, during the first days of Farwardin, the whole of the month of Aban (the month in which Akbar was born) and on several other days. Akbar had issued these orders as a concession to Hindu sentiments and extended them to the entire kingdom. Any one who acted against the orders, was punished and his property confiscated. During these days the Emperor abstained from taking meat altogether and extended the practice to six or seven months in the year. Eight years afterwards, it was forbidden to use the flesh of cows, buffaloes, sheep, horses and camels.[99] The flesh of goats and sheep was used in the royal kitchen at the time when the *Âîn* was compiled and its price is recorded in the *Âîn*.[100]

Jahangir continued the practice of his father of abstention from slaughter of animals on Sundays and Thursdays.[101] Sunday was Akbar's birth day and Thursday was Jahangir's day of accession.[102] Those who violated these orders were seriously punished. Once a *kotwâl* who failed to get these rules observed, was flogged by Jahangir's orders.[103] In Gujarat certain animals were not killed as the Jains there had agreed to pay highly for this concession.[104] It was on account of the scarcity of cattle that Jahangir at the request of th Brâhmins, issued an edict forbidding the slaughter of grazing animals for a certain number of years.[105]

To some extent Shahjahan continued the practice of prohibiting the slaughter of animals on certain days.

Manrique relates the story of the killing of two pea-cocks by a Muslim who was one of the party which was travelling from Bengal to the imperial court. The inhabitants of the nearby village were roused to fury at such a sacrilege. Finding themselves unable to wreak vengeance on the offenders, they petitioned the judge or the *kotwâl* of the city of Nârângor.

At the dead of night, twelve soldiers raided the *serâi* where the travellers were enjoying sound sleep. With their hands and feet tied, they were led to an underground dungeon. After a harsh confinement of twenty-four hours, they were led in the morning to the court. The *qâzî* addressed himself to the culprit, a Bengali Muslim, and reprimanded him for the infringment of the Hindu religious practices in a predominantly Hindu locality. Manrique appealed to the religious fantacism of the *qâzî* and requested him not to show any regard for the religious scruples of the

Hindus. The judge explained to the Portugese the law of the realm where offences against the Hindu religion were to be punished by whipping and the amputation of the hand. The Emperor, explained the *qâzî,* had promised the Hindus the freedom of following their own laws and customs. He assured him, however, that he would inflict a milder punishment.

All except the offender were set free and the latter was shut up in the public prison. Bribery at last saved him. Through the mediation of a eunuch, Manrique supplied the wife of the judge valuable presents and secured the liberty of his companions.[106]

Aurangzeb was requested by the Brâhmins to stop the slaughter of grazing animals.[107] He refused to follow into the footsteps of his predecessors. The liberties of the Hindus were curtailed. The law prevailing in the previous reigns allowing the Hindus their freedom had lost its rigidity. The killing of animals, sure to excite the religious feelings of the Hindus was not considered crime now. In the Hindu states, however, none could dare to do so as the people could take the law into their own hands and deal out a severe punishment to the culprit. The Hindus in the Mughal territories did take offence at such an outrage and protested to the authorities.

Near Burhanpur, Manucci tried to kill a peacock when suddenly two persons with bows and arrows advanced towards him. He saved himself with some difficulty.[108]

A rich Persian merchant, passing by the territory of the Râjâ of Dantivar in Gujarat killed a peacock with his gun. Enraged by this 'horrible sacrilege', the local people seized the Persian, tied him to a tree and whipped him for three days till he gave up the ghost. They, moreover, seized his entire money amounting to three lac of rupees.[109]

A report came from Burhanpur on 22nd January, 1700, that Nasrûllâ, grandson of the late Ilhâm Khân, had gone to the preserved jungle of the Emperor and killed with his gun one *nîlgâo.* He was arrested and sent before Mu'taqid Khân, the governor of the province. The Khân handed him over to the *kotwâl* to be thrown into prison.[110]

CONVERSIONS TO ISLAM

It was the usual practice of the Muslim rulers to convert non-Muslims to Islam. In the beginning of his reign, even Akbar did not form an exception, and made many converts from Hinduism.[111] Under Akbar, it became however, criminal to make forcible conversions.[112] In his sixth year, Jahangir issued an order against forcible conversions to Islam.[113] However, as protector of the faith, he wanted to save it from outside attacks.

Shahjahan was touched to the quick to discover the practice of the marriages of Hindu youths with Muslim girls in Bhadauri and Bhimber. These girls were converted to Hinduism and cremated at their death according to their rites. An order was at once issued to stop this practice. Such marriages were declared unlawful, the converted girls were to be taken away from their husbands who were to be fined. The fine could be remitted in case they became converts to Islam. Full orce was allowed to be used in the suppression of this practice.[114]

Dalpat, a Hindu enthusiast from Sirhind, married a Muslim girl, Zinab, renamed her as Gangâ, and naturally brought up their children as Hindus. Moreover, he converted to Hinduism six Muslim boys and six Muslim girls. Shahjahan ordered to seize from Dalpat his wife and children. He was asked to choose death or Islam. Dalpat preferred to die as a martyr and was put to death with all show of cruelty.[115]

Shahjahan made it unlawful for the Hindu soldiers to enslave Muslim prisoners of war and for the Hindu public to buy Muslim prisoners of war. He was afraid of the fact that the Hindus might not convert them to their religion.[116]

A Portugese who had become a Muslim, expressed a wish to the *qâzi* of Aurangâbâd to be reconverted to his faith. The *qâzi* kept him in prison and held out to him various promises and threats. When he spoke against Islam, he received thrashing. The matter was reported to Aurangzeb who ordered that if the Portugese did not give up his resolve for reconversion, he was to be executed.[117]

PUBLIC WORSHIP IN HINDU TEMPLES

Early in his reign Aurangzeb seems to have ordered against the construction of new temples and the repairs of the old ones.[118] In the beginning of 1670, he sent orders to all the governors and local officers 'prohibiting the practice of Pagan religion throughout the country and closing down all the temples and sanctuaries of Idol worshippers.......in the hope that some pagans would embrace the Muslim religion.'[119]

Thus image worship came to be regarded as an evil practice and a crime necessary to be suppressed. Reports of the 'illegal' activities in this respect claimed the immediate attention of Aurangzeb. The Jaipur News-Letters are replete with instances of the wanton destruction of

Hindu places of worship throughout the country from 1667 to 1705. Below are given a few cases where demolition of such places was ordered on receipt of complaints against this 'evil practice' of the Hindus, as their public worship came to be seen by the orthodox Muslims.

A report came from Ajmer on 23rd June, 1694, that in the village of Jalmahrâh, Bijai Singh and other Hindus were indulging in image worship. The Emperor ordered that they should write to the governor of the province to get the temple in that village demolished.[120]

At the *dîwân-i-mazâlim,* held on 3rd December, 1701, in the village of Malkapur in the south, it was brought to Aurangzeb's notice that the Hindus were practising image worship in the temple at Bijaigarh. Mîr Bakshi Rûhullâh Khân was ordered to write to the governor of the province about this.[121]

On 1st January, 1705, Aurangzeb was at the village of Panditpur in the south. Khwâjâ Mohammad Shâh *muhtasib* submitted that there was a temple in the village of Bandhârpur where the Hindus collected in large numbers and performed image worship. The Emperor sent for Mohammad Junail, Khidmat Râo, *Daroghâ-i-Beldârân,* and Mohammad Amîn, deputy *kotwâ.* He ordered them to demolish the temple and to send the butchers from the army to go there and slaughter oxen inside the temple.[122]

SATI

Akbar issued an order against forcible Sati and appointed inspectors to see that no widow was to be permitted to be burnt against her will. Whenver he heard of an impending case of Sati, he went in person, or sent special officers, saved the widow and punished the offenders. When he learnt that the widow of Jaimal, the son of Mâldeo, was being forced by her son and Udai Singh to burn herself alive, he forthwith reached the place on horseback and saved her. Some of the party offered resistance, but later submitted. They were ordered to be placed in confinement.[123]

Under Jahangir also it was unlawful to burn an unwilling widow, and so was it during the reigns of Shahjahan and Aurangzeb.

FORBIDDEN HINDU PRACTICES

Aurangzeb ordered in 1665 the discontinuation of *Holi* and

Dîpâvali.[124] The men of Râjâ Bhim and Râja Kishan Singh, *zamindâr* of Hânda, and posted to the army of Prince Mu'iz-ud-din, were accused of playing *Holi.* When the *muhtasib* tried to stop them, they threatened fight. Hearing this report on 28th March, 1693, Aurangzeb ordered that letters be written to both the Râjas to see that such a thing did not occur in the future.[125]

The pilgrimages of the Hindus were also stopped.[126]

The burning of the dead on the banks of the Jumna had been prohibited. A serious quarrel occurred between an imperial servant and some merchants when they tried to burn the dead there. The merchants were ordered to be imprisoned for wounding the mace-bearer in this connection.[127]

Similar restrictions were imposed on the burning of the dead on the banks of the Sâbarmati also.[128]

Sayyid Amjad *muhtasib* submitted that the Hindus were dressed in *dhoti* (in court or for official business). Ihtimam Khân was ordered by Aurangzeb to announce by the beat of the drum that the Hindus were not allowed to wear *dhoti;* instead, they were to use *pyjâmas.*[29]

Barring the exception of the Râjpûts and the Marâthâs, the Hindus were fobidden to ride on *'Irâqi* or *Tûrâni* horses, elephants and palanquins.[130] When a person infringed these rules, his saddle and horse were confiscated.[131] An order was issued on 11th December, 1694, that no Hindu but the Râjpûts Maratha and the Deccanis might use Iraqi or Arabi horses and Palanquins. Two days later his order was repeated. No other Hindu excepting the Rajputs and Marâthas were permitted the use of elephants.[133] They were also prohibited from wearing arms.[134]

Yâr 'Ali Beg *kotwâl* submitted on 18th April, 1696, that as the Hindus were prohibited from riding on *'Arabi* and *'Irâqi* horses, Mohammad Amin *kotwâl* had seized from a Hindu in Multan a saddled *'Irâqi* horse on which he was riding and sent the same to the Emperor, who, after viewing it, ordered that it be kept in the royal stable.[135]

REFERENCES

1. Hughes' Dictionary of Islam, p. 670.
2. Ma'âlim-Al-Qarbâ, p. 11.
3. Ma'âlim-Al-Qarbâ, p. 11, Fatâwâ-i-Âlamgîrî, II, p. 688.
4. Mîrât-I-p. 280; Mughal Administration, 4th ed. p. 113.
5. Akbar Nâmâ, III, p. 31.
6. Badâûnî, Text, II, p. 302;
   Lowe, II, pp. 311-12.

7. Tuzk, Text, I, pp. 6 & 76; Tr., I, p. 8. Eliot & Dowson, VI, pp. 284-86; Muntakhib-ul-Lubâb, Text, I, p. 249; Cf. Religious Policy p. 84.
8. Tuzk, Text, I, p. 76; Tr., I, p. 157; Eliot & Dowson, V. p. 351.
9. Qazvini, p. 405.
10. Tuzk, Text, I, p. 6; Tr, (Rogers & Beveridge), I, p. 8.
11. Roe's Journal, p. 265.
12. *Ibid.*, p. 99.
13. Roe's Journal, p. 150.
14. *Ibid.*, p. 191.
15. Roe's Journal, pp. 222, 223, 224; 225.
16. Tuzk, Tr. I, p. 371.
17. *Ibid.*, p. 377.
18. *Ibid.*, II, p. 43.
19. *Ibid.*, II, pp. 165.
20. *Ibid.*, II. p. 218.
21. *Ibid.*, II. p. 291.
22. *Ibid.*, II. p. 126.
23. Roe's Journal, p. 265.
24. Early Travels, p. 67.
25. Roe's Journal, pp. 265-6.
26. *Ibid.*, pp. 264-65.
27. *Ibid.*, 18th January, 1618.
28. Manucci, I, p. 265.
29. Manucci, I, p. 227.
30. *Ibid.*, p. 231.
31. *Ibid.*, p. 224.
32. Manrique, I, p. 55.
33. *Ibid.*, pp. 55-56.
34. Ovington : A Voyage to Surat, p. 230.
35. Indian Travels of Careri, p. 212.
36. Manrique : Travels. I, pp. 58-60.
37. Ovington, p. 140; Tavernier, ii, p. 249; Manucci, ii, p. 6-7; Letters, No. p. 90; Âinâ-i-Gujrat, i, p. 149; Religious Policy, p. 122.
38. Manucci, II, p. 6, cf. Religious Policy p. 122.
39. Manucci, II, p. 7; Ma'âsir-i-Âlamgîrî, p. 385; Âînâ-i-Gujrât, i, p. 148-49; Khâfi Khân, II, p. 8, Kâzim, p. 391-92.
40. Religious Policy, p. 122.
41. *Ibid.*
42. *Ibid.*
43. Manucci, II, p. 5-6; Fatâwâ-i-Âlamgîrî, II, p. 687, Ma'âlim-Al-Qarba, p. 12.
44. Manucci, II, p. 7.

45. *Ibid.*
46. *Ibid.*, II, p. 393-94.
47. *Ibid.*
48. Anecdotes, p. 120.
49. Manucci, pp. 463-64.
50. Letters, No. lxxi, 69-70.
51. Religious Policy, p. 122-22.
52. Munta Khib-ul-Lubâb, II, p. 220.
53. Manucci, II, p. y.
54. Munta Khib-ul-Lubâb, II, p. 6.
55. News letters, 28 February, 1703, Religious Policy, 122.
56. News letters, May 6, 1702, Cf. Religious Policy, 121.
57. Manucci, II, p. 108.
58. Manucci, II, p. 393-94.
59. Akhbârât, 12.11.1679.
60. Akhbârât-i-Darbâr-i-Mu'allâ, 28.10.1692.
61. Akhbârât-i-Darbâr-i-Mu'allâ, 21.4.1693.
62. *Ibid.*, 14.3.1694.
63. *Ibid.*, 14.7.1695.
64. *Ibid.*, 22.4.1699.
65. *Ibid.*, 7.8.1701.
66. *Ibid.*, i.i.1701.
67. Akhbârât-i-Darbâr-i-Mu'allâ, 17.8.1701.
68. *Ibid.*, 1.12.1703.
69. Badâûnî, II, Text, p. 338, cf. Religious Policy, p. 32.
70. Tuzk, Text, I, p. 76; Beveridge, I, p. 157. cf. Religious Policy, p. 84.
71. Mîrât-i-Gujrât, p. 280. cf. Religious Policy, p. 124.
72. Letters, p. 37.
73. Akhbârât-i-Darbâr-i-Mu'allâ, 15.12.1681.
74. Badâûnî, Lowe, II, pp. 310-12; Text, II, pp. 30; 380.
75. Manucci, II, p. 9. Rel. Policy, p. 123.
76. Orme, p. 85; Ma'âsir, p. 385. Aînâ-i-Gujrat, I, p. 156.
77. Ovington. p. 153.
78. Manucci, IV, pp. 118-19.
79. Hughes' Dictionary of Islam, p. 42.
80. Religious Policy, p. 111.
81. Manucci. II, p. 409.
82. English Factories, 1665-66, p. 284.
83. Târikh-i-Kâshmir, p. 165; cf. Religious Policy, p. 126.
84. Ma'âsir-i-Âlamgîrî, p. 120; cf. Religious Policy, p. 127.
85. Târikh-i-Kâshmir, p. 166; cf. Religious Policy p. 127.
86. Manucci, IV, 120-21.
87. Tuzk, Bev, I, p. 77; Text, p. 37.
88. Religious Policy, 80.

89. Tuzk, Bev, I, p. 171, Text, I. p. 83.
90. Âînâ-i-Gujarat, I, p. 132-33.
91. *Ibid.*, I, p. 170.
92. Eliot and Dowson, VII. p. 179, p. 246.
93. Letters, No. CVII, pp. 106-7.
94. Akhbârât-i-Darbâr-i-Mu'allâ, 16.11.1692.
95. *Ibid.*, 6.7.1694.
96. Manucci, I, p. 223, *Ibid.*, IV. p. 427; Bernier (Constable), p. 316.
97. Manucci, II, p. 185.
98. Badâûnî, Lowe, II, p. 312; p. 403.
Text, II, p. 302; p. 391.
99. Badâûnî, Lowe, II, pp. 312; 331; 388; Text, II, pp. 302, 321-22; Tuzk, Text, p. 22.
100. Âîn, I, p. 58.
101. Tuzk; pp. 5, 90, Text; Tuzk, Tr. I, 9.
102. *Ibid.*
103. Payne. op. cit. p. 38, Religious Policy, pp. 85-86.
104. Roe, 124; Religious Policy, p. 86.
105. Bernier, Travels in Mogul Empire (Constable), p. 326.
106. Manrique, II, pp. 105-15.
107. Bernier : Travels in Mogul Empire (A. Constable), p. 327.
108. Manucci. I, p. 67.
109. Tavernier, I, pp. 70-71.
110. Akhbârât-i-Darbâr-i-Mu"allâ, 22.1.1700.
111. Eliot & Dowson, VI, pp. 60-61.
112. Akbar Nâmâ, (Text), II, p. 159.
113. Tuzk, Text, I, p. 101; Tr. I, p. 205.
114. Qazvînî, pp. 444-45; Lâhori, I. II, p. 57, Muntakhib-ut-tawârîkh, I, p. 510; Salih, II, p. 64. Cf. Religious Policy. 2nd ed. p. 88.
115. Qazvînî, p. 262; Lâhori, I, II, pp. 57-58; Cf. Religious Policy, 2nd ed. p. 89.
116. Qazvînî, p. 405; Cf. Religious Policy, 2nd ed. p. 89.
117. Manucci, II, pp. 159-60.
118. Religious Policy, Second Edition p. 131.
119. Orme's Fragments, Notes, 85.
120. See Religious Policy, p. 132.
121. Akhbârât-i-Darbâr-i-Mu'allâ, 3rd December, 1694.
122. Akhbârât-i-Darbâr-i-Mu'allâ, 2nd January, 1705.
123. Akbar Nâmâ, Bev., III, p. 594. Text, III, p. 402.
Badâûnî, Lowe, II, pp. 376-78; 388. Text, II, pp. 365-66; 376.
124. News-Letters, 20th November, 1665; 1st April, 1692;
Manucci, II, p. 154; Mirat, I, pp. 154-55.
125. Akhbârât-i-Darbâr-i-Mulk-i-Iqtidâr, 28th March, 1693.
126. Muntakhib-ul-Lubâb, Text, II. p. 212.

127. Akhbârât-i-Darbâr-i-Mu'allâ, 16th April, 1694.
128. Religious Policy, p. 150.
129. Jaipur Akhbârât, 29th April, 1682.
130. Mîrât, I, pp. 154-55.
131. *Ibid.*
132. Akhbârât-i-Darbâr-i-Mu'allâ, 11th December, 1694; 13.12.1694.
133. *Ibid.*, 13th December, 1694.
134. *Ibid.;* Ma'asîr-i-'Âlamgîrî, pp. 262-63.
135. Akhbârât-i-Darbâr-i-Mu'allâ, 18th April, 1696.

IX
CONVERSIONS OF HINDUS TO ISLAM DURING AURANGZEB'S REIGN
(Based on *Akhbarat-i-Darbar-i-Mu'alla*)

The conversion of Hindus to Islam was almost an obsession with Aurangzeb. There is a long list of Hindu converts recorded faithfully in the Jaipur Newsletters. The proselytising activities of Aurangzeb started from the outset of his reign and continued till the end of the period. We learn from these original Persian sources that the new converts were encouraged to come to the court where they received robes of honour and their new Muslim names from the Emperor. The Akhbarat, moreover, make no secret of the fact that these people embraced the new faith for monetary gain, forthe sake of jobs, and in case of dismissed persons, for the restoration of their previous posts. There was inducement to criminals as well to abjure their faith and accept conversion by assurances of release from prison or escape from punishment. There are also cases on record in the Akhbarat where a sort of compulsion was eercised in the matter of conversion. Reconversion from Islam to Hinduism was a grave offence deserving serious punishment.

Professor Sri Ram Sharma has already dealt with the subject in an exaustive manner in his scholarly work, **"The religious policy of the Mughal Emperors".** Every care has been taken in the present article to exclude the cases mentioned in his book and to refer only to new ones.

AWARD OF ROBES OF HONOUR TO THE NEW CONVERTS

In 1666 A.D., Dehra Jat (8th September), Râm Chandra *Thânedar* of Bihar (1st November), Bairâgi of Karkhoda (16th December) became converts and received robes of honour at the hands of the Emperor. Gulâm Sheikh, a new convert to Islam was awarded a robe of honour on 30th November.

In 1667 A.D. the following new converts were given robes of honours by Aurangzeb :

Karam Se, Ram Se, Rupse, Man Singh (1st April); Bihari Lal (9th April); Sakar etc., four servants of the qanungo of Hawar; Bijay Singh and Hem Raj (17th May); Jagannath (23rd May); Ganga Ram (26th May); Sanwal Das, son of Rai Duni Chand (1st June); Anup Rai Chaudhari and Kair Chaudhari (12th June); Dalip Chand and two others (19th June); Bhoj Raj and three others (27th June); Sekha, son of Kesar Singh of Fatehgarh (6th July); Harkishan Singh *Baqal* of Etawa (18th July); Kesho Ram, renamed Kamal-ud-din (17th September).

Murli was converted and awarded a robe of honour on 2nd July, 1679.

Those who became coverts and received robes of honour in 1680 A.D. were the following :

Sujan Singh Sirhind (19th April); Ghasi Ram, son of Ganga Ram of Etawa (17th May); Anup Singh Bahdoriya (7th August); Garib Das and Man Singh (18th September). They were sent by Man Singh Rathor and later on managed to escape from the custody of Ruhulla Khan and fled away. One Gharib Das, a new convert, received a robe of honour on 22nd September, 1680.

Below are the names of those who became converts in 1681 A.D. and were awarded robes of honour by Aurangzeb :

Jhâbu Singh, son of Hari Singh *zamindar* of Bhangarh (25th April); Gujar of Kot Fatehulla (15th June); Rup Narain, son of Daulat Ram Bahdoriya (28th June). He had been converted by Qazi Sheikh-ul-Islam. On 29th June, 1681, Rup Narain Bahdoriya was christened as Bakht Buland.

On 2nd May, 1682, Sunderkar and two others became converts along with their wives and received the robes of honour.

On 23rd March, 1685, Sabha Chand, son of Sa'adat Yar, embraced Islam and was awarded a robe of honour by the Emperor.

The *Akhbarat-i-Darbar-i-Mu'alla* have recorded the cases of the following Hindus who abjured their faith to become Muslims. The Emperor was pleased to confer robes of honour on them on the dates mentioned below : 7th November, 1693; Tulsi Raj; 13th November : Tej Ram and Ram Chand; 1st Dec., 1693 : Sahib Rai.

1694—Banwar and Lokraj (11th March); Asu Ji (14th March); on 26th July, a Hindu convert was given the name of 'Abdul Qaul, a shawl and a post. Lachhman became a Muslim on 10th September and Debi Chand on 19th September. Both of them were awarded robes of honour.

1695—Jawab Singh (30th May); Narain Das (12th June); Punjab Rao *Qanungo* of Shamsabad in Lahore province; Rama Rao and Malho (5th July); Amin, son of Kalyan barbar (14th July); Human (17th July); Narain Das (23rd August); Ikhlas Keesh, a new Hindu convert (10th November).

On 1st May, 1700, a Hindu was converted, was christened Raja Islam Khan and given a standard and robe of honour. On 20th July of the same year Bahrji Deshmukh became a convert and received a robe.

On 19th March, 1701, Haibutullah, a new convert, came to the court to receive a robe.[1]

Sarna and Rao became converts and received robes from the Emperor on 17th November, 1702.[2]

Four new converts, Babu, Buddu Chand, Kuddo Ji and Kirpa Ram, nephew of Sheikh Ghulam Mohammad, received robes from the Emperor on 9th March 22nd March, 7th July and 9th November 1703, respectively.[3]

The keen interest evinced by the Emperor in the proselytising activities encouraged the imperial officers to follow his example in this respect. They naturally vied with one another in their enthusiasm in the spread of the faith. In their desire to earn the good will of the Emperor, these officers presented the converted Hindus to him. He used to give them a Muslim name, a robe of honour and in certain cases new posts or promotions. The following are such cases recorded in the *Akhbarat-i-Darbar-i-Mu'alla* and not included in the *Religious Policy of the Mughal Emperors.*

On 7th January, 1704, 'Abdul Ma'dud came to the court after circumcision and presented to the Emperor five rupees as offering.[4]

It was reported to Aurangzeb on the night of 15th February, 1704, that the wife of Sheikh Ghulam, formerly Bali Ram, had given birth to two sons. He sent for the Sheikh in the morning of 16th February in the *diwan* and asked him to give the infants the names of Allah Aman and Mohammad Aman.[5]

On 2nd March, 1704, Sayyid Qutb-ud-din, *Pirzada* Talkokan, brought at the time of the *zuhr* prayer Nem Raj and Sahib Ram, sons of Bhoyat Ram, the *vakil* of Mu'tabir Khan, into the royal presence. The Emperor himself made them read the *kalma* and gave them robes and reward. Nem Raj was renamed Mohammad Ikram and Sahib Ram as Mohammad Islam. Qutab-ud-din submitted that their mother too had been converted and deserved to be given a Muslim name. The Emperor was gracious enough to change her name from Gulabo to Gulab Bano.[6]

On 9th May, 1704, Islam Kunwar, the wife of Sheikh Ghulam Mohammad, formerly Bali Ram, was renamed as Rahim-un-nisa and her daughter as Halim-un-nisa.[7]

On 7th June of the same year, Mohammad Muhi-ud-din, son of Sikandar Khan Bijapuri, was betrothed to the daughter of Sambhaji.[8]

Maya Ram had become a convert through Mohammad Ikhlas, *vakil* of Prince Mohammad Mu'azzam. The Emperor awarded him a robe of honour on 29th July.[9]

Yet another Maya Ram received a robe and the name of Islam Yar from the Emperor on 5th September, 1704. He was the *kotwal* of matchlockmen and had been converted through Amir Khan.[10]

Bir Singh, son of Sujan Singh, who had become a convert to Islam with the efforts of Hafiz 'Ambar, was christened by the Emperor as 'Abdul Salam and awarded a robe.[11]

On 18th November, 1704, a Hindu convert was renamed by Aurangzeb as Dindar.

CONVERSION FOR THE SAKE OF MANSABS AND ZAMINDARI

On 25th June, 1667, Fidai Khan submitted that a Baluchi had expressed his wish to become a Musalman if he could receive royal pardon. The Emperor ordered Abdul Makaram, son of Qazi 'Abdul Wahab, to go to the Baluchi and tell him that in case he became a Muslim, he would be given the rank of 3,000 *zat* and 2,000 *swar* and posted in Kabul. 'Abdal Makaram met the Baluchi and returned to the Emperor to inform him that he had read the *kalma* and become a Musalman. He was renamed Mohammad Quli.[12]

Nilkanth and others, four servants of the *zamindars* of Etawa, came of their own accord and got converted to Islam on 7th February, 1667. They were awarded the robes and *Zamindari* was restored to them.[13]

Debi Chand Khatri of Kalanor came along with Sheikh 'Abdulla in the hope of getting a mansab. He was converted on 4th April, 1681.[14]

A letter was received on 18th December, 1684 from Salih Khan *faujdar* of Bareli, that he had sent under royal orders Dharareri (Dharm Raj?) and other dismissed *zamindars* of Indore to Gwalior. Dharm Rai had expressed his desire to become a Muslim in case the *zamindari,* conferred on his uncle Ram Rai, was transferred to him. The Emperor replied that if he wanted to embrace Islam without any condition, he was to be sent into the royal presence. In this connection a letter was received on 22nd January, 1685, from Mohammad Fazil, commandant of Gwalior, to the effect that Dharm Rai had given his consent to be converted to Islam unconditionaly and accordingly he had read the *Kalma* as required in the *Shara'*. He was ordered to be sent to the court.[15]

Hari Singh, a *zamindar* in the province of Burhanpur, was converted to Islam. He received the rank of 100 *zat* and 20 *swar* and the title of Daulatmand on 19th March, 1685.[16]

'Abdul Qaul, a new convert to Islam, was given a post on 6th July, 1694, vacated by Balram.[17]

Sadr-ud-din Mohammad Khan, *faujdar* of Loharu, wrote to the Chief Bakshi Mukhlis Khan that Kal Singh, the second son of Kishan Singh, Raja of Chanda, was prepared to pay a large tribute and become a convert to Islam, if he were appointed the *zamindar* of Deogarh, now renamed Islamgarh. On hearing the contents of this letter on 15th April, 1696, Auragzeb asked the Chief Bakshi to write to Sadr-ud-din to send for Kal Singh and his mother, convert them to Islam and then confer the zamindari of Deogarh along with the title of Raja and a robe on him.[18]

Sheikh Ghulam Mohammad was an enthusiastic neo-Muslim and helped others come into the fold. Matruk was one of them, who, on being converted, received a *mansab* of 10 *zat* on 14th May. Kesari was another who also received a *mansab* and robe of honour on the same date.[19] Some months later, on 4th September, his brother, Jwala Nath, became a convert and received a *mansab* of 50 *zat*.[20] Yet another recipient of his benevolence was Sheo Datt who received the name of 'Abdulla, robe and a *mansab*.[21]

Mohammad Ghaus, *amin jizya,* brought to the royal presence Madhoji, son of Kahandoji. He was renamed Ghalib Islam, given robe and reward and a mansab of 200.[22]

CONVERSIONS FOR THE SAKE OF PROMOTIONS

The brother of Khwaja Danish (a neo Muslim), was converted to Islam, christened as Buland Bakht and given a promotion of 50 *zat* and 200 horse in his rank on 18th April, 1696.[23]

Haibat Rao who held the rank of 800 *zat* and 600 *swar* was converted to Islam on 29th January, 1700, and given a promotion of 200 *zat* and 200 *swar*.[24]

Lachhman, *Qanungo* of Sialkot, who had earlier embraced Islam through the efforts of Khawaja Izzat Quli Khan, received promotion on 26th June, 1703.[25]

Tika Ram, Qanungo of Moradabad, a new convert to Islam, was renamed 'Abdul Rahim, and promoted in rank on 3rd December, 1704.[26]

CONVERSIONS FOR THE SAKE OF MONEY

Cash rewards in lieu of conversion and conferment of daily allowances on new converts served too great temptations to be resisted by many persons. On 6th April, 1685, Aurangzeb ordered Umdtulmulk Asad Khan to issue *firmans* to all the *faujdars* and *diwans* in the kingdom to award four rupees per man and two rupees per woman to all the Hindus who embraced Islam. This benefit of cash reward was to be conferred on all the new converts in the future.[27]

This was a sufficiently high remuneration and handsome amount in those days and provided a strong temptation to weak-minded persons. Even highly placed, greatly honoured and learned Muslim divines did not receive such a high allowance in all cases. Sheikh Razi-ud-din, who belonged to the nobility of Bhagalpur and was one of the celebrated authors of the *Fatawa-i-Alamgiri,* received a salary of three rupees a day.[28] Khwaja 'Abdul Satar, son of Khwaja 'Abdul Qadir, who was recipient of a grant of two rupees a day, got increase of one rupee a day on 19th February, 1704.[29]

The following are the cases of persons who, after their conversion, received handsome amounts of money by way of reward.

Gharib Das and Rai Singh, two new converts to Islam, were awarded Rs. 2,00 each as reward in September, 1680.[30]

Sabal Nath, son of Naroji, who was sent by Harnath, *thanedar* of Mandal, became a Muslim. He received one thousand of rupees on 18th September, 1680.[31]

Fazal Khan submitted in the same month that Bhawani Das, son of Rama Nand, had expressed readiness for conversion in lieu of some concession. The Emperor ordered him into royal presence for the purpose of conversion.[32]

Inayat Khan, the *faujdar* of Ajmer, recommended to the Emperor the cases of 2,000 Rathor men, women and children for conversion and for monetary rewards in lieu thereof. There were other similar cases of the helpless persons deserving succor. The merciful Emperor ordered a letter to be written to the *faujdar* concerned to give to each man three and to each woman two tankas daily. He was, moreover, exhorted to work for the conversion of other persons as well.[33]

A Hindu convert was given a cash reward on 11th January, 1693.[34]

Mansa Ram, who became Sheikh Hidayatuallah, was given 20 *huns* and a robe as a reward for the change of his faith (14th March, 1696).[35]

Shambhu Nath, Deshmukh of Sultanpur, was awarded 10 *charans* and 20 *huns* after his conversion to Islam in 1704.[36]

OTHER CASES OF CONVERSION

The following are the cases of conversion in the reign of Aurangzeb not included in the *Religious Policy* of *the Mughal Emperors.*

Raja Rup Singh's daughter, who was being brough up in the palace after conversion,was married to Prince Mu'azzam in 1661.[37]

Rikhi Ram, Chaudhari of Surat, had promised to become a Muslim. A mace-bearer was despatched by the Emperor who returned after converting him. Another mace-bearer was sent to fetch him to the court.[38]

The *faujdar* of Ajmer wrote to Aurangzeb that in the neighbourhood of the pargana and in the territory of Maharaja Jaswant Singh there lived a people called Bishnaui who were neither Hindus nor Muslims. Orders were at once issued in June, 1667 for their conversion to Islam.[39]

On 22nd July, 1667, Fidai Khan submitted that one of the wives of Mohammad Quli *alias* Netaji had remained in the Deccan; and the other two who had come along with him had refused to embrace Islam. Mohammad Quli was ordered to exhort them to become converts. In case of their refusal, he was ordered not to marry them.[40] Fidai Khan submitted two days later that Mohammad Quli had succeeded in persuading them for conversion. The Emperor expressed his approval and ordered the performance of *nikah* ceremony of Mohammad Quli with these two ladies.[41]

The son and daughter of Gokul Jat were handed over to Jawahar Khan to be brought up. The daughter was married to Shah Quli Chela.[42]

The *qanungo* of Sodhara in *Suba* Lahore was charged with the offence of having used abusive language. As per orders he was ushered into the royal presence on 8th October, 1667. Aurangzeb offered him the choice of Islam or prison.[43]

It was ordered on 16th July, 1680, that 35 men of the village Mawal were to be entrusted to Ihtimam Khan to be converted to Islam and initiated in the Muslim prayers. In obedience to the orders, the *kotwal* went and converted these persons.[44]

A report came from Kabul that Kunwar Kishan Singh had reconverted some women and eunuchs to Hinduism which faith they had already abjured. He had, moreover, kept them in his own house. Ruhulla Khan was ordered on 18th May, 1682, to write to Raja Ram Singh who had been posted in Kabul, to see that these women were got released and sent to the *qazi* and the two eunuchs were to be despatched to the court.[45]

The case of Dalpat Kamboh was interesting. He was the *faujdar* of Mandal and *diwan* and *amin* of Pur and Badhnaur. One day in September, 1682, while a *hafiz* was busy reading the Qur'an in the *majlis,* Dalpat was alleged to have said that he had also read the *kalma* during his childhood. When the *hafiz* asked him to read it again, he kept quiet. The hafiz felt duty-bound to bring this to the notice of the Emperor. On hearing the news on 30th September, he ordered that Dalpat be converted to Islam, and, on his refusal to do so, be removed from his post and put into prison. Dalpat refused to embrace Islam. He was dismissed in November, replaced by Dindar Khan and put into prison. On 4th December, Fazail Khan placed Dalpat's representation before the Emperor. He had submitted that Umdatulmulk had made investigation against him and found the alleged charges to be baseless. He was prepared to face The charges and any further inquiry against him. On this, Bahrahmand Khan suggested that as the charges against Dalapat had failed to be proved, he deserved to be restored back to his post. The Emperor accepted the proposal and ordered the release from custody and restoration of Dalpat to his post.[46] In case the statement of the *hafiz* was found to be true, his punishment was to be upheld unless he showed readiness for conversion. There is no mention of any punishment to the *hafiz* for making a false charge against an innocent official.

The Chief *qazi* Akram Khan submitted that the *Patel* of village Son in the province of Ahmadabad had taken a vow that in case he were blessed with a son, he would present him to the Emperor. Aurangzeb acceded to the request of the parents to present the child in person. It was 2 years and five months old and was sent inside the palace to be brought up there as desired by the Emperor. The parents were also offered conversion. They, however, declined to do so.[49]

On the night of 23 January, 1704, the Emperor sent for *Qazi* Akram and the *Shari' vakil* Fazil Khan, and asked them to perform the *nikah* ceremony of Raja Ram's daughter with Shamsher Beg. He rewarded the bidgroom with a robe and three rings studded with jewels and asked him to have the regular marriage ceremony after *Idul fitr* and take away the bride from the palace to his house.

Next day, the Emperor sent for Raja Nek Ram, son of Islam Bai, wife of the deceased Raja Kishan Singh of Chanda and rewarded him with a *Doshala.* He had been betrothed to a daughter of Raja Ram. He again presented himself on 27th January. The Emperor awarded him a robe and a horse with a saddle costing 1,000 gold *muhrs.* He ordered a *sehra* to be tied on his forehead. Then Auranzeb ordered Mohammad Akram Khan and Fazil Khan *vakil shari'* into royal presence for the performance of the marriage ceremony.[50]

REFERENCES

1—11. Akhbarat-i-Darbar-i-Mu'alla.
12. Jaipur Akhbarat, 26-6-1667.
13. Ibid., 7-2-1667.
14. Ibid., 4-4-1681.
15. Akhbarat, 18-12-1684; 22-1-1685.
16. Ibid., 19-3-1685.
17. Akhbarat-i-Darbar-i-Mu'alla.
18. Akhbarat-i-Darbar-i-Mu'alla.
19-26. Akhbarat-i-Darbar-i-Mu'alla.
27. Ma'asir-i-Alamgiri, Text, p. 94.
28. Ma'asir-i-Alamgiri, Text, p.94.
29-32. Akhbarat.
33. Jaipur Akhbarat, 9-2-1682.
34. Ibid., 11-1-1693.
35. Akhbarat-i-Darbar-i-Mu'alla, 14-3-1606.
36. Ibid., 1704.
37. Ma'asir-i-Alamgiri, p. 37.
38. Jaipur Akbarat, 11-4-1667.
39. Jaipur Akhbarat, 1-6-1667.
40. Ibid., 18-5-1682.
41. Ibid., 24-7-1667.
42. Ma'asir-i-Alamgiri, Text, p. 107.
43. Jaipur Akhbarat, 8-10-1667.
44. Ibid., 16-7-1680.
45. Ibid., 18-5-1682.
46. Jaipur Akhbarat, 30-9-1582.
47. Akhbarat, 30-9-1582; 29-11-1682; 4-12-1682.
48. Akhabarat-i-Darbar-i-Gitimadar 22-3-1702.
49. Akhbarat-i-Darbar-i-Mu'alla, 24-1-1704.
50. Ibid., 25-1-1704; 27-1-1704.

SEXUAL CRIMES

FORNICATION

ELOPEMENT OF A HINDU WOMAN BY AN ENGLISH-MAN

Bulchand, the Chief Customer of Hugli and Qasimbazar in the reign of Aurangzeb, sent to Hedges in February, 1682, 9 Hindu with the complaint that an important Englishman and founder of Calcutta, Job, Charnock, had kept a Hindu woman "of his kindred", and had been living with her for the previous 19 years. In case, he failed to return her, he would be obliged to bring the fact to the governors notice. Hedges learnt from others that while Charnock was at Patna, he had got in his house a Hindu woman who had run away from her husband with money and jewels. The Governor had sent a dozen soldiers to apprehend Charnock who managed to escape by bribing the men. They took his vakil and kept him in prison for 2 months, the soldiers lying all this time at the gates of English factory till Charnock compounded the business for Rs. 3,000, 5 pieces of broadcloth and some swords blades.

The Diary of William Hedges, p. 52. 1.2.1682.

According to Muslim Law, the word *zinâ'* includes fornication with an unmarried person by a man who possesses a wife in lawful marriage. The sin of fornication was to be established, as in the case of adultery, either by confession or by proof by four witnesses.[1] It was not easy to furnish evidence for this sort of crime.

A fornicator, according to Islamic Law, was to be awarded a hundred strokes in view of the people. The punishment in case of a slave was to be fifty strokes. The scourging was to be inflicted with moderation with a whip without knots.[2]

A man, while receiving punishment, was to remain standing. He was neither to be tied, nor stretched. Each member of the human body was to receive its share of beating except the head, the face, the genital organs, and other sensitive parts.[3]

The punishment was to be inflicted by men only. The stage where it caused wounds and made blood flow, was not allowed to reach.[4]

A woman was to be beaten while sitting. She was not to be stripped.[5]

A fornicator was to suffer statutory penalty as well as expulsion. The Muslim doctors are divided on the subsequent question of banishment. Abu Hanifa is not in its favour. According to Mâlik, man and not woman, was to be banished. Shâfi'î views that both man and woman are to be banished from their city for all purposes to a distance of at least a day's journey. The magistrate, maintains the Fatâwâ-i-Âlamgiri, can expel the culprit from the city for any length of time at his discretion.[6]

If a man who was a *muhsan,* committed adultery with a woman who was a *bikr*, or a *bikr* with a *mushan,* the *bikr* was to be beaten and the other party to be stoned. If the culprit committed the offence repeatedly before the punishment, that one punishment should suffice for all offences.[7] A *muhsan* was a person who possessed a wife in lawful marriage.

ADULTERY

The term *zinâ'* includes both adultery and fornication, but a difference was observed in the punishment of the two offences. Adultery was defined as a man having sexual intercourse with a woman unlawful to him. It was essential to prove that the offender knew this fact. An adulterer, as distinguished from a fornicator, was a *muhsan.*[8]

Adultery was established before a *qâzi* by confession or proof. According to Abu Hanifa, punishment was to be inflicted only if the confession was repeated four times. The penalty, however, lapsed if a man retracted his own confession before the punishment was inflicted.[9]

To establish it upon proof, at least four competent witnesses should declare in clear terms that they witnessed the parties in the very act of carnal conjugation.[10]

It was no evidence if they could not make the declaration specifically, as for instance, 'Thou has committed adultery', or 'I saw you commit adultery.' The *qâzi* might accept this clear evidence either separately or jointly.[11] Abu Hanifa, on the other hand, would not accept the separate statements. If the witnesses could not make four in number, they were slanderers. If four persons appeared before a *qâzi*, and gave evidence against an adulterer, and some of them pronounced statements against him, while others not, then, according to the Muslim doctors, those who gave evidence were slanderers and liable to punishment.[12]

The punishment for a *muhsan* who committed adultery, was lapidation. For being stoned, an adulterer was to be carried to a barren place. The lapidation was to be executed, first, by the witnesses, then by the *qâzi,* and afterwards by the by-standers. The punishment lapsed if the witnesses refused to take the initiative. The punishment was not to be inflicted in case the weather was too hot or too cold. The accused was not permitted to compound for the penalty by a sum of money.[13]

A farmân issued by Aurangzeb in 1672 had laid down that if any person entered another man's house for the purpose of commiting adultery, he was to be severely chastised and confined till he showed signs of repentance.[14] This order, however, is silent about the punishment for those who were actually charged with the commission of adultery.

Our authorities fail to provide us with enough material about the commission of adultery and fornication. It does not follow that these cases were rare in Mughal India. It may be that on account of the social odium which surrounded the victim in case of proved adultery, many cases might not have been made public and brought before the courts. Out of the few instances that have come down to us, no where do we come across a single case being tried in the court of a *qâzi.* These cases seem to suggest that the relatives concerned managed to punish the guilty parties.

During the reign of Akbar, Jâlâ, the best horse-dealer of the day, was accused of the crime of adultery. The Emperor ordered his imprisonment and also an inquiry against him. His offence was proved and he was awarded capital punishment in 1583 by strangulation.[15]

Mullâ Badâuni is bold enough to record that at one time he fell a prey to Cupid and committed a 'terrible case of impropriety' in the shrine of Shâh Madâr at Mânakpur in Qannauj. As a punishment 'for that transgression, and chastisement for that sin even in this world', 'God granted to some of the relatives of the beloved to overcome' the Mullâ who received nine sword-wounds on his head, hand and back. They all grazed his skin excepting one on his head which penetrated the bone of the skull and rendered him unconscious.[16]

ADULTERY

We learn from Hawkin that once a high Mughal officer Muqarrab

Khan took a Bania's daughter by force, and after deflowering her, gave her to a Brahmin. When the matter was reported to Jahangir, he ordered a probe. When the case was proved he awarded Muqarrab Khan a prison sentence and ordered the privies of the other culprit to be cut off (William Hawkin' Journal), p. 406.

Fryer records that a rich Muslim merchant murdered his wife, when he caught her with her paramour. a pecuniary mulct excused him. (Fryer, p. 245).

MURDER FOR RAPE (Of Surat Governor Ali Akbar Khan)—Ali Akbar Khan was appointed Governor of Surat in the end of 1646 in place of Mirza Amin, against whom the English had complained to the higher authorities. There is an interesting story of his murder by a Rajput for the rape of his sister entered in the Factory records, vide letter dated Jan 6, 1648, from President Breton and Council at Surat to the Company. It reads :

The Governor Ali Akbar Khan was 'an ancient and very good friend of our nation whilst he continued a merchant, but since changed both in quality and condition, became as very a villaine to all in general as ever officiated that charge, being also Governor of Cambayett, the 30th November left this place to visit that; where practicing his insufferable terrinyes was the 21st following was stobbed in three several places by a Rashoote, content to part with his own life to bereave him of his, if revenge of his father injust sufferences (whom he had long kept prisoner), and in vindication of is sisters honour, by him violently ravished; and so of the said wound the 23rd departed this life, to a general excess of joy in all that had any relation to his government; wherein also we hope for better times then could otherwise have been expected.'

When Akbar left Kâbul in November, 1589, he encamped at Safed Sang in the environs of the city. There it was reported to him that 'a base fellow had dishonoured a peasant's daughter.' The Emperor awarded the culprit capital punishment.[17]

Roe mentions that a woman belonging to Nur Jahan was caught in the place 'in some action' with a eunuch. Another person who loved the woman killed the eunuch. The poor woman was set up to the 'armpitts in the earth ramed', her feet tied to a stake. She remained in that conditions three days and two nights without anything to eat or drink. Her bare head and arms were completely exposed to the sun. If she survived, she was to be pardoned. The murderer was condemned to be trampled under the feet of an elephant.[18]

Edward Terry relates a similar story where a woman and a

eunuch had to pay with their life for their love. The fault of the woman was to kiss the eunuch who was cut to pieces before her own eyes. She herself lived a day and a half, 'crying out most lamentably......which horrid execution, or rather murder, was acted near our house.'[19]

Didâh Khân, one of the principal eunuchs of Shahjahan, became enamoured of the sister of a Hindu scriviner. His advances were responded to by the young woman and deep affection sprang up between the two. Rumours were set afloat in the city and the scriviner was naturally excited. No longer able to exercise restraint on himself, he, one day, finding them closeted together, stabbed the eunuch to heart and left his sister for dead.[20]

A rich Muslim merchant got enraged one day to find his wife in bed with another person. He put her, along with a child of three, to death. The lover, perhaps, made good his escape.[21]

A Muslim woman of low character, who had married an Englishman, developed an illicit connection with a servant. The Englishman finding them one day in the very act of the crime, showed signs of giving them an exemplary punishment. The cunning woman set up a cry and shouted to the people who had gathered there that the Englishman had cursed the Holy Prophet. It was with considerable difficulty that the unlucky fellow escaped the terrible punishment reserved for the alleged crime, though he received from the people a good deal of thrashing.[22]

SODOMY

In the Islamic law sodomy is forbidden even more strictly than adultery (fornication). There was divergence of opinion as to the punishment of the offence. Shâfi'i declared that there was a dispute between 'Ali and 'Abdulla if stoning was the punishment both for *muhsan* and *bikr*. Mâlik and Ahmad were in favour of lapidation as penalty of the crime. According to another opinion, sodomy is like adultery (*zinâ'*) : a *muhsan* is to be stoned and a *bikr* flogged. Abu Hanifa maintains that there was no legal punishment for it. After the decision of the *qâzi,* the offender was to be punished and imprisoned for life.[23]

Sodomy was not unknown in Inda. The casual remarks made by the travellers help us form some opinion about the prevalence of this crime. Fryer writes that the unnatural crime was common in Mughal India. Because of this fear, the Muslims did not trust the tutors of their children.[24] According to Manrique, the 'unmentionable vice' was very common in Inda.[25] Catamites dressed and adorned themselves as women, and paraded the streets soliciting other persons as dissolute as themselves.[26]

Shâh Quli Khân Mahram, a court noble of Akbar, loved a boy named Qabûl Khân. As the Emperor did not like any of his servants indulging in such improper acts, he ordered the noble to desist from this evil deed. Shâh Quli failed to give up the practice. Akbar ordered that the boy should be taken away from him and made over to the guards. Unable to bear the separation, the noble, giving way to anguish, put on the dress of a *jogi,* and sought retirement. Later, he solicited and received pardon (1559).[27]

There was a similar story of yet another noble, Muzaffar Khân, who had unnatural relations with a beautiful boy Qutb Khân. Akbar ordered the boy to be separated from him and entrusted to the guards. Muzaffar Khân, like Shâh Quli Mahram, felt the separation too much to bear became an ascetic, and fied to jungles. The Emperor summoned him to his presence and remonstrated with him.[28]

Mirzâ Sharf-ud-din Husain had an Indian boy named Mahmûd for whom he had an unnatural affection. Mirzâ's enemy, Ma'sûm Khân Kâbuli, used the boy to poison the Mirzâ.[29]

Khân Zamân, a powerful noble at Akbar's court, developed a strong passion for Shâhim Beg, who was 'pre-eminent for beauty of disposition and appearance, the beau Ideal of the age'. Upon Akbar's accession to the throne, Khân Zamân secretly called Shâhim from Delhi and developed a passionate love for him. He called him 'my king', and waited upon him like an ordinary servant and remained standing in his presence. As Shâhim became attracted to Ârâm Jân, lawfully married to himself, Khân Zamân even entrusted that dancing girl to him. When the news of Khân Zamân's conduct was conveyed to Akbar, he became exceedingly angry and issued orders to Khân Zamân to rack Shâhim Beg. The fief-holders of that district were ordered that in case Khân Zamân was dilatory in this matter, he should be brought to punishment.[30]

Mirzâ Momin and Daryâ Khân had rebelled against the imperial authority and joined the rebel Mûsâ Khân in Bengal. When they had been deputed to the Mohânâ of Isâmati at Jatrapur, there came to them their *pîrzâdâ* (some of their common spiritual guide) with a handsome eunuch named Phundnâ. Daryâ Khân became enamoured of him and tried to get him by gold and messages. Failing in his efforts, he brought him to his house by some trick, made him drunk, behaved improperly with him and confined him to his house. The sons of Mirzâ Momin who already bore him a grudge for his past behaviour, felt enraged at this, and formed a conspiracy to murder him. The Mirzâ called him to hold a council of war and himself went out. His sons attacked him with a sword and dagger and finished him.[31]

Suspecting the evil designs of the governor of Burhanpur, a handsome servant boy stabbed him three times and ended his life. Shahjahan did not punish the offender. Rather he bestowed on him a small appointment.[32]

Mirzâ Ibrâhim Adham from Îrân had attained such a fame in learning that Shahjahan was inclined to have him as his son-in-law. The Mirzâ, however, always spurned the offer as he was opposed to such a relationship. He became notorious as a confirmed sodomist which made the Emperor very unhappy.[33]

Tavernier has narrated the story of a young boy who was disgraced by his master. The boy became overwhelmed with grief, and, in order to take his revenge, killed his master in a fit of rage. After the commission of the offence, he reported the matter to the authorities and confessed his guilt. In spite of the persistent demands of the murdered man's relatives for retaliation, the authorities did not award death punishment on him. They were afraid of the populace of the city who regarded the boy to be in the right.[34]

Nauras Bâno, the wife of Shâh Nawâz Khân, petitioned Aurangzeb inside the palace that Khânzâd Khân was falling on evil ways. She requested the Emperor to take her son under his own care. Aurangzeb ordered Fûlâd Khân and Rahmat Khân to make inquiries and report as to why the said Khân who had a rank and a *jâgir,* was practising sodomy and indulging in drinking.[35]

They marry but one Wife, except in Cases of Barrenness or Adultery, tho' there are no laws against Polygamy. They abhor Buggery and Sodomy, and the Mahometans for that Account, because they use them. They eat twice a Day, but the Husband and Wife eat separate; and they wash before and/after Meat. And the Europeans there follow that cleanly Custom.

A boy killed a sodmist with a Kataree. The Boy came out with commendation. Though three is nothing more frequently committed annual them (he means Moores) than the natural in 7 Buggary).

Saifulla Khân, the *khidmatgâr* of Sayyid Lutf, held the rank of one hundred with Prince Kâm Baksh. He came to the house of the Sayyid and always did improper things. He was dismissed from *mansab* and Ihtrâm Khân was ordered to commit him to prison and administer him a warning.[36]

INCEST

We come across one case of incest, sexual commerce of near kindred. A Brâhmin of Chakor village in Bengal had his own daughter as mistress and had a son by her. According to the Brâhmin, his son-in-law had been killed in a battle. Bâbâ Khân Kâkshâl, the *jâgirdâr* of the *pargana,* arrested the Brâhmin and imprisoned him for the offence; but released him after realizing from him a fine of two hundered rupees. When Akbar was on his way to Bengal and passed through Chakor, the matter was reported to him. The 'accursed man' submitted that if his daughter was left to him, he would become a çonvert to Islam.

Akbar summoned *Qâzi* Yâqûb of the Imperial army to the boat in which the *Dîwânkhâna* was held and asked him the law of *sharî 'at* in this matter. The *qâzi* submitted that according to the concurrent opinion of all the *imâms* of Islâm, such a crime was liable to death punishment. for non-Muslims there were two opinions : he should not be or should be put to death. Akbar accepted the latter view and ordered both of them to be committed to prison by Khidmat Râi, in charge of the prisons. Next day, the Emperor ordered that 'the means of his vice and wickedness' should be cut off from the roots and roasted before his eyes. 'That eternally accursed and forever condemned man ate that thing with great appetite' in the belief that after this punishment he would probably be released. Next day, he was ordered to be executed. His daughter, who repented of the offence, escaped with her life.[37]

REFERENCES

1. M'aâlim Al-Qarbâ, p. 69. Hughes, p. 130, IV, p. 1227.
2. *Ibid.*, p. 68; Fatâwâ-i-'Âlamgîrî, II, p. 667. Hughes p. 131; Ency. IV, p. 1227.
3. *Ibid.*, II, p. 667-68, Hughes, p. 31.
4. *Ibid.*, p. 69.
5. *Ibid.*, Hughes, p. 131.
6. Fatâwâ-i-Âlamgîrî, II, pp. 668; 667 Ma'âlim Al-Qarba, p. 69; Hughes pp. 131.
7. *Ibid.*, p 68-69.
8. *Ibid.*, Hughes, p. 11.
9. Fatâwâ-i-'Âlamgîrî, II, p. 663; *Ibid.* Hughes p. 11.
10. *Ibid.*, p. 662; Hughes, p. 11.
11. Ma'âlim Al-Qarbâ, p. 69; p. 72.
12. Ma'âlim Al-Qarbâ, pp. 69-70; Fatâwâ-i-'Âlamîrî, 13, p. 675.
13. *Ibid.*, p. 72; *Ibid.*, pp. 665, 666, 669. Also see Hughes, p. 11.

14. Mîrât-i-p. 282, cfs arkar's Mughal Adminisration, p. 114.
15. Akbar Nâma, Beveridge, III. pp. 577-78. Text, iii, pp. 390; 391; 392. Muntakhib-ul-Lubâb, ii, p. 124; Monserrate's Commentary. p. 210.
16. Badâuni, Lowe, II, pp. 140-41; Text, II, pp. 136-38.
17. Akbar Nâmâ, Bev., II, p. 861. Text, III, p. 569.
18. The Embassy, pp. 190-91, Roe's journal, pp. 190-91.
19. Early Travels, p. 407.
20. Bernier, I, pp. 146-47.
21. Fryer, I, p. 245.
22. Manucci, III, p. 217.
23. Ma'âlim Al-Qarbâ, p. 70.
24. Fryer, I, p. 282.
25. Manrique, p. I, 240.
26. *Ibid.*
27. Akbar Nâma, Bev., II, p. 121, Text, p. 79.
28. Akbar Nâmâ, Text, p. 286. II.
29. Akbar Nâmâ, Bev., III p. 478. Text. b. 32.
30. Akbar Nâmâ, Bev., II pp. 104-7, 127; Text, 67-69; 83 Tabâqat, De, II. pp. 225-27.
    Farishta, II, 320, Tabaqât, Text, ii, pp. 136-38; Farishta, Text, i, p. 4.
31. Bahârtstân, I, p. 55.
32. Tavernier, I, pp. 53-54.
33. Muntakhib-ul-Lubâb (Urdu Translation), I, p. 274.
34. Tavernier, I, pp. 122-23.
35. Jaipur Akhbârât, 10th year, 31st August, 1667.
36. Jaipur Akhbârât, 13th October, 1684.
37. Tabaqât-i, Akbari, De, II, pp. 436-38;
    Text, II, pp. 285-86.
    Akbar Nâmâ, Beveridge, III, p. 124.
    Text, III, p. 88.

XI
OFFENCES AGAINST THE SAFETY OF THE STATE

In Mughal India the ruler was the state and offences against him were considered crimes against the State. We shall take up the subject under the following heads :—

Attack on the life of the Emperor.
Rebellions; prisoners of war.
Espionage.
Correspondence with the enemy.
Helping the enemy.
Desertion or flight.
Neglect of duty.
Disobedience and Disrespect to the Emperor.
Attack on or Disobedience or insult of imperial officers.
Criticism of Government by public servants.
Leave without permission.
Infringement of royal prerogatives.
Disturbance of Peace; and Riot in the Realm.
Fights among imperial officers.
Breach of court etiquettes.

ATTACK OF THE LIFE OF THE EMPEROR

When on 11th January, 1564, Akbar, on return from hunt, entered Delhi and reached in procession near the *Madarsa-i-Begum,* a slave named Fûlâd aimed an arrow at him from the balcony of the *madarsa.* This slave had been set free by Mirzâ Sharf-ud-din Husain before he had fled and gone to Mecca. The arrow, according to Badâûni, did not more than graze the Emperor's skin. Abul Fazl and Farishta, however, make us believe that it penetrated the right shoulder about the length of a span.

The Emperor's attendants wished to examine Fûlâd and investigate the matter, in order to find out if it was the result of a conspiracy. Akbar did not, however, favour the idea and ordered that the offender be immediately put to death.[1]

Four years later in 1569, when Akbar was again returning from hunt to Agra, some body gave the information that the rebel Deo Sultân, the son of Darbâh Khân, was hiding in his father's tomb, possibly to attack the Emperor. In accordance with orders, he was arrested and made over to Jagmal Panwâr. He died in prison.[2] It is not known if he was tried for this suspected attack on the Emperor.

In 1580, a number of persons such as 'Ali 'Âlamshâhi, Mîrâki and others hatched a conspiracy against Akbar and then fled to Bengal in order to join the rebels there. The plan was discovered and an inquiry was instituted first by the imperial officers and then by the Emperor himself. There is no mention of any trial. As a result of the inquiry, Mirâki was executed and others were put into prison.[3]

During his journey to Kabul in 1606, it was discovered that some officers like Fatehullâh, Nûr-ud-din, Âsaf Khân and Sharif Khân, had, at the instigation of Khusrow, formed a conspiracy to murder Jahangir. The Emperor ordered the chief insurgents to be captured. After perhaps their guilt was established, Jahangir punished them according to the gravity of the crime. Fatehullâh was imprisoned while others were executed.[4]

In the 16th year of his reign, while Aurangzeb was riding back after the performance of the *'Id-uz-zuhâ* sacrifice, a mad-looking person came near and struck the Emperor with a stick which fell on his knee. The man was arrested and brought before Aurangzeb by the mace-bearers. Instead of punishing him, he, however, ordered his release.[5]

On another occasion Aurangzeb was returning from the *Jâma masjid,* While he was getting down from the boat in order to sit on the revolving throne, a disciple of Guru Tegh Bahâdur, threw two brickbats on him, one of which fell on the throne. The foot-soldiers took the offender into custody and handed him over to the *kotwâl.*[6]

A petitioner threw a stick on the Emperor during his ride and it fell on the *chhatar*. The man was arrested and handed over to the *kotwâl.*[7]

While one day Aurangzeb was riding back from the *Jâma' masjid,* a 'wretched fellow' reached near him with sword in band. When he was being arrested by the guards, Mukarram Khân received injuries on his hands. The mace-bearers had the intention of putting him to death. The Emperor, however, forbade them to do so. Rather he bestowed on him a daily allowance of half a rupee, though, at the same time, sent him to Ranthambor.[8]

While on 9th April, 1680, Aurangzeb was returning from Friday prayers, seven persons threw stones towards him. They were arrested and questioned as to the purpose of their action. They replied that 15,000 rupees had been earmarked for the distribution of alms. As they had been excluded from the list of recipients, they had become broken-hearted and resorted to this step. They had no intention to kill the king. They were ordered to be handed over to Ihtimâm Khân *kotwâl* to be thrown into prison.[9]

Tahawur Khân who had been *faujdâr* of Ajmer in 1679, made an attempt on the life of Aurangzeb in 1681.[10]

In 1692, in the *Jâma' masjid,* a mad-looking man rushed towards Aurangzeb with a naked sword in his hand. The guards on duty arrested him and handed him over to Sa'âdat Khân.[11]

The use of abusive language by Mohammad Tâhir Diwân cost him his life. As per advice of Mulla 'Ivaz Wajih, he was considered worthy of capital punishment and was accordingly executed.[12]

REBELLIONS

To rise in rebellion against the ruling monarch was considered a grave crime. The Mughal royal princes were in many cases heads of different provinces. Vast resources at their disposal enabled them to risk such undertakings. Almost all of them were pastmasters in warefare, as they had the opportunity, at one time or another, of leading armies and directing campaigns. Hindu *râjas,* anxious to regain their freedom, would rise up in arms against the Mughal Emperor. Their motive was not to overthrow the reigning monarch; their anxiety was to release themselves from all obligations to the Central Government. Their risings were taken by the Government with all seriousness. Full preparations seemed necessary to nip the evil in the bud. Influential imperial generals sometimes took up arms against the sovereign. Organized bands would at times fling down the gauntlet to the provincial authorities and disturb the peace of the locality by their unlawful activities. Peasants would refuse to recognize the Government and cease to pay revenue, and thus incur the wrath of the Emperor.[13] Against all these, he took immediate measures, and, according to the need of the moment, sent either large armies under the command of experienced military officers, or levies under the *faujdârs.* Then there were the religious heads whose *fatwâs* against the Emperor could be a source of great nuisance. Very often such leaders deserved and received death punishment, transportation for life or imprisonment as the following cases will show.

In 1558, Bairam Khân, the all-powerful minister of Akbar, charged Musâhib Beg with the offence of rebellion and awarded death punishment on him. Musâhib Beg was executed in Delhi without the knowledge of the Emperor. The other nobles raised an outcry against the arbitrary decision of Bairam Khân.[14]

The rebel Khân Zamân 'Ali Quli Khân was killed in the battle-field in 1567. His brother Bahâdur Khân was produced before the Emperor who did not favour his execution; but after urgent solicitations from his officers, Shâhbâz Khân and Banârsi Dâs Kamboh were ordered to behead him.

At Mânakpur, a number of associates of Khân Zamân 'Ali Quli Khân were produced before the Emperor in 1567. They included rebels like Khân Quli Uzbeg, 'Âlam Shâh Badakshi, Mir Shâh Badakshi, Yahiyâ Bakshi and Kalma Khân. They were ordered to be trampled under the feet of wild elephants before the eyes of the Emperor. An elephant was let loose against Mirzâ Mirak Rizvi of Meshed. He had fled from the court and had become a special confidant of 'Ali Quli. The elephant caught him in his trunk and squeezed him from one side to the other. For five successive days he was brought out and tortured in this manner in the place of execution. Later on he was pardoned at the intercession of the nobles. At this time Jai Tiwâchi brought to court Shâh Nâsir Khwâja, a ring-leader of the rebels. He was awarded capital punishment.[15]

I'timâd Khân and other Gujarati officials, accused of conspiracy in Gujarat in 1572, were produced by Shâhbâz Khân before the Emperor. Akbar ordered all of them to be handed over to an officer in order to be placed in confinement.[16]

The rebels who fell into the hands of the royal army after the defeat of Khân Zamân and the capture of Sûrat in 1573 were ordered to be imprisoned.[17]

Quli Khan in 1574. His brother Masud Husain was imprisoned The famous rebel Ibrâhim Hussain Mirzâ was defeated by Husain Quli Khan. He was imprisoned.[18] Husain Quli Khân brought along with him to the capital Fatehpur the rebel Mas'ûd Khân and 300 other prisoners who were presented to Akbar with the skins of asses, hogs and dogs drawn over their faces. Some of them were put to death by ingenious tortures and the rest were released.[19] Mas'ûd was sent to the fort of Gwalior as a prisoner. He died there the same year.[20]

In that very year another rebel noble Mohammad Husain Mirzâ was defeated and captured in Gujarat. Akbar handed him over to Rây Râyân to be kept in safe custody. The Rây Râyân became afraid of the fact that the Mirzâ might not fall into the hands of Ikhtiâr-ul-Mulk, whose army had appeared on the scene just at that time. He killed the Mirzâ on the advice of Râja Bhagwân Dâs, though without the express orders of the Emperor. Akbar did not mind the action of the Rây Râyân. He himself was in favour of awarding the Mirzâ capital punishment. Mirzaâs *kîkâ,* Shâh Madâd, was taken prisoner on the battle-field. He was a *faqîr.* Akbar cast him on the ground with his spear and the others cut him to pieces by the blows of sharp-edged swords.[21]

In 1577, the Gujarat rebels were ordered to be executed.[22]

Some Sheikhs and Imâms got enraged with Akbar and started preaching against him in the mosques. The *Qâzi-ul-qazzât,* Mullâ Mohammad Yazdi of Jaunpur, gave the *fatwâ* that as Akbar had become irreligious, *jehâd* should be started against him. Thus a number of rebels raised their head in Bengal in 1581 A.D., *mullâs* fanned the embers of rebellion, and the nobles joined them.

Akbar was determined to stamp out the revolt and mete out an exemplary punishment to the ringleaders among the *mullâs.* He summoned *Mullâ* Mohammad Yazdi and *Mullâ* Mu'iz-ul-mulk on some pretext to the court. At Ferozabâd near Agra they were separated, in order to be sent to Gwâlior. The guards placed them in a broken boat and drowned them in the river. All the *Sheikhs* and *mullâs*, suspected of treason, were put to death. The *Amîrs* who were their associates were transferred to distant places. Old families of the *mullâs* were exiled and otherwise punished. Hâji Ibrâhim Sirhindi, the *sadr* of Gujarat, was, on charge of rebellion, ordered to be kept in custody.[23]

Roshan Beg, the collector of exchequer lands in Bengal, embezzled money and fled to Kâbul. At the instigation of some persons, he returned to Bengal and there joined the rebels in 1581 A.D. He was caught, and, on the orders of Akbar, awarded capital punishments. Mir 'Ali Akbar, another rebel in Bengal, was brought in chains in the court and ordered to be cast into prison.[24]

Two years later, Bahâdur, the son of Sa'id Khân Badakshi, became a rebel. He made the hill country of Tirhut the 'abode of turbulence', and, finding an opportunity, plundered and distressed the peasantry in the neighbourhood. Gâzi Khân Badakshi, the *jâgirdâr* of the *pargana,* attacked him, plundered his home and captured his children. Bahâdur came to Gâzi Khân and sued for mercy. The latter took him to

Khân-i-Â'zam at Hâjipur and he sent the rebel to the court with chains round his neck. He was awarded capital punishment.[25] Another rebel, Nûr Muhammad, sent by Khân-i-Â'zam to the court in the same year, was ordered to be executed.[26]

In the first year of Jahangir's reign, his eldest son, Khursrow, raised the standard of revolt against his father and fled towards the Punjab. Later on he was caught, and, with his hands bound and with fetters on his legs, was brought before Jahangir in Lahore. He was ordered to be put in custody.

Two of his special associates, Hussain Beg and Abdul 'Aziz, were ordered to be enclosed in the skins of a cow and an ass respectively face to the tail, and to be paraded through the city. As the skin of the cow dries quicker than that of the ass, Husain Beg died near the fourth watch. Abdul 'Aziz, however, survived.

Prior to Khusrow's defeat, five of his associates were captured and brought before Jahangir. The Emperor ordered one of them to be cast before the elephants and the others to be put in custody.

As to Khusrow's punishment there are different theories. According to Du Jarric and De Laet, he was blinded at Jahangir's orders. William Finch says, "there were two stories prevalent at that time. One makes us believe that he was blinded on the battle-field with glass. The other has it that Jahangir merely caused a handkerchief to be tied over his eyes and that he sealed it with his own seal." Terry mentions that his eyes were sealed up for the space of three years, after which time the seal was taken away. In 1617, Thomas Roe saw Khusrow with his eyes intact.

As for other rebels, they were punished more severely. Nearly 300 of them (according to Price's Text) were impaled on the stakes, set up between the city of Lahore and the gardens of Mirzâ Kâmrân, on both sides of the road. 'Than this', writes Jahangir in the Tuzk, 'there cannot exist a more excruciating punishment, since the wretches exposed frequently linger a longer time in the most agonising torture, before the hands of death relieves them', and the 'spectacle of such frightful agonies' served a warning to others.[27]

Guru Arjun Dev, the head of the Sikh religion at that time, who was living at Govindwâl on the Beas, was reported to have waited on the rebel Prince Khusrow, paid him homage, and put *tilak* on his head. Thus he was, in the eyes of Janagir, guilty of treason. Moreover, he had earned the displeasure of the Emperor by his proselytising activities. He was ordered in 1606 to be produced before Jahangir who awarded him capital punishment. His children were imprisoned and his property was confiscated.[28]

The rebel *zamindârs* of Bengal captured by the imperialists were kept in safe custody in fetters by the governor Islâm Khân.[29]

Dulip, the son of Rây Singh, was a rebel. He was seized by the *faujdâr* of Khost and sent as a prisoner to the court in 1613. He was awarded death punishment.[30]

Chaupar Mal, the son of Râja Bâsu, who was sent for the conquest of Kângra in 1620, rebelled. Shortly afterwards, the Râja was made prisoner and executed under orders of Jahangir.[31]

In 1623, Nûr-ud-din Quli brought in chains to the royal court forty-one of the rebels who had been taken Prisoners at Ahmadabad. Their ring-leaders, Sharzâ Khân and Qâbil Khân, were ordered by the Emperor to be trampled under the feet of warlike elephants.[32]

MINARS OF THE HEADS

Mundy saw on the way minars of heads of men killed by government troops for rebellion etc.

(Mundy, II, pp. 166; 185; 186.)

Aurangzeb had ordered that rebels were to be confined till penitence, in case they were seized before taking up any position. If they took up a position for fight, they were to be attacked and extirpated. All among them were to be slain mercilessly.[33]

The fictitious Shujâ‘ who raised the standard of revolt against Aurangzeb, was awarded capital punishment.[34]

When it was proved that Mohammad ‘Ali ‘Âlamshâhi and his accomplices were guilty of conspiracy in a revolt, they were ordered to be imprisoned. As they failed to show any improvement in their behaviour, they were ordered to be executed.[35]

On a charge of conspiracy with Abul Hasan of Golconda, Shâh ‘Âlam and his sons were ordered to be taken into custody. Shâh ‘Âlam and his sons were ordered to be taken into custody. Shâh ‘Âlam was deprived of his *mansab* and also of the reward of a crore of *dâms* bestowed on him earlier. A eunuch in the service of his wife was also imprisoned and his property was confiscated. Two eunuchs of Shâh ‘Âlam were imprisoned and put to death.[36]

PRISONERS OF WAR

The Marâtha prisoners of war often received capital punishment at the hands of Aurangzeb.

The 112 servants of Sambhâji who were prisoners of war at the *chabûtra kotwâli,* were ordered to be executed in 1684.[37]

On 24th January, 1700, Aurangzeb summoned Khwâja Mahram Khân into his presence and ordered that 14 Mâvel prisoners who had been handed over to Mohammad Amin, the deputy *kotwâl* and three Marâtha prisoners already imprisoned in the fortress, be executed on the banks of the river Krishnâ. Mahram Khân submitted that one of the prisoners was a boy and he sought orders about him. The Emperor sent for *qâzi* Mohammad Akram and asked his opinion in this matter. The learned *qâzi* replied that the execution of even the boy prisoner was justifiable. Accordingly, all the prisoners of war, including the teenage boy, were ordered to be taken to the banks of the Krishnâ and were executed there.[38]

On 22nd February, 1703, Aurangzeb ordered 11 Marâtha prisoners of war detained at the *chabûtra kotwâli* to be beheaded.[39]

Khânzâd Khân brought on 12th April, 1704, four prisoners of war under orders in the Emperor's presence. Aurangzeb asked Mohammad Amin, the deputy *kotwâl,* to convey his message to Sarbrâh Khân *kotwâl* that two of the prisoners be given capital punishment.[40]

ESPIONAGE

Spying was a serious crime and was punished as such.

During the reign of Akbar two Portugese were caught by the Customs-officer of Sûrat. After they were interrogated, they confessed that they were spies. They were given the choice of Islam or death. They refused to become converts and were immediately put to death.[41]

In 1666, the commandant of the fortress of Ghazni arrested eight persons, and, on charge of espionage, sent them to the governor of Kâbul. They were sent for inquiry to the governor of Lahore, and from there to the Court. The Emperor entrusted them to I'timâd Khân for investigation. One of them wounded the said Khân fatally, and, consequently, seven of them were put to death by I'timad Khân's men. The one who survived was ordered to be permanently kept in confinement and the whole truth ascertained from him.[42]

In 1667, the ruler of Bukhârâ sent along with the ambassador a woman as a spy. On her own confession she was ordered on 3rd September, 1667, to be imprisoned and closely watched.[43]

On 14th June, 1682, the ten spies of Sambhâ, who had made their confession in prison, were executed, at the Emperor's orders, in front of the *chabutra kotwâli*.[44]

During his stay in Goâ, Prince Shah 'Âlam had given orders that every one entering or leaving the camp at night should be killed without fail. This step had been taken to frighten the spies and hinder their movements round about the royal camp.[45]

CORRESPONDENCE WITH THE ENEMY

It was a serious crime to correspond with the enemy and the offender merited grave punishment.

Shâh Mansûr, the *diwâni-i-kul,* was suspected of carrying on correspondence with Mirzâ Mohammad Hakim, who had revolted against Akbar. A number of letters were intercepted from which it appeared that Shâh Mansûr was in correspondence with Mirzâ Hakim. As a matter of fact some powerful nobles at the court were set upon his ruin. Near Shâhâbâd, on his way to Kâbul, in 1581, Akbar received letters written by the Mirzâ to Shâh Mansûr. Suspicion became confirmed, and, on the suggestion of the nobles, the Emperor ordered the Captain of the Guard to hang him by a tree near Shâhâbâd. At Kâbul, when the Emperor learnt that the said letter was a forgery on the part of the Amirs, he felt grieved.[46]

Jahangir came to know in 1622 that the eunuch Muhtarim Khân, the Master of the Ceremonies, Fidâi Khân, and Khalil Beg Zul-qad, had allied themselves and corresponded with the rebel Prince Shahjahan. They were imprisoned, and, after inquiry, awarded capital punishment.[47]

'Ârif had written with his own hands a letter to the rebel Prince Shahjahan, professing his own and his father's loyalty to the Prince. The letter fell into the hands of Mahâbat Khân who showed it to the accused. 'Ârif could make no excuse and Mahâbat Khân ordered him to be executed in 1624. His father and two brothers were kept in confinement.[48]

With the illness of Shahjahan, the virtual power had passed into the hands of Dârâ Shikoh. Aurangzeb's supporters were over-vigilant and kept him informed of the situation. This was more than Dârâ could put up with. Orders for the arrest of such persons were issued and immediately carried into effect.[49]

Aurangzeb's reign was full of battles. The latter half particularly was an unbroken spell of continued warfare. The imperial generals did not always wish a speedy end of the campaigns. They stood to gain by their prolongation. Sometimes they communicated their intentions to the enemy who made a prompt reply. Constant endeavours were made to conceal the proceedings from the Emperor.[50]

Letters exchanged between the rebel Prince Mohammad Akbar and the royal Princes Zeb-un-nisâ were intercepted and brought to the Emperor's notice in 1681. The Princess was deprived of the annual grant of 4 *lac* of rupees awarded to her earlier and also of her entire property and was confined in the fortress of Salimgarh.[51]

HELPING THE ENEMY

Shâh Nawâz Khân, the governor of Gujarat and the father-in-law of Aurangzeb, handed over Ahmadâbâd to Dârâ without any resistance. Aurangzeb ordered Daler Khân to inflict death punishment upon the old man. After Dârâ's defeat in the battle of Ajmer, when Shâh Nawâz was sitting on a carpet spread under the trees, a little distant from the battle-field, Daler Khân hastened his elephant's pace towards that side and killed the old man 'impiously and cruelly by repeated arrow-shots'.[52]

Fâzil Khan, the Chief Officer of Royal Wardrobe, had begun to put into execution the plan of despatching secretly to Prince Mohammad Akbar in Persia a sum of five lac gold coins. The Sûrat governor discovered the attempt and informed Aurangzeb. Learning that his secret had come to the knowledge of the Emperor, Fâzil Khân swallowed poison and died. 'He thus avoided the torture which would, no doubt, have been inflicted upon him.'[53]

DESERTION OR FLIGHT

Desertion in the face of the enemy or flight from the battle-field were considered crimes sometimes punished very seriously.

Tardi Beg had fled from the battle-field in the fight against Hemu. As a matter of fact Bairam Khân had an old grudge to settle with him and was in search of an opportunity to get rid of him. According to Badâûni, he got a sort of permission from the Emperor to finish him off. Bairam Khân was all powerful at that time and took important decisions himself. By treachery he took Tardi Beg to his tent where in 1556 he was clubbed to death or stabbed in a barbarous manner.[54]

While returning from Burhânpur in 1562, the imperial general, Pir Mohammad Sherwâni, was drowned in the Narbada when crossing it. The other nobles reaching Mâlwa found that Bâz Bahâdur had reconquered the province. They fled away from Mâlwa and came to the court without permission. For this they were punished and committed to prison.[55]

During Akbar's campaign in 1581 against his half-brother, Mirzâ Hakim, in Kâbul, twelve deserters to the enemy were captured in an ambush and brought before the Emperor. Some of them were ordered to be kept in custody for a more thorough investigation of their cases and others were executed. Those imprisoned were, however, released on account of the witty remarks of one of the convicts about his singing.[56]

In December 1590 it was reported to Akbar that Shâhbâz Khân had come from Swâd without orders. He was committed to prison for three years.[57]

Mirzâ Sharf-ud-din Husain had fled from Nâgor. He fell into the hands of Bahâr Jiv, the *Râja* of Baglâna. The *Râja* presented the Mirzâ before Akbar while the Emperor was at Ahmadâbâd after the conquest of Sûrat. He was ordered to be flogged and sent as a prisoner to the Gwalior Fort where he died.[58]

It was reported to Jahangir in 1605 that Abhay Râj, son of Akhay Râj, son of Bhagwân Dâs, was desirous of despatching his wives and children to his own country without permission, and afterwards himself running away to the Rânâ. When nobody was prepared to furnish security for him and his two brothers, they were ordered to be handed over to Ibrâhim Khân Kakar. When they tried to disarm them, they began to quarrel and fight. Jahangir ordered that they should be punished 'according to their deeds'. They were killed after fighting bravely.[59]

It was reported that Badi'uz—zamân, the son of Mirzâ Shâh Rukh, had started at the head of a body of rebels with a view to joining the Rânâ of Mewâr. 'Abdulla Khân, the governor of Mâlwa, gave them a chase, took Badi-'uz-zamân a prisoner, and slew several of his associates. An order was given by Jahangir that Ihtirâm Khân should start from Âgra and bring the Mirzâ to the court.[60]

As Sheikh Banârasi and Ghiâs Zain Khân and some other *mansabdârs* had failed to protect Patna against the impostor Qutb, and had fled from there, Jahangir summoned them to the court in 1610 and punished them. Their hair and beards were shaved off, they were clad in women's dress and paraded round the city.[61]

Dârâb, the son of Khân-i-Â'zam, who had deserted the imperialists and joined the rebel Shahjahan, was caught by imperial forces. Under orders from the Emperor, Mahâbat Khân cut off his head and sent it to the imperial court in 1624.62 About 1,000 deserters from the rebel Prince Shahjahan's army in 1624 were killed by Mahâbat Khân's officers.[63]

Aurangzeb felt disgusted at the cowardly act of Mahârâjâ Jaswant Singh when he deserted the imperial side in the thick of the battle of

Khâwajâ in January, 1659, and joined the enemy. Aurangzeb ordered a punitive expedition against him. The order was withdrawn only at the intercession of Râja Jai Singh. Jaswant Singh's apologies calmed the impending storm.[64]

Learning that his chief noble Allâhvardi Khân had planned to desert to Aurangzeb during the War of succession, Shujâ' ordered his public execution. His younger son Saifullah and two *mansabdârs* who were his partners in the crime, shared the same fate.[65]

In June, 1659, Prince Sultân Mohammad deserted Mir Jumla and went to his uncle, Shujâ' who offered him the hand of his daughter, Gul Rukh Bâno. The unlucky Prince could not develop a liking for his father-in-law, and, after eight months, returned to join the imperial forces in Bengal. From there he was sent to his father, Aurangzeb, who ordered him to be sent to prison where he sighed away the rest of his life.[66]

In case a commander fled from the battle-field (or did not perform his duty), he was severley punished. Even his wives and daughters were not spared. In order to disgrace and frighten them and serve as a warning to others, rats were placed in their trousers.[67]

NEGLECT OF DUTY

Neglect of duty was regarded as a serious crime and punished according to the nature of the offence.

Shâh Abul Ma'âli who failed to attend the court on the day of Akbar's accession, was arrested and imprisoned in Lahore. Due to the negligence of the *kotwâl,* Pahalwân Gulguz, he fled away. From fear of punishment, Gulguz committed suicide.[69]

In order to ensure that the attendants did not fail to do their duty in a proper manner, Akbar had laid down rules and regulations for the proper care of the horses and elephants. Those who failed to do their duty towards these animals were to be fined and a whole list of fines has been mentioned in the *Âîn.*[69]

Mahmûd, the son of Iskandar Afghân, had been made over to Shâhbâz Khân, in order to be placed in confinement. The prisoners escaped from his guards in 1572 and fled to the Deccan. Shâhbâz Khân was severely censured and chastised.[70]

While Akbar was in the eastern provinces in 1574, in connection with the conquest of Bihar, it was reported that the special elephant, Lâl Khân, was drowned at the Chausa ferry. Sâdiq Khân, who along with Yusuf Khân, held charge of the camp, had not taken sufficient care while leading the elephants across the river. He fell out of royal favour and got his fief confiscated. He was not permitted to perform the *kornish* and was transferred to Thatta. Moreover, he was required to produce a choice elephant of the calibre of Lâl Khân before he could be permitted to perform *kornish.*[71]

Imperial commanders were sent against Chandra Sen, the son of Râjâ Mâldeo, in 1574. They gained partial victory, and, thinking that his flight was the end of the task, they returned to the court without being summoned. The Emperor degraded them from the post of trust.[72]

Qutb-ud-din Khân and Râja Bhagwân Dâs were sent against Rânâ Pratap in 1576. They failed to encounter him and returned hastily and without orders to the court. They were forgiven when they showed signs of repentance.[73]

Jahangir recalled the Khân-i-Khânân from the Deccan in 1610 for his failure of duty there.[74]

Husain Khân, brother of Anwar Khân, ally of Mûsâ Khân, was captured by the imperialists and thrown into prison at Dâca. One day he gave bread and sweets mixed with *dhatûra* to the guards and the custodians of the prison and after they had become unconscious, he fled after one *pahar* of the night. Reaching his country Baniachung he killed his wives and daughters and began to mobilise his fleet and artillery against the Mughals. When Islâm Khân heard the news of his escape from the prison, he grew furious and ordered all the thirty-five gate-keepers and guards to be torn to pieces limb by limb. Husain Khân, however, was again captured with the help of Mûsâ Khân, and thrown into prison.[75]

Râja Kalyân, the governor of Orissa, led an expedition against Râja Puroshottam Dev of Khurda. The Râja sent envoys to tender apologies and submission. He was prepared to offer his daughter to the Emperor along with one lac of rupees and his best elephant *Shesnâg.* The Râja sent the *dola* along with the *peshkash* in cash and kind to the court. When the came to Akbarnagar along with the bride, the administrator there Sheikh Ahmad did not allow the *dola* to depart till he received the permission of the governor Islâm Khân. When the news was brought to the notice of the Emperor, he punished Sheikh Ahmad by cancelling his *jâgir* and *mansab.* He was also recalled to the Court. When Islâm Khân failed to send him there, His Majesty censured the governor.[76]

During his rebellion in Bengal, Prince Shahjahan got displeased with Mohammad Sâlih, the Inspector of Buildings, for his failure to complete the construction of the fort of Garhi. He ordered the *Kotwâl*

Nowbat Khân, to punish the *Dârogha* by inflicting one hundred lashes on him in the market-place. Mirzâ Nathan represented to the Prince that it was not the fault of the *Dârogha* and asked for the remission of the punishment. By the time the order of pardon reached, Mohmmed Sâlih had already received forty strokes of the whip.[77]

A captain of guard who allowed a prisoner to escape, received capital punishment in 1617.[78]

It was reported to Jahangir in 1618 that Jahângir Quli Khân, the governor of Bihar, was showing neglect in performing his duty. He had failed to restrain his brothers and sons-in-law from exercising oppression on the people. The Emperor issued orders dismissing Jahângir Quli Khân from the governorship of Bihar and appointing Muqarrab Khân in his place.[89]

In 1643, it was brought to the notice of Shahjahan that Prince Aurangzeb had determined to retire from the worldly affairs and pass his days in seclusion. The Emperor absolutely disapproved of the idea. The Prince was punished with the loss of *mansab* and dismissal from his office as the Viceroy of the Deccan.[80]

Shahjahan dismissed NawâbÂ'zam Shâh, the governor of Bengal, for his utter failure against the invaders from Assam.[81]

Sheikh Farid, the governor of Balkh, was ordered by Shahjahan in the 19th regnal year, to join Bethal Dâs, who had been appointed governor of Lahore. As he was jealous of the Râja, he showed delay. For this neglect of duty, he was deprived of his rank and *jâgir*.[82]

Shahjahan had ordered Sa'âdat Khân, the rich slave in charge of the betel-leaves, to desist from distributing these to any noble at the court. He did not pay heed to the royal orders and continued the practice. One day the king caught him in the act of giving the betel-leaf to a noble. At the end of the audience, he went into the garden and ordered the slave to be beaten to death.[83]

The Chief *Qâzi* who had objected to the confirmation of Aurangzeb as Emperor during the life-time of his father, was removed from his post.[84]

Orme writes that the customs-officer of Sûrat who held charge of the fort during the second raid of Shivâji was suspected of connivance and neglect of duty. Aurangzeb got rid of him by administering him poison.[85]

In the beginning of his reign, when Aurangzeb started from Burhânpur for Delhi, the gunners had left some thirty sacks of gunpowder in a cellar of the citadel. It remained there till 1681 when one day it burst, blew off the roof and burnt several men. The officers responsible for this were censured for their neglect of duty and degraded in their ranks.[86]

Munârâm was accused of neglect of duty. He was degraded. Similar treatment was meted out to other officers.[87]

A charge was levied against Ibrâhim Khân for having shown delay in carrying out orders. Aurangzeb at once ordered the reduction of one thousand in his rank.[88]

Prince Bedâr Bakht was entrusted with the command for reducing the fort of Sinsani belonging to Râja Râm Jât. The length of the campaign exhausted his patience. He sent a verbal message to the said chieftain asking him to give him (the prince) his brother's daughter, and himself to go out of the fort. The knowledge of the matter annoyed Aurangzeb who punished the Prince for his neglect of duty by reduction of his rank.[89]

An enemy Marâtha commander plundered some merchants on the highway of Sûrat, 80 miles from Ahmadâbâd. When the matter was brought to the notice of the provincial governor, Prince Mohammad Â'zam, he evinced lack of concern as it had occurred within the jurisdiction of Amânat Khân, the collector and *faujdâr* of Sûrat. For this neglect of duty his rank was reduced. His agents were required to compensate the merchants.[90]

Bhagwant Singh, the son of Pahâr Singh, and the sons of Champat Bundela were creating trouble round about Îraj. The *gumâshta* of Râja Jaswant Singh Bundela had been asked by the Mughal commandant to render help in defeating the rebels; but he paid no heed to this. The Emperor ordered on November 26, 1685, that the rank of the Râjâ be reducted.[91]

A Marâtha servant who was imprisoned at the *chabûtra kotwâli*, fled from custody. Aurangzeb ordered on 8th January, 1693, the transfer of the *dârogha* and the dismissal of the guards.[92]

Sa'di Sâlam Khân was reported to have failed to defend Balârak against the attack of 100 horsemen and 500 foot-soldiers belonging to the rebel forces, to have deserted the place and fled away. For this offence his transfer was ordered on 24th April, 1693.[93]

A resident of Chakla Jalna put up a petition through Yâr 'Ali Beg to the effect that a Hindu of the same place had demolished the house of the complainant and also the mosque adjacent to it. When he brought the matter to the notice of the *faujdâr* of the area, he expressed his inability to chastise the accused. The Emperor ordered Yâr 'Ali Beg to ask Bahrahmand Khân to issue transfer orders of the said *faujdâr*.[94]

In 1701, Rao Budh Singh of Bûndi suffered diminution in his

rank under Aurangzeb's orders as his *gumâshta* had failed to render assistance to the royal forces sent to chastise Gopâl Singh rebel.[95]

Abdur Rahman and others posted to the army of Zulfikâr Khân had their *jâgirs* transferred under royal orders for absence from duty.[96]

Dâd Prabhu posted to the army of Khân Nusrat Jang suffered diminution of rank of 1000 *swâr* for his absence from duty.[97]

It was reported that Hamid-ud-din attached to the same command had gone to and not returned from Râvati since a month. He held the rank of 5,000 *zât* and 5,000 *swâr*. He was puhished with the diminution in his rank of 1,000 *zât* and 1,500 *swâr*.[98]

Jai Singh held the rank of 2,000 *zât* and 1,000 *swâr*, and was attached to Bedâr Bakht. It was reported that he had failed to chastise the Marâtha raiders in Burhânpur. His rank was reduced by 500—*zât*.[99]

The *mutsaddi* of Sûrat, I'tizâr Khân, was removed from his post on 28th November, 1703, for dereliction of duty.[100]

It was reported to the Emperor that in *pargana* Kâkori, in the *sarkâr* of Lucknow, there were no '*âmils* and *mutsaddis* on duty. The *zamindârs* of the area appropriated to themselves the revenue of the *pargana*. As the responsibility for this state of affairs lay on Mohammad Yâr, the *dîwân* of Prince Mohammad Khajasta Akhtar, orders for his transfer were issued.[101]

On the morning of 25th January, 1705, Aurangzeb, accompanied by Prince Kâm Baksh, went out for hunting.During the journey he expressed a desire for dry fruit. The *kahâr* deputed for the purpose arrived a *ghari* late. The Emperor ordered that for his neglect of duty the *kahâr* should be severely chastised. The poor man was given such a furious thrashing that he fell unconscious. Aurangzeb had taken this affair so seriously that he ordered the dismissal of the entire *kahâr* fraternity along with their *jama'dâr*.[102]

DISOBEDIENCE AND DISRESPECT TO THE EMPEROR

During his march against Mirzâ Hakim, Akbar ordered an official to proceed upstream to a particular place and find out if the Indus could be forded there by the cavalry. The official returned with incomplete information without having reached the required place. He was ordered to be seized and dragged to that particular point, bound prostrate on an inflated bag of ox-hide and launched upon the Indus. He was released after he had undergone terrible misery and agony. He was, however, 'entered in the inventories as royal property, exposed for sale in all the *bâzârs,* and finally auctioned as a slave.' One of his friends purchased him for eighty pieces of gold. Later on, he was pardoned.[103]

Mirzâ 'Aziz Koka opposed the enforcement of the branding orders and put up an insolent behaviour. For this offence he was ordered by Akbar to be interned in his own garden.[104]

Hakim Nûr-ud-din of Tehrân, a *mansabdâr* of 500, was awarded capital punishment in 1623 for using disrespectful language towards Jahangir. He was executed in the presence of the Emperor.[105]

The governor of Bengâl Islâm Khân defied with impunity the royal orders of despatching to the imperial court his best musicians and placed the imperial envoy into confinement.[106]

The despatch of a false report to the Emperor could be regarded as an offence. The Bengal governor Qâsim Khân reported wrongly to the Emperor that his son Sheikh Farid had attained victory over the Mâg Râja. He was censured for this.[107]

A person in charge of drinking water showed calculated misbehaviour to Aurangzeb by greeting him loudly near the staircase of the mosque in 1676. He was taken into custody and handed over to the *kotwâl.*[108]

Threat of resignation from service could earn a person royal displeasure. Mohammad Ikhlâs, the *vakîl of Prince Mu'azzam,* was reported to have tendered resignation. Commenting on the news Aurangzeb remarked that in case Mohammad Ikhlâs persisted in his design, he was liable to incur royal displeasure.[109]

During the last days of Aurangzeb's reign, the officers who were at a long distance from the imperial court; paid little attention to his orders and acted in accordance with their own whims with impunity.[110]

DISOBEDIENCE TO THE EMPEROR'S ORDERS

Khafi Khan writes that two years after accession to the throne, Aurangzeb ordered the collection of a number of taxes, particularly the one charged on grain and corn which amounted approximately 25 lac rupees. Despite the confirmation of such orders, the Faujdars and jagirdars in places far away from the capital, continued collecting these forbidden taxes and cesses. One reason for this, according to Khafi Khan, was that these officials had completely shed off all sort of fear or fright of punishment for their misdeeds. These officials used the excuse that the collection of these taxes was included in the orders of their salaries and used all sorts of excesses and rigours in their collection. All this was being done in open defiance of the Emperor's orders. Whenever such reports came to the Emperor's notice, he ordered a diminuition in the officials' rank. But the disease continued unabated throughout his reign.

ATTACK ON OR DISOBEDIENCE OR INSULT OF IMPERIAL OFFICERS

A Turkish slave and door-keeper of Pir Mohammad Sherwâni insulted Bairam Khân in 1559. Pir Mohammad's apologies did not satisfy Bairam Khân. He was shorn of all powers, then imprisoned in the fort of Biâna, and afterwards ordered to be exiled to Mecca. Shortly afterwards, however, the Mullâ heard of Bairam Khân's fall and returned to the court where he was favourably received by the Emperor.[111]

After the defeat of Bairam Khân at Gunâchor on 23rd August, 1560, one of his associates, Wali Beg, was wounded and sent to prison where he died. His head was cut off and sent to the eastern provinces as a warning. When it was brought to *pargana* Etâwa by a Twâci, the *jâgirdâr* of the *pargana*, by the name of Bahâdur, murdered the Twâci. Bahâdur was saved by his loving companions who induced him to feign madness.[112]

Râja Ganesh of Nadaun in the Punjâb attacked Jân Mohammad, the *jâgirdâr* of Birkâ, in 1562. His exploit did not meet with success. On the other hand, his property was confiscated, his beautiful wife was dishonoured and killed. From the Punjâb, the imperial officers were sent to inflict 'suitable punishment on him.' It was through Râja Birbal that he was presented before Akbar and received into royal service.[113]

Hamid Bokhâri, one of the equerries, in a fit of intoxication, tried to shoot another servant of the threshold. When the matter was reported to Akbar in Lahore in 1567 by the complainant Qulij Khân, he grew angry, gave a special sword to Kulij Khân, and ordered him to kill Hamid Bokhâri with it. Qulij Khân twice struck him with the sword, but did not injur a hair of his head. Then the Emperor relented and ordered to shave off his head only.[114]

In the same year, Mohammad Amin Diwâna encountered and shot an arrow at one of the Superintendents of the royal elephants as he was riding on an elephant. When the matter was reported to Akbar, he ordered him to be put to death. The courtiers attached to the *harem* interceded for him. The Emperor granted him life, but ordered corporal punishment. After receiving punishment Mohammad Amin fled away the next day and joined the rebel 'Ali Quli. On his way a *mansabdâr,*

Shahâb Khân Turkhân, offered him refuge in the *pargana* of Bhojpur and then gave him horse and money in order to enable him to go to 'Ali Quli Khân. When Akbar was going from Agra to Lahore some time later in the same year, he ordered Shâh Fakhr-ud-din-Meshedi to produce Shahâb Khân at Palwal where he was given capital punishment.[115]

In 1572, Bâbâ Khân Kâkshâl behaved towards Shâhbâz Khân, the Amir-i-Tuzk, in a rude and presumptuous manner. He was severely punished,[116] though the manner of punishment is not mentioned.

In 1573, Shujâ'at Khân, who used improper language about Mun'am Khân, Khân-i-Khânân, was severely rebuked by Akbar. He was handed over to the Khân-i-Khânân for punishment or forgiveness according to his choice. The Emperor pardoned him at the intercession of Mun'am Khân who treated him with respect.[117]

A Râjpût who came as an ambassador in 1573, struck Khân-i-Kalân with a sharp weapon that pierced his breast and came out at the shoulder blade. The wound, however, did not prove fatal. The Râjput was killed instantaneously.[118]

In 1585, Mirzâ 'Aziz Kokaltâsh, the governor of Gujarat, handed over to his servant, Tâlib, his *dîwân,* who was suspected of dishonesty and embezzlement. Tâlib, on score of old enmity, beat the *Diwân* 'Alâ-ud-din so severely that he died. Khân-i-Â'zam awarded capital punishment on Tâlib by way of retaliation.[119]

On the night of 28th July, 1587, when Râjâ Todar Mal was going from the palace to his house, a person came out of ambush and struck him with a sword. He was seized and killed by the Râjâ's attendants. His accomplices were seized and awarded (capital) punishment.[120]

Ghiyas Khân who was engaged in a conflict against Mûsa Khân in Bengal, complained to the governor Islâm Khân against the misbehaviour of Bâz Bahâdur, a naval officer. Islâm Khân wrote to Bâz Bahâdur to come to him with his entire fleet. On the third day of his arrival the governor invited Bahâdur Khân to a feast of mangoes and there got him arrested. The governor then sent a report of the whole matter to the Emperor. Subsequently, the prisoner was sent to the royal court with the reports of his repeated misbehaviour. The Emperor ordered that Bâz Bahâdur Qalmaq be entrusted to some reliable officers and sent to Afzal Khân, the Bihar governor, and a letter of acknowledgment brought from him concerning the transfer of the prisoner.[121]

Mirzâ Saif-ud-din was accused of saying improper things to Sheikh Ghiyâs Khân, a Mughal *mansabdâr* in Bengâl. He indulged in jokes. He also tried to force his entry into the private chamber of the

Sheikh at night. The Sheikh put him to disgrace and in charge of trustworthy persons to be confined and carried to governor Islâm Khân. The governor cancelled his *jâgir* and put him in prison.[122]

Qulij Khân, the commander of the army in Kâbul and an important imperial officer, complained against the misbehaviour of Ahmad Beg Khân, an old retainer. Jahangir ordered that he be imprisoned in Gwalior.[123]

Sheikh Husain, the imperial envoy to Orissa, came to Akbarnagar and from there he was asked to come to Jahangirnagar (Dâca) to see the governor, Islâm Khân. Because of his intimacy with Islâm Khân from his childhood, he could not bear the arrogant attitude of the governor and indulged in a behaviour which appeared to Islâm Khân unbecoming. When brought in, he refused to perform *kornish* to Islâm Khân. Under the Governor's instructions, two officers made him bend his neck and then threw him down on his feet. When they tried to embrace each other, the governor caught hold of his beard, pulled him vehemently to his feet and gave severe blows on his shoulder. The Sheikh's beard was placed under Islâm Khân's feet and he was given a good thrashing. The report of the Sheikh's braggings was sent to the imperial court and he was kept in prison.[124]

When Sheikh Husain arrived at the imperial court and narrated his experiences to the Emperor, Islâm Khân incurred royal displeasure. The Emperor issued an ordinance in the 6th year of his reign to be observed by all the provincial governors and particularly by Islâm Khân.[125]

The *zamindârs* of Chandrakûnâ, Bayda and Jhakra submitted to Mirzâ Nathan in Bengal. He appointed his brother Murâd as a *faujdâr* of that region and ordered the *zamindârs* to accompany him to an expedition against another *zamindâr*. Chandrasen and other *zamindârs* proved disloyal, and, because of this Murâd sustained defeat and injury in leg. Mirzâ got naturally angry. When they came to see Murâd, his driver set one of the elephants upon them, as a result of which many of them were wounded or killed.[126]

Mirzâ Nathan, an important army and naval officer in Bengal, and the author of Baharistân-i-Ghâyabi, was ordered by the governor Islâm Khân, to proceed against the Mâgs. He refused to carry out the orders and instead turned a mendicant. Some thousands of his followers also became *faqîrs* and *qalandars*. He advised them to refrain from mendicancy. He put a chain round his own legs and allowed himself to be escorted to Islâm Khân under guard. To a mesenger of Islâm Khân he used harsh words and Islâm Khân kept him in confinement. He was released at the intercession of Shujâ'at Khân.[127]

After the failure of the Mâg campaign by the governor Qâsim Khân, Mukhlis Khân *dîwân,* refused to sanction any expenditure without an order from the Court. Upon this, Qâsim Khân insulted the *dîwân* and his men severely scourged one of the *dîwan's* soldiers. Mukhlis Khân reported the matter to the imperial Court. The Emperor issued orders on 8th April, 1617, for the dismissal of Qâsim Khân and the appointment in his place of Ibrâim Khân Fateh Jang as the governor of Bengâl. Ibrâhim Khân upto that time was the governor of Bihar. Qâsim Khân was directed to be sent to the imperial court to receive retributive punishment for his actions.[128]

In 1616, 'Abdulla Khân Bahâdur Firoz Jang, the governor of Gujarât, querrelled with the Bakshi 'Âbid Khân (the son of the historian Nizâm-ud-din). The ground of the quarrel was the fact that the *Bakshi* had recorded and sent to the court the account of certain events that were unpleasing to the governor. The governor sent a body of men against the *Bakshi* and insulted him by carrying him away to his house. Jahangir took the matter seriously and sent Dayânat Khân to inquire into the matter. The charge against him being proved, 'Abdulla Khân was dismissed from governorship and Muqarrab Khân was appointed in his place.[129]

Sâbit Khân was always addressing unbecoming speeches and making palpable allusions to I'timâd-ud-daulâ and his son Âsaf Khân. One night, without rhyme or reason he began to speak unpleasánt words to him and repeated them to such an extent that I'timâd-ud-daulâ felt annoyed. Next morning, Jahangir sent Sâbit Khân in the custody of a servant of Court to Âsaf Khân. He was to be shut either there or in the fort of Gwalior and was not to be released unless he made amends to Âsaf Khân's father. According to orders, Âsaf Khân sent him to the Gwalior fort.[130]

Shahjahan gave a signal for the murder of *Râo* Amar Singh Râthor, who, when offended by an imperial officer in the royal court had flung his dagger into his (officer's) breast.[131]

Sharf-ud-din, the brother of Bahrahmand Khan, holding the rank of 400 *zât* and 20 *swâr*, was removed from service for disrespect shown to Prince Mohammad Kâm Baksh.[132]

It was reported to Aurangzeb at Burhânpur on 14th December, 1681, that a day earlier, Sheikh Sa'âdatmand, brother of the Bakshi of Baklâna, had gone to the court of the imperial *dîwân* Rashid Khân was demanded from him Rs. 5,000 that fell due from him. Later on, the

Sheikh went to the house of the *dîwân,* entered into on argument with him and used harsh language. The Emperor inquired as to why the *Darogha-i-Katechery* had not chastised the Sheikh then and there. He issued orders for putting the Sheikh under the custody of Bahrahmand Khân, and for the realization of the dues from him.[133]

A mace-bearer of Prince Rafi'ul-Qadr tried to forbid some merchants to burn a dead man on the banks of the Jumnâ. The merchants attacked and wounded him. They were ordered to be put in jail till the recovery of the mace-bearer.[134]

CRITICISM OF GOVERNMENT BY PUBLIC SERVANTS

Mirzâ 'Aziz Koka criticised the branding of horses and used 'unbecoming' language. For this presumptuousness he was degraded in 1575 and was sent to Agra to be kept under surveillance in his own garden.[135]

Shâhbâz Khân, while incharge of the capital Âgra in 1581, used disrespectful language against the servants of Akbar's mother. Abul Fazl calls him 'foul-tongued' and Jahangir terms him as 'foul-mouthed and scurrilous'. Under Akbar's orders she was sent to prison in the custody of Râl Sâl Darbâri for three years.[136]

In Jahangir's time a letter was discovered which was alleged to have been written by Khân-i-Â'zam Mirzâ 'Aziz Koka to Râja 'Ali Khân, the governor of Khândesh. The letter was full of abusive language against Akbar and Jahangir. After confirming the truth, Jahangir punished him by depriving him of his *jâgir*. According to De Laet, he was treated with the greatest ignominy, loaded with chains, and sent off as a prisoner to the Gwalior fort. He was released and restored to favour after two years.[137]

In 1623, 'Abdulla, the son of Nûr-ud-din, was accused of using disrespectful language against Jahangir in 'assemblies and companies'. After the charge was confirmed in his absence, he was summoned to the Court by the Emperor and ordered to be executed.[138]

In 1667, Mukarram Khân enjoying a *mansab* of 5,000 *zât* and 4,000 *swâr* was replaced by Mâ'sum Khân, as the *faujdâr* of Oudh, and given a *mansab*of 2,000 and 1,200. Mâ'sûm Khân refused the offer on the ground that though having the same nature of work to do, he was to hold a lower rank. Fo raising this objection, Aurangzeb punished Mâ'sûm Khân with diminution of rank.[139]

LEAVE WITHOUT PERMISSION

In 1615, Qizalbâsh Khân, a Gujarât official, came to the court without permission of the governor. In order to set an example to others, Jahangir ordered him to be put in confinement and sent back to the governor of Gujarât.[140] There is no mention of the treatment meted out to him by the governor.

In 1621, 'Abdulla Khân went to his father without the permission of Shahjahan, the governor of the Deccan. Jahângir ordered the Chief *Dîwân* to deprive him of his *jâgîr.* I'timâd Râi was ordered to act as a *sazâwal* and send him back to the Deccan.[141]

It was ordered by Jahangir that as Qâsim Beg had left Bengal without imperial permission, he was to be put in chains and in that condition was to be taken to the governor of Bihar who was to send him on to the *subedâr* of Bengal in the same manner. After some time Qâsim Beg petitioned the Emperor for mercy. His appeal was accepted and orders for his release issued. On receipt of the orders, the governor of Bengal Qâsim Khân, removed the chains of Qâsim Beg, conferred the rank of 100 personnel and 50 horse and a *jâgîr* upon him.[142]

Some of the officers of the *thânas* came to the capital of Bengâl, Jahângirnagar (Dâca), without permission of the governor. Qâsim Khân ordered them to go back. They replied that the previous governor Islâm Khân, had increased their *mansab* and yet assignments had not been made. They would go back only after the needful had been done. Qâsim Khân (governor : 1614-16) reported the matter to the imperial court. Jahangir punished both the officers, Mubâriz Khân and Mirak Bahâdur, by cancelling their titles of Khân and Bahâdur respectively. Moreover, it was ordered that if before the arrival of that peremptory order, both the *thânedârs* did not return to their *thânas,* the officiating governor, Khwâjâ Mohammad Tâhir (provincial Bakshi) was to confiscate their *jâgîr* and was to go personally as a *sazâwal* and imprison both of them in the *thâna* and report the matter to the imperial court. The *thânedârs*, however, had returned to the *thânas* before the arrival of the royal *farmân.* Under orders of the governor. Khwâjâ Tâhir Mohammad, reinstated their *jâgîrs* and reported the matter to the imperial court.[143]

At a *ghusalkhâna* court at Dipâlpur in Mâlwa on 25th October, 1681, it was reported to Aurangzeb that horsemen, foot-soldiers and servants had gone to Delhi without obtaining regular permission. The emperor ordered Bahrahmand Khân that the *faujdârs* and *zamindârs* of the districts falling on the way should be warned that only those persons should be allowed to pass who had in their possession the written permission of Ihtimm Khân. Any person trying to pass without such a document (*dastak*) was to be sent to the royal court.[144]

Previously it had been ordered that the written permission for Delhi and other places should be given by Ihtimâm Khân *kotwâl*. Now it was decided that it could bear the seal of Umdtul-mulk Asad Khân also.[145]

INFRINGEMENT OF ROYAL PREROGATIVES

The infringement of royal prerogative was considered an offence. The charge of the commission of the crime was usually levied against the governors of the provinces who seemed anxious to play the king. An offender found it difficult to escape the punishment if his guilt was brought to the notice of the Emperor.[146] Usually he was punished by degradation in rank. Some time only censure would do.

The wearing of umbrella was a royal privilege and none could violate it without meriting punishment.[147]

It was a Mughal regulation that no one could carry his quiver in his hand. His hunting ground was also a taboo for others. Any one entering it was made a slave.[148]

It was an established convention that after a victory the articles of plunder and the women belonging to the enemy, came in the possession of the Emperor. Some time royal commanders infringed this rule, and, without the knowledge of the Emperor, kept the elephants, valuables and women to themselves. This was done by Khân Zamân 'Ali Quli Khân and Bahâdur Khân after their victory over Sher Khân in Jaunpur (1561), by Adham Khân after defeating Bâz Bahâdur in Mâlwa (1561) and by Âsaf Khân after the Garha victory. As soon as the matter was reported to the Emperor, the generals were usually obliged to part with their prizes.[149]

It was ordered by Jahangir that Mahâbat Khân should return all the elephants captured in Bengal in 1624.[150]

To give the Emperor uninvited advice was also regarded as an offence and was punished accordingly. A royal servant Khâksâr Sultân, had the audacity of suggesting to Akbar in 1564 that he should give up expedition against 'Abdulla Khân Uzbeg in Mâlwa. The Emepror became furious and attacked him with a sword. Somehow Akbar overpowered his anger and spared his life.[151]

Qâzi Tawaisi represented to Akbar in 1567 that to capture and kill

Khân Zamân's people and to confiscate their goods and chattels after the victory, was not in accordance with the Holy Law. (A similar advice was tendered by Badâûni to Mullâ Pir Mohammad Sherwâni in 1562). For this unsought-for advice the *qâzi* was removed from his post.[152]

Qâzi 'Abdulla pleaded with Aurangzeb to stop the war of aggresson against Golconda and avoid unnecessary bloodshed. As this advice was not sought for and was unpalatable to the Emperor, the *qâzi* was forbidden the court.[153]

Hunting of lion was a special royal prerogative.[154]

During a royal hunt in 1610, when Jahangir had got within a shot of a *nîlgâo,* a groom and a carrier appeared suddenly. In a fit of rage the Emperor ordered to kill the groom on the spot and to hamstring the carrier. They were to be mounted on asses and paraded through the camp, so that no one in the future might infringe the royal prerogative in this manner.[155]

In 1666, the hunters complained to Aurangzeb that Bahâdur Khân had pitched his tents in hunting ground and as a result the game had dispersed from there. The Emperor ordered Himmat Khân to send twenty mace-bearers in order to remove the tents and the men of the army from there.[156]

In 1667, hunters reported to Aurangzeb that the large number of cultivators had cultivated the land earmarked for the royal hunt. They, moreover, had cut down the jungle. Orders were given to Niâz Beg, the mace-bearer, to bring them bound to the court. He accordingly brought some of these persons who were entrusted to Dârâb Khân.[157]

When Mandelslo was at Ahmedâbâd, a new kind of cloth which was a mixture of silk and cotton, interwoven with flowers of gold was being manufactured there. None was allowed to use it as it was reserved for the special use of the Emperor.[157a]

After a successful campaign against 'Usmân of Bukainagar, Islâm Khân, the governor of Bengâl, assumed imperial prerogatives. He ordered a platform to be constructed which was higher than the height of two men and built a small house on it and called it *jharoka.* He, moreover, ordered that the high officers who could not mount guard, were to send one of their sons or near relatives in their place for the purpose. They were to pass their time in the night at the royal house-guard. He ordered that the other officers should make their obesiance at the *qûr* (standard). Mirzâ Saif-ud-din refused to do so and was imprisoned by Islâm Khân's Bakshi. Despite the strict orders of the Emperor against such malpractices, Islâm Khân continued the infringement of the royal prerogatives with impunity.[158]

In the sixth year of his reign, Jahangir issued regulations known as the Âin-i-Jahângiri with regard to the royal prerogatives. The border officers were ordered not to sit in *jharoka,* to see elephant fights or to confer titles. They were asked not to trouble their officers with keeping guard and saluting them. They were forbidden to inflict punishment of blinding and cutting off ears and noses of criminals. They were not to force Islam on any person. They were prohibited from ordering royal servants from doing *kornish* or *taslîm*. They were asked not to force singers to remain on duty in the manner customary in the royal court. They were not to beat drum when they went out or when they gave horses or elephants to others. They were not to place reins or elephants' goads on their backs and make them perform obeisance. While going in procession they were ordered to see that they did not take with them on foot in their retinue the royal attendants. When they wrote to their subordinates, they were to avoid affixing their seal.[159]

The use of scarlet tent by any one except the king was regarded an offence.[160]

Shahjahan had granted Prince Dârâ special royal prerogatives which he had denied to any other Prince. He could cause elephants to fight according to his desire. He was authorised to display in his presence gold and silver maces. Dârâ was permitted to sit on a small throne placed near his own, though the Prince did not use it out of respect for his father. The officers had been ordered first to go to the heir-apparent Dârâ for their morning bow and to come to the king's audience only after that.[161]

To award capital punishment was an important royal prerogative. In case the offender was at a distant place, the crime was thoroughly determined before the pronouncement of the punishment.[162]

It was reported to Aurangzeb that while holding court, Prince Mu'azzam had ordered four kettle-drums to be beaten. For this offence he was censured.[163]

He was reprimanded for having ordered an elephant fight.[164]

Ibrâhim Khân, governor of Gujarât, infringed the royal prerogative by going to the *jâma'* mosque in a *pâlaki.* He was administered rebuke by Aurangzeb.[165]

Aurangzeb learnt that while holding court, Prince Bahâdur Shâh used to sit on a platform raised one yard above the ground. Mace-bearers were ordered to go and force him to come down from his seat in the open court and pull down the platform.[166]

Another report regarding the same Prince came from Kâbul. It was alleged that during the performance of traditional prayers in the *jâma masjid,* the Prince used to set up canvas screens. Aurangzeb ordered that an inquiry be made into the matter, and, in case the report was confirmed the Prince be removed from the governorship of the province and be sent into the royal presence.[167]

Aurangzeb ordered on 26th February, 1701, that none should hoist a flag in the imperial army.[68]

DISTURBANCE OF PEACE; AND RIOT IN THE REALM

To cause disturbance of peace or riot constituted an offence and was punished as such.

During Akbar's expedition to Gujarat in 1572, some mischief mongers spread the false news that the Emperor had issued an order for the plundering of the camp of the Gujartis. The royal soldiers started plundering the camp and a great commotion ensued. When the matter was reported to Akbar, he summoned the high officers and ordered them to inflict punishment on the plunderers and put to death those who were found in possession of the loot. He himself held a public court and ordered that fierce elephants be brought there. The rioters were taken before the Emperor and trampled under the feet of the elephants. The goods were returned to the owners and order was restored.[169]

In the Deccan where Prince Parwez was the governor, an incident occurred in 1623, which led to a serious quarrel between the Sayyids of Barah and the Râjpûts. The servants of Sayyid Kabir Barah, an attendant of Prince Parwez, struck a cutler some blows with a stick after exchange of a few hot words about the charges of sharpening the sword of Sayyid Kabir. The men of Râja Girdhar who happened to be there, used their whips on the Sayyid's servants. More Sayyids came from the neighbourhood and a regular fight started between the Sayyids and the Râjpûts, with arrows and swords. Hearing this, Sayyid Kabir came with thirty or forty horsemen in order to assist his people. At this time, Râja Girdhar and his people, all bare-bodied, were taking their meals in their house. Becoming aware of the violence of the Sayyids. Râja Girdhar brought his men inside the house, and closed the door. The Sayyids came and set fire to the door, forced their way in and attacked the inmates. They killed the Râja along with twenty-six of his men and wounded forty more. Four of the Sayyids were killed. After this, Sayyid Kabir took from the Râja's stable all his horses and returned to his house. On learning of this tragedy, the Râjpûts came out of their houses and from the other side the Sayyids began to collect in the plain outside the citadel, in order to have a pitched fight. Immediately afterwards Mahâbat Khân came on the spot, brought the Sayyids inside the citadel, soothed the Râjpûts, took their chief men and went to the house of the Khân-i-Khânân nearby. The Prince also reached there and calmed the Râjpûts. Mahâbat Khân became a security for an inquiry into the matter. Next day he contrived to get hold of Sayyid Kabir and put him into confinement. The Râjpûts were satisfied only when Sayyid Kabir was executed by way of punishment.[170]

During Aurangzeb's reign, a terrible famine occurred in 1685 A.D. in the province of Gujarat. One day the crowd attacked Mohammad Amin Khan, the governor of the Province, when he was going in a procession to the mosque for the *'Îd* prayers. The people accused him of indifference to the terrible misery that had befallen them. The mob under one Abu Bakr attacked the procession. The soldiers put up a brave defence but the foresight of the governor prevented them from committing excesses. Aurangzeb felt incensed at the news of the incident and ordered that the offenders be executed. Mohammad Amin took resort to wisdom, only picked up Abu Bakr and treacherously made him swallow poison.[171]

When four years later another famine visited Gujarat, the angry mob attacked Sheikh Muhi-ud-din, the *Sadr,* while on his way to the *Jâma'* Mosque and tore his *pâlaki* to pieces. He himself reached home unhurt. The Sheikh while reporting the matter to the Emperor, accused Khwâjâ 'Abdulla, the *qâzi* of the city, of having stirred the trouble.[172] Nothing came out of the complaint.

Riots between *Shi'as* and *Sunnis* were not unusual occurrences. Thevenot witnessed such a quarrel in Golcunda. A Târtâr spoke against Husain. *Shi'as* fell upon him. In the melee that ensued seven persons were killed outright. 'At that time there is no inquiry made into man-slaughter, because the Moors believe that, during these ten days, the Gates of Paradise are open to receive those who die for the *Musselman* faith.[173]

Referring to a *Shi'a* procession witnessed by him during his ıtenary of India, Fryer writes that when in the streets two 'Companies encounter, they seldom apart without bloody Noses.'[4]

Khâfi Khân has referred to a *Shi'a-Sunni* riot in Burhânpur in 1669 A.D. between the residents of Ahdipura and Khirkipurâ. A rivalry and hostility between the two had been a regular feature since long. This time a serious fight took place near the *Jâma' Masjid.* A large number of spectators also joined the Khikipurâ people. The crowd climbed upon the roofs of the houses and rained the tiles upon their rivals in such abundance that the houses became tile-less. This attack resulted in the death of about 50 and injury to about 100 Ahdipura people. Their property worth Rs. 50,000 in the form of precious clothes and pearls spent on the *ta'zia* tombs was completely damaged. When the report of the riot was conveyed to the *Sunni* Emperor, he stopped the making of tombs of the martyers and carrying them in procession.[174]

FIGHTS AMONG IMPERIAL OFFICERS

There are frequent references in the News Letters to the mutual quarrels among the royal officers requiring the intervention of the Emperor.

In the *dîwân-i-khâs* of 17th May, 1695, Sharif Khân submitted to the Emperor the petition of Sarâji, *thânedâr* of Kâkil, adjacent to the *thâna* of Kolhapur. The complainant had gone to fetch ammunition for the artillery of Lutfulla Khân. In his absence, Anwar Khân, the *thânedâr* of Kolhapur, came to his *thâna,* killed some persons and captured a large number of others. He also carried away cash and grain and cattle to the amount of Rs. 25,000 and set up his own *thâna* there. The Emperor ordered that Lutfulla Khân should be asked to investigate into the matter and report.[175]

In the *dîwân-i-khâs* of 2nd June, 1695, the *vakîl* of Jamshed Khân submitted that 'Izzat Beg, son of Jahângir Quli Khân, had ravaged the *jâgir* of his client and carried away cash and grain. The Emperor ordered that the Chief Bakshi Bahrahmand Khân should write to Jahângir Quli Khân to get the *jâgîr* restored to the complainant and see that the offence was not repeated again.[176]

A matchlockman quarrelled with the son of commandant 'Abdul Ghafâr, killed him and wounded two persons. He was in turn killed by the servants of the commandant. The Emperor acceded to the request of the commandant for the transfer of all the matchlockmen from there.[177]

Three *mansabdârs* accused of having fought with some persons, killing three and wounding two, were deprived of their ranks under the orders of the Emperor.[178]

As a result of a fight between the men of Khân Bahâdur and those of 'Ali Mardân Khân at Burhânpur in November 1703, a number of casualties were reported of dead and wounded. As punishment, Khân Bahâdur suffered diminution of 200 *zât* in rank.[179]

On 26th October, 1703, the applicaton of Sayyid Zain-ul-'Âbdin was placed before the Emperor. He had complained therein that Aurang

Khân, commandant and *faujdâr* of Fateh Ahad alias Dahâru, had collected revenue from his *jâgir*. The Emperor ordered that one mace-bearer be posted to see that whatever amount of money had been seized, was to be returned to the *gumâshta* of the said Khân.[180]

On a news of a quarrel between 'Abdul Salâm *kotwâl* of Delhi and 'Abdul Qâsim *dîwân,* orders were issued on 24th March, 1704, for the transfer of the *kotwâl* and of the appointment in his place of 'Ali Mir *kotwâl* of Âgra.[181]

A quarrel was reported to have taken place between Mubârakrû Suhbat Yasâwal and Shukarullâh Khân. The former was holding the rank of 400 *zât* and 40 *swâr*. He was punished with the reduction of 100 in his *zât.*[182]

Again, there was a fight between the two in September 1704. This time he was deprived of his rank along with his brother. Sarbrâh Khân *kotwâl* was ordered to seize from them arms and horses, and to deposit arms in *Morkhâna* and horses in the stable.[183]

An argument between Dayânat Râo and Munirâm over arrears of pay developed in a serious quarrel resulting in an attack with *jamdhar* by Munirâm's son on Dayânat Râo and another person. Orders for investigation and report were issued.[184]

On the report of a civil war between Suleimân Khân *thânedâr* of Karâbâd and *thânedâr* Khwâja Khân resulting in the death of many persons and injury to four others, their ranks were reduced.[185]

I'tibâr Khân, the dismissed *mutassadi* of Surat, was accused of causing obstruction to his successor, Najâbat Khân. Muttalib Khân, the *dârogha* of mace-bearers, was ordered to send one mace-bearer to fetch the offender to the court.[186]

BREACH OF COURT ETIQUETTES

In 1560, while Akbar was on his way to the Punjab, Shâh Abul Ma'âli, in the *pargana* of Jhajar, wanted to saluet him while seated on his horse. Akbar felt annoyed and handed him over to Shahâb-ud-din Ahmad Khân to be kept in custody as a prisoner.[187]

In 1571, Lashkar Khân came to the court drunk and made a disturbance. When the matter came to the knowledge of Akbar, he ordered Lashkar Khân to be tied to the tail of a horse, to be led around and then sent to the prison.[188]

REFERENCES

1. Akbar Nâma, Text, II, pp. 201-2; Beveridge, II, pp. 312-13.
   Badâuni, Lowe, I, p. 60; Text, II, p. 62;
   Tabaqât, II, pp. 275-6; Text II, p. 167.
   Farishta; II, p. 337.
2. Akbar Nâmâ Beveridge, II, p. 509; Text p. 349.
3. Akbar Nâmâ, Bev., III, p. 441. Text, III, p. 298.
4. Tuzk, R. & B., I, pp. 122-23; Text, J. p. 59;
   Iqbâlnâmâ, p. 20; Text, pp. 28-29; De Laet, p. 177.
   Eliot & Dowson, VI, pr. 315-16.
5. Ma'âsir-i-'Âlamgîrî, Text, p. 127.
6. Ma'âsir-i-Âlamgîrî, Test, p. 127.
7. *Ibid.*, p. 154.
8. *Ibid.*, p. 155.
9. Jaipur Akhbârât, 23rd year.
10. Manucci, II, pp. 247; 248; 249.
11. Ma'âsir-i-'Âlamgîrî, Text, p. 344.
12. Ma'âsir-i-'Âlamgîrî, Text, p. 120.
13. Manucci, II, pp. 223-24; 319-20.
14. Akbar Nâmâ, Bev, II, pp. 107-8, Text, p. 70. Tabaqât, II, Text, p. 138.
    Eliot & Dowson, VI, p. 257.
15. Akbar Nâmâ, Bev., II, pp. 107-8, Text, p. 70. Tabaqât, II, Text, p. 138.
    Eliot & Dowson, VI, p. 257.
16. Akbar Nâmâ, Text. III, p. 9-10; 11; Beveridge, III, pp. 13-15.
17. Badauni, ext, II, pp. 51; 97-100; p. 148-49; Lowe, II, pp. 38,48, 149.
18. Akbar Nâmâ, Text, III. pp, 36-38.
    Badâûni, Text, II, pp. 151-61; Lowe, II, pp. 158-59;
    Tabaqât, Text, II, p. 255; p. 260;
    Farishta, Text, I, p. 496.
19. Akbar Nâmâ, Text, III, pp. 36-38.
    Badâuni, Text, II, pp. 15161; Lowe, II, pp. 158-59.
    Tabaqat, Text, II, p. 255; p. 260.
    Farishta, Text, I, p. 496.
20. *Ibid.*
21. Tabaqât, Text, II, pp. 271-72; De, II, p. 417;
    Farishta, Text, I, p. 496; (Urdu), II, pp. 356-58;
    Badâuni, Text, II, pp. 167-68;
    Tuzk, Text, I, p. 21; Bev, I, p. 44.
22. Akbar Nâmâ, Text, III, p. 213, Bev, III, p. 300.
23. Badâûni, Text, II, pp. 277-77; Lowe, II, pp. 284-85.
    Akbar Nâmâ, Text, III, p. 309; Bev., III, p. 455.
24. Akbar Nâmâ, *Ibid.*, Badâûnî, Text, II, p. 280; Lowe, II, p. 289.
25. Akbar Nâmâ, Text, III, pp. 374-75.

26. *Ibid.*, Text, III. p. 397.
27. Tuzk, Beveridge, I, pp. 51-59; 61-62; 64; 66-68; 70; 72; 174; Iqbal Nâmâ, pp. 7, 11; pp. 16, 17, 19; Tuzk, Text, pp. 24, 35; 84-85; De Laet, pp. 173-76; The Embassy, p. 236; Khâfi Khân, Text, p. 253 Eliot & Dowson, VI, pp. 267-68; 273-74; 292-96; 300; 401, 448-49.
28. Tuzk, Bev., I, pp. 72-73; Persian Text, p. 35.
29. Bahâristan, I, pp. 107; 114.
30. Tuzk, Tr., I, pp. 258-59.
31. Eliot & Dowson, VI, p. 374.
32. Tuzk, Tr. II, p. 276.
33. Mirât-i-Ahmadi, . 280;
Âinâ-i-Gujârât, I, pp. 168-69;
Mughal Administration, p. 126.
34. Manucci, II, pp. 193-94;
English Factories, 1665-67, p. 287.
35. Muntakhib-ul-Lubâb, Text, II, p. 124.
36. *Ibid.*, pp. 331-33.
37. Ma'âsir-i-'Âlamgîrî, Text, p. 243.
38. Akhbârât-i-Darbâr-i-Mu'allâ, 24th January, 1700.
39. *Ibid.* 22nd February, 1703.
40. *Ibid.*, 12th April, 1704.
41. Monserrate, p. 189.
42. Jaipur Akhbârât, 30th Oct. 1666.
43. Jaipur Akhbârât, 3rd Sept. 1667.
44. *Ibid.*, 25th year, 14th June, 682.
45. A Pepys of Moghul India, p. 189.
46. Akbar Nâma, Bev., III, pp. 501-3, Text, III, pp. 342-43.
Badâûni, Lowe, II, p. 301; Text, II, pp. 292-93,
Farishta, II, p. 365; Text, I, p. 502.
Monserrate, pp. 64, 68, 98-99.
47. Tuzk, Tr., II, p. 249. Text, II, p. 362.
48. Tuzk, Tr., II, p. 297, Text, II, p. 391.
49. Manucci, I, p. 255.
50. Manucci, III, pp. 270-72.
51. Ma'âsir-i-'Âlamgîrî, text, p. 204.
52. Manucci, I, pp. 325, 344;
Ma'âsir-ul-Umarâ, p. 670.
53. Manucci, III, p. 270.
54. Akbar Nâmâ, Bev., II, pp. 51-52; Text, pp. 32-33;
Tabaqât, De, pp. 215, 654; Text, II, pp. 130-31;
Badâûni, Lowe, II, pp. 6-7; Text, II, pp. 14, 50;
Farishta, II, pp. 315-316; Text, I, pp. 363-64.
55. Akbar Nâmâ, Bev., II, pp. 258-59; Text, pp. 162-63.
56. Monserrate, pp. 209-10.

57. Akbar Nâmâ, Bev. III, 585-86; Text, p. 396; Eliot & Dowson, V, p. 467.
58. Badâûni, Lowe, II, p. 151; Text, II, p. 147.
Farishta, II, p. 355. Text, I, pp. 493-94.
59. Tuzk, Tr., I, pp. 29-30. Text, I. p. 13.
60. *Ibid.*, p. 127. Text, I, p. 61.
61. *Ibid.*, p. 173. Text, pp. 84-85, Eliot & Dowson, VI, p. 32.
62. Iqbal Nâmâ, Text, pp. 239-40; Urdu : pp. 166-67.
63. Bahâristan, II, pp. 784-85.
64. Peter Mundy, II, pp. 202-203.
65. Sarkar's Aurangzeb, Vols. I & II, pp. 574-76.
66 Bernier, I, pp. 97-98; Manucci, I, pp. 337-38; English Factories, 1665-69, p. 289; Eliot & Dowson, VII, pp. 249-51; Ma'âsir-i-Âlamgîrî, pp. 17,m 20, 22; Tavernier, I, pp. 360-61, 367; Riâz-ul-Salâtîn, p. 216.
67. Manucci, I, p. 198.
68. Akbar Nâma, Bev, II, p. 28-30; Text, pp. 16-17.
Tabaqât, De, II, pp. 276-79; Text, II, p. 127.
Eliot & Dowson, V, p. 264; Farishta, II, p. 313, Text, I, p. 261.
69. Âîn, (Blochman), p. 139; pp. 148-49.
70. Akbar Nâmâ, Bev, III, p. 23; Text, III, p. 15.
71. *Ibid.*, p. 149. Text, III, p. 107.
72. *Ibid.*, p. 155; Txt, III, p. 111.
73. *Ibid.*, pp. 274-5. Text, III, pp. 194-95.
74. Tuzk, R., & B. I, p. 180.
75. Bahâristân Vol. I, pp. 140-41; 142.
76. *Ibid.*, I, pp. 144-45.
77. *Ibid.*, II, pp. 770-71.
78. Tuzk, I, Tr. p. 373.
79. Tuzk, Bev, II, pp. 37-38. Text, II, p. 246.
80. Eliot & Dowson, VII, p. 69.
81. Riâz-ul-Salâtin, pp. 207-8.
82. Muntakhib-ul-Lubâb, I, pp. 583-84.
83. Manucci, I, p. 202.
84. Manucci, I, p. 381.
85. Orme, p. 25.
86. Eliot & Dowson, VII, pp. 310.
87. Letters, XIC, p. 108-9.
88. Letters, CXIX, p. 119.
89. Anecdotes, p. 68.
90. Anecdotes, p. 74.
91. Akhbârât, 29th yar.
92. Akhbârât-i-Darbâr-i-Mu'allâ, 8th January, 1693.
93. *Ibid.*, 24th April, 1693.
94. *Ibid.*, 27th November, 1693..

95. *Ibid.*, 26th February, 1701.
96. *Ibid.*, 8th June, 1701.
97. *Ibid.*, 11th September, 1701.
98. Akhbârât-i-Darbâr-i-Mu'allâ, May 6, 1701.
99. Akhbârât-i-Darbâr-i-Mu'allâ, 3rd March, 1703.
100. *Ibid.*, 28th November, 1703.
101. *Ibid.*, 12th June, 1704.
102. *Ibid.*, 25th January, 1705.
103. Monserrate's Commentary, pp. 82-83.
104. Akbar Nâmâ, Text, III, p. 147;
Ibid., Tr., III, pp. 208-9.
105. Tuzk, Tr., I, pp. 286-87.
106. Bahâristan, I, p. 224.
107. *Ibid.*, p. 374.
108. Ma'âsir-i-'Âlamgîrî, Text, p. 155.
109. Jaipur Akhbârât, 25th November, 1706.
110. Manucci, IV, p. 170.
111. Akbar Nâmâ, Bev., II, pp. 131-32; Text, p. 86;
Tabaqât, De, p. 132; Text, II, p. 146.
Farishta, II, pp. 321-22; Text, I, p. 370.
112. Akbar Nâmâ, Bev., II, pp. 175-76; Text, p. 114.
113. *Ibid.*, pp. 261-62, Text, pp. 169-70.
114. *Ibid.*, p. 417; Text, p. 282; Tabaqât, De, II, pp. 328-29; ext, II. p. 207.
115. Akbar Nâmâ, II, p. 420; Text, p. 284; III, p. 387, ev., Text, III, p. 266.
Tabaqât, De, II, p. 328-29. Text, II, p. 207.
116. Akbar Nâmâ, II, Bev., p. 538. Text, p. 370.
117. *Ibid.*, Bev. III. pp. 89; 120. Text, pp. 64; 85.
118. Badâûni, Lowe, II, p. 144. Text, II, p. 140.
119. Akbar Nâmâ, Bev. III, p. 387. Text, III, p. 266.
120. Akbar Nâmâ, Bev. III, pp. 792-93. text, III, pp. 519-20.
Badâûni, Lowe, p. 377. Text, II, p. 365.
121. Bahâristan, I, pp. 91, 96.
122. *Ibid.*, p. 125-126.
123. Tuzk, Tr., I, p. 279.
124. Bahâristân, I, pp. 132-33.
125. *Ibid.*, pp. 213.
126. *Ibid.*, pp. 139-40.
127. *Ibid.*, pp. 147-63.
128. Bahâristân, pp. 409; 419.
129. Tuzk, Bev., I, pp. 330-31. Text I, pp. 162-63.
130. *Ibid.*, pp. 278-79. Text, I, p. 137.
131. Manucci, I, pp. 207-8;
Ma'sr-ul-umarâ, II, pp. 230-732.
132. Akhbârât-i-Darbâr-i-Mu'allâ, 14th November, 1681.

133. Akhbârât-i-Darbâr-i-Mu'allâ, 14th December, 1681.
134. *Ibid.*, 16th April, 1696.
135. Akbar Nâmâ, Bev. III, p. 209; Text, p. 148.
137. *Ibid.*, pp. 550-51, Text., p. 375.
137. Tuzk, Bev., I,pp. 79-81; Text, p. 39.
Badâûni, Lowe, II, p. 333, Text, II, p. 323;
Iqbâlnâmâ, pp. 19-20, Text, p. 14; De Laet, p. 179;
Muntakhib-ul-Lubâb, I, p. 256.
138. Muntakhib-ul-Lubâb, I, pp. 286-87. Iqbâlnâmâ, p. 147; Text. p. 213
Tuzk, Tr. II. pp. 286-87.
139. Jaipur Akhbârât, 3th April, 1667.
140. Tuzk, Text, I, I, p. 143; Bev., I, p. 289.
141. *Ibid.*, p. 342; Bev., II, p. 217.
142. Baharistân, I, pp. 264; 320.
143. Bahâristan I. pp. 271-72.
144. Akhbârât-i-Darbâr-i-M'ullâ, 25th October, 1681.
145. *Ibid.*
146. cf. Sarkar's Mughal Administratioı for a description of prerogatives, pp. 129-31.
147. Ovington, pp. 185-86.
148. Akbar Nâmâ, Bev., III, p. 974; Text, p. 635.
149. Farishta, II, pp. 320-32, 339.
150. Iqbâl Nâmâ, Bev., III, pp. 17-73. Text, pp. 252-53.
Akbar Nâmâ, pp. 215, 323-30, Text, II, pp. 208-13.
151. Akbar Nâmâ, II, p. 347, Text, p. 226.
152. Badâûni, Text, II, pp. 100-101;
Lowe, II, p. 104.
153. Muntakhib-ur-Lubâb, Text, II, p. 343.
154. Bernier, II, p. 115. Roe's Journal, p. 365,
155. Tuzk, Bev., I, p. 164.
156. Jaipur Akhbârât, Oct., 23, 1666.
157. *Ibid.*, Aug., 20, 1667.
Mandelslo, pp. 26-27.
158. Bahâristân, I, pp. 120; 213-15.
159. Tuzk, Tr., I, p. 205; See Bahâristân, I, pp. 213-15.
160. Manucci, I, p. 137.
161. Manucci, I, p. 224.
162. Ovington, p. 138.
163. Ancedotes, p. 58.
164. *Ibid.*, pp. 59-60.
165. *Ibid.*, pp. 123-24.
166. *Ibid.*, p. 60.
167. *Ibid.*, pp. 58-59.
168. Akhbârât-i-Darbâr-i-Mu'allâ, 26.2.1701.

169. Akbar Nâmâ, Beveridge, III, p. 11.
170. Tuzk, II, Bev., pp. 283-84.
171. Mirât-i-Ahmadi, I, pp. 182-82.
172. *Ibid.* p. 186. text, II, p. 383.
173. Indian Travels of Thevenot, p. 149.
174. Fryer, p. 273.
Muntakhib-ul-Lubâb, Text, II, pp. 213-14.
175. Akhbârât-i-Darbâr-i-Mu'allâ, 17th May, 1695.
176. *Ibid.*, 2nd June, 1695.
177. *Ibid.*, 15th November, 1695.
178. Akhbârât-i-Darbâr-i-Mu'allâ, 17th April, 1696.
179. Akhbârât, 25th November, 1703.
180. Akhbârât-i-Darbâr-i-Mu'allâ, 27th Nov., 1703.
181. *Ibid.*, 27th March, 1704.
182. *Ibid.*, 15th July., 1704.
183. *Ibid.*, 20th September, 1704.
184. *Ibid.*, 7th Oct., 1704.
185. Akhbârât-i-Darbâr-i-Mu'allâ, 20th Oct., 1704.
186. *Ibid.*, 19th January, 1704.
187. Tabaqât, De. II, p. 242; Text, II, p. 146.
Farishta, II, pp. 324-25. Text, I, p. 469.
188. Akbar Nâmâ, Bev., II, pp. 534-35; Text, p. 368.

BIBLIOGRAPHY

1. (a) PERSIAN MANUSCRIPTS (National Library Calcutta)

AKHBÂRÂT-I-DARBÂR-I-MU'ALLÂ AND THE 'ARÂIZ-O-FARÂMÎN

Court bulletins or the Imperial gazettes (*Akhbârât*) of the Mughal Government containing brief records of daily occurrences at the Mughal *darbâr* and the news-letters (*'Arâiz-o-farâmîn*) from the Imeprial Court despatched by the representatives of the Princes, Râjas and governors. These volumes are copies of the original preserved in the following libraries :

1. Royal Asiatic Society of Great Britain and Ireland.
2. Jaipur State Archives, which forms a large portion of such *Akhbârât.*
3. Raghubir Library, Sitamau (M.P.)

Volume I It consists of 427 pages and contains records of the following dates—
November, 1679; September 1680; Oct., 1681; March 168 Feb. 1695; May 1696; March 1703; July, November, December, 1704., May-sept. 1705.

Volume II 542 pages, 20 cm.
1681 July-December.

Volume III 146 pages 20 cm.
1658 May-June.
1688 April-August-October.
1689 July and November.

Volume IV 162 pages 22 cm.
1692 Oct.-December.
1693 January-October, December.
1694 March-April.

Volume V 224 pages 20.5 cm.
1692 November

1693 March, April, May, October.
1694 March
1695 January, February, March.
1696 March, April, May.

Volume VI 542 pages, 20 cm.
1694 June-December.
1695 January; April-June
The 38th year of Aurangzeb's rule.
A transcript of the Royal Asiatic Society of London Manuscript.

Volume VII 199 pages, 20.5 cm.
1695 April-December.
1696 January-March.
The 39th year of Aurangzeb's reign.

Volume VIII 92 pages, 20.5 cm.
1696 March-June.

Volume IX 350 pages 21.5 cm.
1699 April-December.
1700 January-February.

Volume X 402 pages, 22 cm.
1700 February-December.
1701 January.

Volume XI 374 pages 20 cm.
1701 January-December
1702 January

Volume XII 565 pages, 23.5 cm.
1702 January-December.
1703 January-October.

Volume XIII 696 pages, 21 cm.
1703 January-December

Volume XIV 362 pages, 21 cm.
1703 June
1704 October-December.
Pages 192-233 in Devnagri Script.

Volume XV 248 pages, 21.5 cm.
1703 December only
1704 January; July.

Volume XVI 284 pages, 22 cm.
1704 July-December.

Volume XVII 126 pages, 22 cm.

	1705	January-April.
Volume XVIII	193 pages, 21 cm.	
	1706	October-December,
	1707	January only
Volume XIX	44 pages, 21.5 cm.	
	1707	February.
Volume XXI	375 pages, 23 cm.	
	Miscellaneous entries of the following years—	
	1665	October-December.
	1666	May; October; December.
	1667	January; March; April.
	1669	February; September; October; December.
	1670	January; April; May.
	1671	January; March.
	1672	October; November
	1674	June; August.
	1676	December.
	1677	February; August.

Volume XXVII 174 pages, 20.5 cm.

Being letters from Prince Dârâ Shikoh, his son Suleimân Shikoh and Emperor Aurangzeb to Mirzâ Râjâ Jai Singh, Jaswant Singh and others.

Volume XXVIII 230 pages, 22 cm.

Being news of the court of Prince Mohammad Â'zam Shâh, governor of Gujarat during the 46th, 47th, 48th and 49th years of Aurangzeb's reign.

'ARÂIZ-O-FARÂMÎN

Volume I **300 pages, 20.5 cm.**

Being news-letters of the Imperial Court referring to the following dates chiefly drafted by Munshi Kanwal Nain, one of the *vakîls* of the court.

1681	July and October.
1683	April; June; July; October.

Volume II 472 pages, 20.5 cm.

Being news-letters from the Imperial court referring to the following dates chiefly drafted by Munshi Megh Râj and Kesho Râi, *vakâls* of the *darbâr*—

1684	August
1688	September; October; December.

1689 December
1690 January
1692 March; April.
1693 March.

Volume III 286 pages, 20.5 cm.

Being news-letters from the imperial court drafted by Munshi Megh Râj, Kesho Râi and Jagjiwan Dâs chiefly to Mirzâ Râja Jai Singh and Râm Singh with reference to Prince Bedâr Bakht and the Jâts. A few pages in Devnagri script. Includes the following dates—

1689 December.
1690 January; March; May.
1693 August.

Volume IV 384 pages 20.5 cm.

Being news-letters from the Imperial Court written chiefly to Mirzâ Râja Jai Singh with reference to the Jâts.

Volume V 138 pages, 20.5 cm.

Being news-letters from Prince Mu'azzam Shâh and Bedâr Bakht, including records of the occurrences of the following dates—

1702 March-May.

Volume VI 592 pages, 20.5 cm.

Being letters and *farmâns* of Aurangzeb during 48th year of his rule (1704) and letters of Prince Bedâr Bâkht and Farrukh Siyar to Râja Jai Singh, Bishan Singh, Gopâl Singh, Thâkur Shyâm Singh, Mir Qâsim Husain, the *dîwân* of Mâlwa, and others.

Volume VII 444 pages, 20.5 cm.

Being news-letters from the imperial court drafted by Munshi Megh Râj, Kesho Râi and others to Râja Jai Singh, Bishan Singh, Prince Bedâr Bakht and others.

Volume VIII 420 pages 20.5 cm.

Miscellaneous letters and *farmâns* of Aurangzeb, Mohammad Shâh and Farrukh Siyar written to different officials of their court.

Volume IX 399 pages, 20.5 cm.

Being news-letters as well as some *farmâns* of Emperor Aurangzeb to Mirzâ Râja Jâi Singh, his son Râm Singh and others with a few pages in Devnagri script.

Volume X 438 pages, 20.5 cm.

Contains news-letters issued from the Imperial Court chiefly written by Kesho Râi,Govind Chand and Megh Râj to Râja Bishan Singh, Râja Jai Singh and others.

Volume X I 212 pages, 21 cm.

Being letters of Megh Râj, a clerk at the Imperial Court, drafted on behalf of the officers of the court as well as on his own behalf to the various officials and nobles of the Government—

1688	August.
1693	April and October
1694	June
1695	January
1695	March and May
1700	February
1702	April; May; August; October
1705	October and November.
Volume XII	304 pages, 20.5 cm

Being news-letters issued from the Imperial Court and some personal letters of Jagjivan Dâs, Bihâri Dâs, Meghrâj, Govind Chand and others chiefly to Mirzâ Râja Jai Singh with a few pages in Devnagri script.

Volume XIII 158 pages, 20.5 cm.

Contains letters from the servants of Sawâi Jai Singh to their master with a few pages in Devnagri script.

1 (b) JAIPUR AKHBÂRÂT (Raghubir Library Sitamau)

AURANGZEB'S REIGN :

1. 9th year	
2. 10 year	Parts I-II
3. 23rd year	Parts I to IV
4. 24th year.	Parts I to II
5. 25th year.	
6. 26th year	Parts I-II
7. 27th year	
8. 28th year	Pars I-II
9. 29th year	
10. 30th to 34th years.	
11. 35th and 36th years.	
12. 36th to 42nd years.	
13. 50th and 51st years.	

Royal Asiatic Society London Collection
(Raghubir Library Sitamau)

Aurangzeb's Reign :

1. 8th to 22nd years.
2. 24th and 25th years.
3. 36th and 37th years.

4. 38th yar.
5. 39th year.
6. 40th year.
7. 42nd year.
8. 43rd year.
9. 44th year.
10. 45th year.
11. 46th year
12. 47th and 48th year
13. 48th year
14. 49th year.

II. PRINTED PERSIAN WORKS

1. Abdul Qâsim Mohammad : *Târîkh-i-Farishta.*
2. Abu'l Fazl : *Âîn-i-Akbari.*
3. Abu'l Fazl : *Akbar Nâmâ.*
4. Badâyuni : *Muntakhib-ut-tawârîkh.*
5. Nizâm-ud-din : *Tabaqât-i-Akbari.*
6. Jahangir : *Tuzk-i-Jahângîrî.*
7. Mu'tamid Khân : *Iqbâlnâma-i-Jahangîrî.*
8. *Letters of Aurangzeb.*
9. Abdul Hye : *Mirât-i-Ahmadı.*
10. Abdul Hamid Lâhori : *Bâdshâh Nâma.*
11. Kâzim : *'Âlamgîr Nâma.*
12. Must'id Khân : *Ma'âsir-i-'Âlamgîrî.*
13. Ghulâm Husain; *Rayâz-us-Salâtîn.*
14. Khâfi Khân : *Muntakhib-ul-Lubâb.*
15. Mohammad Sâlih : *'Aml-i-Sâlih.*
16. 'Abdul Hamid Lâhori : *Bâdshâh Nâma.*
17. Qazvini : *Bâdshâh Nâmâ.*

III. HINDI WORKS

1. Keshav Dâs : *Bîr Singh Deo Charit.*
2. Banârsi Dâs Jain : *Ardha-Kathâ.*
3. Kavi Râj Varinda; *Varinda Satsai.*
4. 'Usmân : *Chhatra Prakâsh.*
6. Bihâri : *Satsai.*
7. Manjhan : *Madhu Maltî.*
8. Jatamala : *Gorâ Bâdal.*
9. Tosh : *Sudha-Nidhî,*
10. Sûr Dâs : *Sûr Sâgar.*

IV. ACCOUNTS OF FOREIGN TRAVELLERS.

1. Francis Bernier : *travels in the Mughal Empire*, 1656-68. Edited by Archibald Constable.
2. John Bapitse Tavernier : *Travels in India.* Edited by V. Ball. 2 volumes.
3. *John Marshall in India*, 668-72. Edited by Sir Shafaat Ahmad Khan.
4. Nicolao Manucci : *Storia do Mogor.* Edited by William Irvine. 4 volumes.
5. Nicolao Manucci : *A Pepys of Mughal India* (abridgement of the four volumes).
6. Sebastien Manrique : *Travels in India* (1629-43). Edited by Eckford Luard and Father H. Hosten.
7. Thomas Roe : *Embassy to India* (1615-19). Edited by William Foster.
8. Thomas Roe : *Roe's Journal.*
9. John Jourdain : *The Journal of a Voyage to the East Indies.* Edited by William Foster
10. Pietro della Valle : *The Travels of Pietro della Valle to India.* Edited by Edward Grey.
11. Francis Pelsaert : *Jahangir's India.* Translated by Moreland.
12. Peter Mundy : *The Travels of Peter Mundy in Europe and Asia* (1608-67) *Edited* by Sir Richard Temple.
13. Thevenot : *Voyage to Europe, Asia and Africa.*
14. Thevenot : Indian Travels of Thevenot. Edited by S.N. Sen.
15. Careri : *Indian Travels of John Francts Gamelli Careri.* Edited by S.N. Sen.
16. Mandelslo : In the *Complete Collection of Voyages and Travels* by John Harris.
17. : Travels in Western India.
18. Foster : *Early Travels in India* containing the accounts of Ralph Fitch (1583-91); John Mildenhall (1603-5); William Hawkins (1608-13); William Finch (1608-11); Nicholas Withington (1612-16); Thomas

Coryat)1614-17).

19. Edward Terry : *A Voyage to East India.*
20. De Laet : *Empire of the Great Mughal.* Translated from Latin into English by Hoyland and annotated by Bannerji.
21. John Fryer : *A new Account of East India and Persia.* Edited by William Crooke.
22. Ovington : *A Voyage to Surat* (1689).
23. Monserrate : *Commentary.* Translated by J.S. Hoyland and annotated by Bannerji.
24. Linschoten : *Voyage to the East Indies.* Edited by A.C. Burnell and P.A. Tiele.
25. Pyrard : *The Voyage of Francis Pyrard of Laval.* Edited by Albert Gray and Purvis Bell.
26. Brij Narain and Sri Ram Sharma : *A Dutch Chronicle of Mughal India.*

V. ENGLISH FACTORIES IN INDIA, (Edited by William Foster.)

1. 1618—1621.
2. 1622—1623
3. 1624—1629.
4. 1630—1633.
5. 1634—1636.
6. 1637—1641.
7. 1642—1645.
8. 1646—1650.
9. 1651—1654.
10. 1655—1660.
11. 1661—1664.
12. 1665—1667.
13. 1668—1669.
14. 1670—1677.

(b) *Court Minutes of East India Company.*

(c) *Letters Received by East India Company from its Servants in the East.*

VI. ENGLISH TRANSLATIONS OF CONTEMPORARY PERSIAN WORKS

1. Henry Beveridge. *Akbar Nâma.*
2. Blochman. *Âin-i-Akbari.*

3. Lowe. *Muntakhib-ut-Tawârikh.*
4. *De.* Tabaqât-i-Akbari.
5. Rogers and Beveridge. *Tuzk-i-Jahângîrî.*
6. Eliot and Dowson. *History of India as Told by its own Historians,* Volumes, V, VI, VII.
7. Eliot and Dowson. Reprinted by Sushil Gupta Ltd. under the following titles :

Akbar.	By Badauni.
Akbar.	By Abul Fazl
Akbar.	By Nizâm-ud-din Ahmad.
Jahângir.	Memoirs.
Shahjahan.	By Qazvînî; Lâhori; 'Inâyat Khân; Wârris; Kamboh; Mohammad Sâdiq; Bharmal.

8. M.I. Borah. *Bahâristân-i-Ghayabi* by Mirzâ Nathan.

VII. URDU TRANSLATIONS AND WORKS

1. *Fatâwâ-i-'Âlamgîrî* (4 volumes).
2. Iqbâlnâma-i-Jahangîrî.
3. Farishta. *Tarikhi-i-Farishta.*
4. Mohammad Husain Âzâd. *Darbâr-i-Akbari.*
5. *Âîna-a-Gujarât* (Translation of Mirât-i-Ahmadi).
6. Mohd. Kâzim : *Ma'âsir-i-'Âlamgîrî.*
7. Khâfi Khân; *Muntakhib-ul-Lubâb* (3 volumes).

VII. WORKS ON ISLAMIC LAW

1. *Encyclopaedia of Islam* (4 volumes).
2. *Shorter Encyclopaedia of Islam.*
3. Hughes : *dictionary of Islam.*
4. Hurgronje : *Mohammadanism.*
5. Mohammad : *Ma'âlim-al-Qarba.* Edited by Levy with extracts in English.
6. Joseph Schacht : *Origins of Islamic Jurisprudence.*
7. Gaudfroy-Demombynes : *Muslim Institutions.*
8. Gibb and Bowen : *Islamic Society and the West.*
9. A.S. Triton : *Islam.*
10. Gustave Von Graunebaum : *Medieval Islam.*

IX. OTHER WORKS.

1.	V.A. Smith	:	*Akbar, the Great Mughal.*
2.	Malleson	:	*Akbar.*
3.	Von Noer	:	*Emperor Akbar.*
4.	Rushbrook Williams	:	*An Empire-builder of the 16th century.*
5.	A.L. Srivastave	:	*Akbar.* Vol. I

6. Du Jarric : *Akbar and the Jesuits.* Translated by Payne.
7. Beni Prasad : *Jahangir.*
8. Guerrerio : *Jahangir and the Jesuts.* Translated by Payne.
9. Banarsi Prasad Saxena : *Shahjahan.*
10. Jadu Nath Sarkar : *Aurangzeb.* (5 volumes).
11. Jadu Nath Sarkar : *A Short History of Aurangzeb.*
12. Jadu Nath Sarkar : *Anecdotes of Aurangzeb.*
13. Jadu Nath Sarkar : *Letters of Aurangzeb.*
14. Jadu Nath Sarkar : *Mughal Administration.*
15. Jadu Nath Sarkar : *Studies in Aurangzeb's Reign.*
16. Sri Ram Sharma : *A Bibliography of Mughal India.*
17. Sri Ram Sharma : *Religious Policy of the Mughal Emperors.*
18. Sri Ram Sharma : *Mughal Government and Administration.*
19. Ibn Hasan : *Central Structure of the Mughal Empire.*
20. P. Saran : *The Provincial Government of the Mughals.*
21. Moreland : *India from Akbar to Aurangzeb.*
22. Moreland : *India at the Death of Aurangzeb.*
23. *The Thought* Quarterly No. 40.
24. Henry Eliot : *Memoirs on the History, Folklore and Distributions of the Racesof NWFP.*
25. M.B. Ahmad : *The Administration of Justice in Medieval India.*
26. *Cambridge History of India,* Vol. IV.
27. Maclagan : *The Jesuits and the Great Mughals*
28. Qanungo : *Sher Shah.*
29. Rushbrooke Williams : *Aurangzeb.*
30. Orme : *A Historical Fragment of Mughal India.*
31. Oaten : *European Travellers to India.*
32. Marshall : *Mughals in India.*

INDEX

A

B

C

D

K

L

M

R